Ambition and Accommodation

AMBITION & ACCOMMODATION

ROBERTA S. SIGEL

*How Women View
Gender Relations*

The University of Chicago Press
Chicago and London

ROBERTA S. SIGEL is distinguished professor emeritus of political science at the State University of New Jersey, Rutgers.

The University of Chicago Press, Chicago 60637
The University of Chicago Press, Ltd., London
© 1996 by The University of Chicago
All rights reserved. Published 1996
Printed in the United States of America
05 04 03 02 01 00 99 98 97 96   1 2 3 4 5

ISBN 0–226–75695–5 (cloth)
       0–226–75696–3 (paper)

Library of Congress Cataloging-in-Publication Data

Sigel, Roberta S.
    Ambition and accommodation: How women view gender
relations / Roberta S. Sigel.
        p.   cm.
    Includes bibliographical references and index.
    1. Sex role—United States.   2. Man-woman relationships—
United States.   3. Sex discrimination against women—
United States.   4. Women—United States—   Attitudes.
I. Title.
HQ1075.5.U6S56   1996
305.3—dc20   95-39468
                                                            CIP

To my best friend—my husband

Contents

Acknowledgments

The data on which this book is based had their genesis in a lunch conversation with my colleague, Professor Cliff Zukin. On that occasion, we were speculating about the extent to which feminist consciousness had penetrated the thoughts and emotions of ordinary men and women and how one could go about measuring such consciousness. Next followed the decision to stop wondering and start investigating. So Cliff Zukin and I developed a research design that the National Science Foundation subsequently funded, and we hereby wish to thank them for their support.

Our overriding concern in preparing the investigation was to find a way of gaining a genuine understanding of the ways the public thinks about today's gender relations and how it frames these thoughts in its own words and metaphors. To gain that understanding, Zukin made what was, at the time, a rather novel suggestion that our research should combine quantitative and qualitative methods of investigation in the same design. Once the instruments were developed and the fieldwork was completed, our respective research paths parted. Cliff returned to his work on public opinion, and I proceeded with the data analysis, the presentation of numerous papers based on it, and the writing of the book. Although Cliff Zukin is to be absolved of any errors and shortcomings found in the book, I would be grossly unfair if I did not acknowledge how much this project owes to him.

Thanks are also due to the Rockefeller Foundation for inviting me to a month's residence at their Conference Center in Bellagio, Italy. The serene surroundings of that lovely place high above Lake Como gave me the quiet and, yes, the inspiration to organize and code the hundreds of pages of focus group transcripts and return home ready to start with the writing of the book.

Throughout instrument development and initial data analysis, I was greatly assisted by Nancy L. Whelchel. Dr. Whelchel, then a graduate student, made a major contribution through her mastery of the feminist literature and her unflagging enthusiasm for the topic. We co-authored three papers, and parts of their contents have found their way into this book. Many thanks are also due to three other Rutgers University graduate students, Laura D. Burnbauer (now Dr. Burnbauer), Loretta A. Sernekos, and Kathleen J. Casey, who assisted me during various phases of the project. I have worked particularly closely with Ms. Casey, whose critical insights and quantitative skills I have come to value very much.

The comments and suggestions of the anonymous reviewers proved very incisive and valuable. Many have found their way into the final version of the book. But to no one am I more indebted than to Professor Jane Mansbridge, who read the whole manuscript and with a keen eye and a sharp green pencil did her level best to improve my writing style as well as my thought processes. No matter how much I thank her for her efforts, it is not enough. Finally I wish to express my appreciation to John Tryneski, senior editor at the University of Chicago Press, for his sage advice and unfailing encouragement.

Introduction

The great question which I have not been able to answer is: What does a woman want?

—Sigmund Freud

I myself have never been able to find out precisely what feminism is: I only know that people call me a feminist whenever I express sentiments that differentiate me from a doormat.

—Rebecca West

Hardly a month passes without one or another of the many popular American magazines devoting an issue to the "New American Woman" and to the dramatic changes in her social position—changes which some characterize as a revolution.[1] This book is about that alleged revolution. But it is not about the *reality* of the revolution; that is, it does not seek to ascertain if changes resembling a social revolution have actually taken place. Rather, it is about people's *perception* of these changes. It asks: How do women and, to a lesser degree, men of all walks of life perceive the position of the American woman in today's society? Do they believe that women's societal position has undergone much change during the past two or three decades? If so, in what domains has it changed, and how satisfied are they with the new arrangements?

The book is meant to serve as a map of men's and women's perceptions about how American women are faring at the close of the twentieth century and to ascertain whether the two genders navigate from the same map. But, above all, it is about the map that guides *women's* perceptions and how these perceptions in turn affect their attitudes, opinions, and behaviors. In short, it is a book about perceptions of reality, not about objective, scientifically verifiable reality. Perhaps it would be more accurate to say it is about reality as the individuals *experience* it. As we all know, what *is* and what people *believe is* are not necessarily

1. This evaluation is not restricted to the popular literature. Social scientists occasionally make similar assertions. For example, a sociologist (Kathleen Gerson) opens her 1985 book *Hard Choices* with the following sentence: "We are in the midst of a 'subtle revolution'" (p. 1). Many others—some of whom are cited in the chapters which follow—also comment on the dramatic changes which are said to have occurred and which can best be captured in the Virginia Slims slogan "You've come a long way, baby."

1

the same. "The pictures inside our heads of the world beyond" (to use Walter Lippman's famous phrase) constitute the world for all of us and guide the encounters with that "world beyond." It is important to learn what humans define for themselves as real if we want to understand how people cope with the "world beyond," what they anticipate from each other, how they determine their own responses, and what form their social interaction takes. Ultimately, it is the tenor of these interactions that shapes the social fabric of civil society. Nowhere should this apply more forcefully than in the realm of gender relations—if for no other reason than that these involve persistent, perhaps daily, interactions for most people and hence assume a directness and salience possessed by few other types of interaction.

Understanding the dynamics of the perceptions and beliefs which fuel the interactions becomes especially crucial during periods of transition and/or social change when old, accustomed ways of thinking about gender relations and each gender's "proper" place coexist and at times come into conflict with some of the newer realities of daily living. Ours is such a period of transition—whether or not it amounts to a "revolution" is another matter—during which many aspects of women's lives, both public (beginning with their massive entrance into the workforce) and private (with the increase in the divorce rate and the so-called sexual revolution), have undergone many changes.

The second American Women's Movement is now over twenty years old; the majority of American women are employed outside of the home, quite a number in occupations previously reserved for men; they have obtained as much education as men, and they vote as much as men do, on occasions even more so. The year of 1992 was declared "The Year of the Woman," but just a few years earlier the fight for ratification of the Equal Rights Amendment was lost; and in 1993 a prestigious military school was challenged in court because it refused to enroll a woman cadet it had admitted before learning of her gender. The picture is mixed and contradictory. Some declare that women now have achieved full equality with men; others are equally certain that women are still subordinate. And so the debate continues. My interest here is not to enter that debate or the larger topic of gender equality. Rather, I want to explore what role that debate plays in the lives of the women who are the subjects in our study. Just how real is the debate about women's liberation to most ordinary citizens? How much does it preoccupy their thoughts? What are the positions of most citizens on these issues? By now, we have much information on how prominent activists on either side of the debate view gender relations and what changes they would like to bring about or prevent. But "between avowed feminists and activist anti-feminists lies the majority of women" (Tolleson

Rinehart 1992:16), and we know much less about their views on the topic. This book hopes to capture the gender perspective of this vast female majority.

The book is based on research conducted in New Jersey late in 1985 with over 650 adult men and women who were interviewed on the telephone or observed during focus group discussions. It describes *their* map of women's place in modern American society, as they drew it for us. Any cartographer's map of the world does not represent the real world but a one-dimensional representation of it, reflecting the cartographer's own knowledge and, indirectly, the current state of knowledge about the world. And as Columbus and others have discovered, maps can be highly inaccurate and therefore misleading. Our participants carried in their heads visions of the way the world works; in our particular case, how gender relations work. These too may be misleading and inaccurate versions, nonetheless, I let the participants serve as my navigators. I listened to them tell me how *they* viewed themselves and their relations to the opposite sex—at work, at home, and in the outside world generally. Because the social position of women is the focal point of the reportage, most of the chapters will deal with women and how they reported experiencing their role and their status, how they viewed the treatment they are accorded because they are women, and what meaning they attach to that treatment. In short, my aim is to report on gender-related experiences and perceptions as seen and felt from the perspective of women from all walks of life.

Because the women in this study became my navigators, the book turned into a different enterprise from what I had anticipated, for I soon found out that the women framed the issues of gender equality and gender relations in terms very different from those customary in political science. For them, issues of equality, of dominance and subordination, and of rights and privileges are played out within the context of everyday living, in the workplace, the home, and the personnel office rather than in the voting booth, let alone the Halls of Congress. Consequently, I made the decision to give prominent place to my informers' own words whenever possible and to emphasize their narrative rather than the statistics. My aim is to reveal how ordinary women view the gendered system and their position in it as the twentieth century draws to an end.

The book begins with a brief overview of the ways social scientists, especially political scientists, have studied gender relations since, roughly, the end of World War II. The chapter does not purport to be a review of the literature but rather a sketch of the changes in investigative approach and conceptualization which have taken place over that period. I begin the chapter with a focus on sex differences, proceed to the stress on cultural determinism, and then move to the more recent focus on gender, gender relations, and questions of empowerment. It is not meant to be a chapter describing the status of today's gender relations; many others have commented on that with great insight. Nor is it a chapter on feminist thought: that too has been covered extensively by others. Instead, this chapter pursues two objectives: (1) to document how the "scientific" ways of studying women have changed over time and (2) to present the theoretical framework from which the book is approached. The approach is derived, though modified, from theories of relative deprivation.

The second chapter then describes the study's methodology, which involves two different investigative techniques. The study is part qualitative and descriptive, relying on focus group observations, and part quantitative and analytic, relying on a sample survey. This chapter also discusses the study design, the sample, the instruments used, and the rationale for the choice of the particular methodologies.

Subsequent chapters substantively analyze how women perceive their situation. Chapter 3 directs our attention to the question of equality and women's perception of progress or lack of progress eliminating or minimizing inequality. It describes the obvious as well as the subtle areas where women perceive discrimination to be widely practiced. Focus group members offer ample, often vivid, illustrations of what they understand by discrimination. The chapter discusses how much improvement in their situation women perceive and what they believe still needs to be done. Chapter 4 then inquires into their reactions to perceived discrimination and seeks to determine if they are angry over it, as relative deprivation theory would suggest. It tries to explain why some who are cognizant of discrimination are angry while others refuse or are hesitant to get angry, or are actually indifferent. The *degree* of discrimination observed by a participant usually has an impact on her expression of resentment and anger. The chapter discusses how women deal with anger and notes how societal norms impact on the expression of anger. The analysis compares focus groups' and survey respondents' descriptions of their emotional reactions to perceived discrimination and asks why they differ.

Chapter 5 focuses in detail on the contexts in which women become most sensitized to and upset over discrimination. Many political scientists may not consider these areas to be political, however, they have serious political implications even though formal politics hardly ever lie at the forefront of most people's consciousness or concerns. The "new woman," in spite of her recently raised consciousness, is no exception to this old rule. For her, as for most citizens these days, the stress and strain of daily living is predominant. "Politics" enters in only when it directly and visibly affects daily life. An example is women's support of governmental policies designed to improve living conditions for women. An important question to be raised in this book is whether or not such support is indicative of women's gender consciousness and, furthermore, does such support translate into political behavior on behalf of women?

The sixth chapter pursues further the topic of group consciousness. It seeks to determine the role that minority consciousness plays in the daily lives of today's women. Minority consciousness, the empathy for disadvantaged groups, does seem to have political implications. Because minority consciousness need not be restricted to members of the minority itself but can be shared by sympathetic others, men's perceptions of the issues of discrimination will be included. This chapter compares men's and women's reactions to discrimination and observes that men take a more detached view of the situation than do women. This detachment is mirrored in men's political preferences as well.

Chapter 7 focuses exclusively on men and notes that male focus group discussions paint a different picture about their receptivity to the currently occurring changes than telephone interviews reveal. The chapter seeks to explain what might account for the difference. A comparison of men's and women's reactions to discrimination reveals different perspectives on gender relations. Social class differences also seem to play a more decisive part in male than in female reactions. The last chapter, building on the previous observations, draws a picture of the ways in which men and women learn to maneuver in a world they both perceive to be unfair to women and speculates why they may have adopted their particular strategies for coping with this unfairness. The concluding section reflects on the importance men and women attach to bringing about egalitarian gender relations.

1

CONCEPTUALIZING GENDER

All societies, from the most primitive to the most modern, use sex as a convenient and preferred attribute to differentiate members of the human race . . . Invariably, this has invited invidious comparisons.

—Cynthia Fuchs Epstein (1988)

Gender relations, the subject of commentary from the days of Adam and Eve to the present,[1] continue to have nearly universal interest. Unlike many topics, this is one on which almost everyone has an opinion and considers himself or herself to be an expert simply by virtue of living in a gendered world. It is also a topic on which opinions and attitudes in the United States currently are in a state of flux, undergoing considerable change in some areas but virtually none in others.

It is the thesis of this book that men and women are changing their traditional expectations with respect to gender relations and that this change is accompanied by a good deal of ambivalence and conflict. It asserts, furthermore, that the genders are changing at a different pace. Women are more anxious for change than men because women believe that current arrangements put them at a disadvantage simply because they are women. How women respond to their sense of deprivation relative to men constitutes the core of my investigation.

To understand why and how our thinking about gender relations has changed over the past decades, this introductory chapter offers first a brief sketch of the ways in which the social sciences, most particularly political science, have studied gender relations and how, over time, they have altered their investigative approach to the topic.[2] I conclude by suggesting that theories of relative deprivation can help explain how

1. A few sections in this chapter are adapted from my presidential address, "How Men and Women Cope When Gender Orientations Change," which was delivered in Helsinki, Finland, at the 1991 Annual Meeting of the International Society for Political Psychology.
2. Even the term "sketch" is probably an exaggeration since the social science scholarship on gender has become so voluminous in the last two decades that it could not possibly be surveyed within the confines of a single chapter.

ordinary men and women, especially those disadvantaged by virtue of their gender, might react to recent changes.

Had I chosen to discuss gender and gender relations twenty years ago, I probably would not have referred to "gender relations" but to "relations between the sexes" or, more likely, to "sex differences." That change in language in itself is of considerable significance in that it indicates that our thinking about male/female roles and relations has undergone a profound change.[3] By changing the nomenclature, we "bear witness to a general change in our characteristic ways of thinking about our common life: about our social, political and economic institutions; about the purposes which these institutions are designed to embody . . . " (Williams 1983: xi). By speaking of gender rather than sex, we seek to indicate that our thoughts about male/female differences have undergone changes. The nomenclature is meant to indicate that many differences commonly attributed to women's biological nature instead are attributable to their position in the social structure and to society's expectations for appropriate female behaviors.

CONCEPTUAL CHANGES IN RESEARCH APPROACH

The way political scientists (as well as the public) think about men and women has undergone major transformation since the days of World War II and especially over the past three decades. Roughly speaking, three stages can be distinguished: During the first, in the rare cases when women were discussed at all, the emphasis was on how women differed from men; the second stage continued to stress male/female differences, but attributed them to socialization rather than to biology; and the third stage looks at "gender" rather than "sex."

THE FOCUS ON DIFFERENCES

Before the last few decades, anyone reading the political science literature in order to find out what role women played in American political life would have come away with the impression that, as far as political science was concerned, women did not exist; they were not significant actors in any public sphere. Women were ignored not because political scientists were mean-spirited misogynists but because in their opinion women did not play a significant part in the formal, visible, "public" life of the nation. Women's contribution to this "public" life, when acknowledged, was considered exceptional (as in the occasional Indira

---

3. The use of the term "gender" in this context is relatively recent. As Conway, Bourque, and Scott (1992: 6) point out, the 1964 issue of *Daedalus* on the "Woman in America," though often credited as having been a precursor to the gender revolution, "had no place at all in the index" for the term gender.

Gandhi or Margaret Thatcher). In part, this can be attributed to political scientists' narrow definition of what constitutes "politics" (Sigel and Hoskin 1981). Most of their attention focused on initiatives by or pressures on the major centers of government and ignored many quasi-political activities (such as communal or school-related engagements) in which women were involved. Moreover, they attributed women's absence from the major centers of political power not so much to the social and political structures which tend to exclude women as to the then common belief that women preferred the domestic sphere over the public one. A sharp distinction thus was made between private and public as though they were two totally distinct spheres, a distinction which, however erroneous, still pervades much political science thought today.

In most instances, the early political science literature failed to examine the extent to which the economic, social, and political structures of the nation contributed to women's lack of participation in traditional political activities. For example, commenting on women's lower voting turnout in the period between the two world wars, political scientists failed to relate it to the recency of women's suffrage and instead offered what was essentially a biological explanation. Men, it was said, were attracted to public life, and women were not. Politics, so the popular phrase went, was men's business. Their "natures" and temperaments differed because their biological make-ups differed. "Biology is destiny," and destiny, it seemed, favored the male of the species.[4] Women were judged to lack the propensity for political conflict or at least the appetite for its competitiveness and aggressivity. Their tender or emotional "nature" caused them to avoid making the tough decisions required in the political process. While political scientists were perhaps not quite as blatant in relying on biological explanations, they shared the public's view of women's unsuitability for political life and favored keeping politics a male sphere.[5] The net effect was that few if any references to women and politics can be found in the mainstream political science literature of the first two decades following World War II.

A related, but equally androcentric, approach to the study of gender emerged in the deliberate search for male/female differences. This approach is perhaps most characteristic of psychology, with its emphasis

4. The literature on the topic is voluminous. Two good reviews, albeit critical ones, of the evidence for biological determinism are: M. Z. Rosaldo's chapter, in a collection edited by her and L. Lamphere (1974), and J. Sayers's chapter in the collection edited by B. H. Hess and M. M. Ferree (1987).

5. Susan Bourque and Jean Grossholtz (1974) asserted: "That politics is a man's world is a familiar adage; that political science tends to keep it that way is less accepted, but perhaps closer to the truth."

on finding statistically significant differences among groups, but with the advent of the so-called behavioral or empirical revolution in political science, the approach became popular there as well. In both psychology and political science,[6] males (and most of the time white males) furnished the norm against which political scientists compared all other populations' capacities and behaviors. The topics chosen for comparisons—voting, running for political office, etc.—were those in which men predominated and where male performance was used as the benchmark against which to compare women—inevitably to the disadvantage of the latter. Male actions, attitudes, and interests became the norm for evaluating women's actions, attitudes, and interests. The verdict often was that women simply did not measure up. Political scientists, for example, documented that women did not vote as much as men and showed less interest in politics; psychologists showed that women performed less well on tests of intelligence and aptitude; sociologists concluded that women displayed less talent for organizational leadership. Seldom did the researchers ask whether anything in the social structure rather than in women's "nature" might account for the differences. Even less frequently did they question whether male norms were the only valid ones, the ones against which everyone's performance should be measured. The myth of the innate difference in interest, talents, and behaviors between men and women was thus kept intact, and again it was nature not society that caused it. This, in turn, permitted the perpetuation of the existing social system with woman in a subordinate position in the hierarchy—a hierarchy many feminists chose to call a patriarchy. As feminist psychologist Rhoda K. Unger (1990: 123) maintains, "[v]irtually all women exist within a social hierarchy in which 'male is greater than female.'"

The Focus on Childhood Socialization

By about 1960, the tenor and emphasis in social science research on women had shifted from biological determinism to a focus on cultural determinants.[7] Instead of looking to biology for explanations of male/female differences in social behaviors, researchers directed their atten-

---

6. The possible exception would be anthropology, which has a long-standing tradition of studying women, although much of the information about women in so-called primitive societies was obtained from male informers rather than the women themselves.

7. The anthropologist, Margaret Mead, focused on culture as early as 1935 with the publication of *Sex and Temperament in Three Primitive Societies*, but this point of view was not widely accepted in many of the social sciences until considerably later, when the paradigm shifted from an emphasis on nature to one on nurture. The nature/nurture controversy, of course, is a perpetual one that never can be fully resolved one way or another since it probably is not an either/or issue.

tion to the social arrangements that caused, in fact demanded, men and women to behave differently. New research demonstrated that almost from the moment of birth adults treat boys and girls differently (Maccoby and Jacklin 1974; Hoffman 1974 and 1977; Marini 1978), and that many adult behaviors can be traced to the impact of socialization. These researchers placed particularly heavy emphasis on early childhood socialization on the assumption that childhood was the period during which adults convey culture's messages, values, and norms to the young and during which youth is most receptive to incorporating these into their personality, attitudes, and enduring habits. Childhood socialization, so the theory went, not only laid the foundation for effective adult functioning at the individual level but also served to maintain the stability of the sociopolitical system (Easton and Dennis 1969; Hess and Torney 1967). Early political socialization studies operated on the assumption—or at least were interpreted as indicating—that young children's political proclivities foreshadowed adult political behaviors (Easton and Dennis 1969; Greenstein 1965; Sigel 1975).[8] The studies found girls less interested in politics than boys and less informed about politics but more trusting of authority (Sigel 1975), although some noted that class and race differences at times offered more meaningful explanations than an individual's gender (Jaros, Hirsch, and Fleron 1968; Greenberg 1970; Jennings and Niemi 1974; Sigel 1965).

One characteristic of this early political socialization literature was to search for the "agent" or "agents" who most determined the course and content of socialization. Different studies singled out the family, the school, the church, and somewhat later the mass media and peers as being most important. One important component of the agents' socialization mission was the training of boys and girls for their respective adult "sex roles."[9]

Some strands of the political socialization literature received their impetus from psychoanalytic theory with its heavy emphasis on childhood experiences. Other strands were more influenced by sociologists and social psychologists, especially in accounting for the acquisition of sex role orientations. Sociologist Talcott Parsons (1951; and Parsons and Bales 1955) particularly encouraged the shift to a socialization paradigm, arguing that gender socialization forged the crucial link between individual personality and societal needs. This early socialization literature more or less took it for granted that men and women would always play different roles in adulthood and that socialization

8. This is an interpretation which several authors held to be unwarranted. See, for example, Searing, Schwartz, and Lind (1973), and Sigel and Hoskin (1981).

9. One could, of course, argue, as did Rhoda Unger, that the concept "sex role" in itself constitutes a paradox since sex is a biological concept while role is a sociological one.

should help them develop personalities suited to these differential roles. Learning to internalize one's sex-appropriate role was seen as central to the smooth functioning of the social system. In Western societies, as in almost all societies, the sex role prescribed for women involved subordination to men, with women tending to the nurturant tasks, especially the care of the family, and with men holding authority over the family as well as assuming the economic and political direction of the polity.

Three characteristics distinguish the early socialization/sex role perspective: (1) it traces gender-based behavioral differences to societal rather than biologically determined origins; (2) it assumes stability of attitudes and behaviors throughout the person's life course (Hyman 1959); and (3) it assigns to women an essentially private role in contrast to men's public one. While today's students of gender relations maintain that this public/private dichotomy resulted in women being relegated to an inferior position, Parsons (1951; Parsons and Bales 1955) and others in this era defended the essentially inegalitarian nature of the arrangement as socially desirable because it permitted the nuclear family to function and society to maintain itself. To their way of thinking, successful childhood socialization constituted a bulwark against societal chaos and individual anomie. This functionalist approach to socialization reflected a conservative outlook, for which it has been heavily criticized (Merelman 1986; Connell 1987; Wrong 1961). In political science, the functionalist approach had the effect of stressing, perhaps even overvaluing, the virtue of system support and individual conformity. The socialization perspective helped to explain how the traditional gendered order had maintained itself from generation to generation, even in countries such as the United States—which, as de Tocqueville observed, has been said to attach relatively great importance to the idea of human equality. It is not surprising, therefore, that for a long time the private/public dichotomy was the prevailing paradigm for explaining gender-based differences and inequalities.[10] Moreover, extolling the virtues of the public/private dichotomy harmonized well with the prevailing traditional views while at the same time providing a much needed antidote to strictly biological explanations.

One great shortcoming of this concentration on childhood socialization is that it tended to overlook adults' capacity for change. Only recently has the literature begun to pay attention to the human potential for growth, development, and adaptation throughout the entire life

10. Recently, however, the pendulum seems to be swinging back to a biological or rather sociobiological explanation which, though not completely ignoring social factors, puts heavy emphasis on biological ones. See, for example, the work of Wilson (1978).

course. This new research refutes the traditional presumption of continuity from childhood throughout the course of an adult's life (Carter 1987; Steckenrider and Cutler 1989; N. D. Glenn 1974; Gerson 1985; Kagan and Brim 1980; Levinson 1971; Sigel 1989; Sinnott 1987). Humans adapt and change in response to altered conditions in their personal lives and to changes in their historical, political, economic, and social environment. They are not frozen into a permanent mold upon completion of childhood, even in gender roles. Socialization and learning can continue right through old age (see especially Neugarten [1968] and Baltes and Schaie [1973]).

The childhood socialization approach also fails to take account of the large repertoire of behaviors at the disposal of individuals which enables them to modify their actions in order to cope with important new life situations. Humans, for example, are perfectly capable of engaging in "sex-appropriate" behavior or discarding it, depending on the context in which it is to be performed. "The individual is not . . . in possession of an absolute unchanging role that is a permanent descriptor of one's identity, but rather is constantly—perhaps even consciously—creating a flexible role defined in relation to individuals and circumstances in one's context. This last—the context—is a shared but also dually created perception of reality" (Sinnott 1987: 158). Female job applicants, for example, have been observed (von Baeyer, Sherk, and Zanna 1981) to vary their behaviors, clothing, make-up, and even their opinions depending on whether they are being interviewed by a traditional employer or a less traditional one. Similarly, women and men have been known to vary their so-called sex-appropriate behaviors depending on whether they acted in private or in public, adopting more sex-appropriate stances in public than in private interactions" (Sheriffs and McKee 1957).[11] The participants in our study, as well as in others (Ballou and Del Boca 1980; Kane and Macaulay 1993), gave more circumspect answers to interviewers of the opposite gender than to same-gender interviewers. And just as people can change behaviors in a given situation, they can also change and internalize for themselves entirely new role definitions. As the following chapters illustrate, many women who had been socialized to traditional sex roles no longer accepted these definitions. To cite one subject, they "had grown into something new."

By overlooking or at least deemphasizing the potential for self-induced change, the socialization approach tends to project a passive,

11. The rich literature on stereotyping is replete with a variety of examples of the ways in which our beliefs about the nature, preferences, and expectations of the other gender shape our behavior. (See Ashmore and Del Boca 1986; Carter 1987; and Deaux 1984.)

"oversocialized" image of women (Wrong 1961) as though all women accepted more or less unquestioningly the lessons of their childhood.[12] Such a perspective overlooks how frequently individuals create their own lives and the extent to which they shape their society. In the rebirth of the Women's Movement, for example, women themselves brought about change, and this change in turn "socialized" other women as well as men.

A related consequence of the early sex role socialization literature was that it exaggerated the degree of homogeneity among women. Women differ among themselves just as much as men do, and on many issues the variability within each gender is as great as or greater than that between the genders—sex role socialization notwithstanding. The many scales and other instruments which purport to measure male and female traits and/or personalities (Bem 1975; Spence and Helmreich 1978) show much overlap. Scholars have consequently concluded that we tend to "underestimate actual variation and 'grossly exaggerate' . . . the degree and importance of gender differences in personality" (Gerson 1985: 36). As G. Rubin (1975: 179) so graphically put it, "from the standpoint of nature, men and women are closer to each other than either is to anything else . . . " In their 1974 landmark survey of male/female differences, Maccoby and Jacklin found no significant differences between the two genders on most of the attributes they studied. Moreover, observable differences, especially in personality, can just as easily be attributed to structural and contextual factors as to socialization or biological ones. Eagly (1987), for example, attributes the gender-based differences she finds (such as aggression, influence attempts, leadership initiation) not to socialization but to the situations in which men and women customarily are found. Because in organizations men tend to hold positions of authority, women are less likely to attempt to engage in leadership behavior. The early socialization literature was notoriously blind to such explanations. Much of the early literature, therefore, exaggerated both the difference between the two genders and the permanence of the difference.

Finally, and perhaps most significantly, the socialization/sex role approach does not come to terms with the central question underlying all gender relations, that of equality. It is able to document society's different expectations for men and women, but does not question—or does not question sufficiently—the justice or fairness of treating one group as less equal than the other. Ironically, as long as the socialization perspective failed to question the moral justification for assigning dif-

---

12. D. H. Wrong's 1961 article made this criticism with respect to the childhood socialization literature, but his message applies equally to studies of gender roles.

ferent sex roles to the genders, this line of research had some of the same consequences as the innate-difference, biological perspective which it rejected. It too strengthened and implicitly justified the status quo and the inequality of women.

THE GENDER PERSPECTIVE

More recently, the gender perspective, especially as it is discussed in the feminist literature, has directly addressed the question of equality and power. That perspective rejects the idea that men and women are fundamentally different in temperament, abilities, and interests. The gender perspective maintains that differences in anatomy, or "sex," "are not gender differences. . . . Sex differences are physiological features related to procreation, to biological reproduction. . . . Gender depends on how society views the relationship of male to man and female to woman. Every culture has prevailing images of what men and women are 'supposed' to be like" (Gailey 1987: 33–34). By referring to gender rather than sex, scholars aim to signify that the alleged or observed differences between men and women are not ordained by nature, and that "'male' and 'female' are cultural constructions; that each person is brought up in a particular society with a rich set of beliefs and expectations about these social categories" (Ashmore 1990: 486). Gender, in short, is a social construct. The gender perspective maintains that in most respects women and men resemble each other far more than they differ from each other,[13] and that within each sex great individual differences prevail while much overlap exists between the sexes. This perspective rejects the traditional polarization of male and female and the notion that men and women are "natural opposites" of each other, even though, as Deaux and Kite (1987: 101) suggest, "the temptation to treat two categories as opposites may be irresistible"; a temptation which they label "the oppositional trap" (p. 102). The gender perspective holds that, with the exception of physiological and reproductive differences, sex-based behavioral differences observable in men and women, especially in their overt public behaviors,[14] are not biologically ordained but are the results of long-standing and complex socially ordained arrangements which, through a division of labor, assign different roles and different spheres of activities to men and women. "Gender," in

13. Recently, some feminist researchers have tended to put a good deal of emphasis on innate temperamental and other differences between men and women and somewhat less emphasis on their essential similarity. Carol Gilligan best represents that approach. Sue Tolleson Rinehart is probably correct when she writes that among feminists "the possibility of important gender differences is no longer flatly denied" (1992: 9).

14. Both males and females act in more sex-typed ways in public than they do in private. For a review, consult A. H. Eagly (1987).

Unger's words, "refers to the cognitive and perceptual mechanisms by which biological differentiation is translated into social differentiation" (1990: 110).[15]

The gender perspective resembles the socialization perspective in its belief that it is society, not nature, which has ordained that men and women should play different roles and should operate in different spheres, assigning the public sphere to men and the private one to women. But where the functionalist socialization school—at least in its earlier formulations—considered this arrangement to be fair and functional in allegedly meeting social and individual needs, the gender approach both rejects its fairness and its functionality. It holds that the artificial division is neither fair nor functional and that it promotes an unfair and unjust system. It is "a system for dividing people into distinct, nonoverlapping categories despite their natural variability on any particular characteristic . . . [and b]ecause the gender system is not a reflection of natural differences, creating gender is a struggle. We all bear 'the traces of conscription' into a system that represses parts of our potential" (Ferree and Hess 1987: 17). Nor is this "system for dividing people" a separation into two groups with equal degrees of freedom and power. Quite the contrary, it creates a system of gross inequalities. Biological characteristics are translated into power differences, with power allocated primarily, on the basis of sex, to males. In almost every society, men exercise most of the authority and control most of the important institutions as well as most of the resources. Women, lacking institutional control and resources, are relegated to a subordinate position not unlike that of other disadvantaged groups. "Gender systems—regardless of the historical time period—are binary systems that oppose male to female, masculine to feminine, usually not on an equal basis but in hierarchical order" (Conway, Bourque, and Scott 1987: xxix).[16] Almost everywhere "gender forms a dichotomized status structure, with the lower status structure assigned to women" (Lopata 1987: 382).

Hierarchy based on gender is an all-pervasive one which penetrates and shapes almost all social structures from the most private to the

15. Social scientists, feminists as well as nonfeminists, differ among themselves as to the precise meaning of the term *gender* and as to the nature of gender relations but all of them make the distinction between sex and gender where the former refers to biological functions exclusively and the latter is seen as the result of social constructions.

16. "Patriarchy is one form of gender hierarchy, but not the only one" asserts Christine Ward Gailey (1987:32). It is generally agreed that until not so long ago patriarchy was *the* familial arrangement in the Western world and still is in many parts of the Third world. Some feminists maintain that it is still the order of the day in the Western world as well.

most public. That hierarchy consequently affects most aspects of the life of the individual—from family relations to childrearing practices, occupational mobility patterns, sex-role conventions, and politics. All such structures have explicit or implicit rules as to how each gender is to perform certain tasks. Indeed, many of the tasks have been designated as gender-specific, appropriate for one but not the other gender, thereby providing for a division of labor and status. In most of these structures men exercise varying degrees of dominion over women. Moreover, those structures where men are particularly dominant (such as public life) are usually accorded greater prestige and value, whereas the "women's spheres" tend to be relatively devalued. Clearly, the gender system is "a structure of great scope, complexity, and consequences in our affairs" (Connell 1985: 260) and, some would argue, its consequences work to the benefit of one gender (the male) and to the detriment of the other, whereas others would argue that it ultimately works to the detriment of both, repressing the potential of both.

The written and unwritten, official and unofficial norms of the gender systems pervade all institutional structures, thereby limiting the options available to women and restricting their capacity to control their own lives. "Individuals make choices but institutional patterns shape the alternatives and make one choice more likely than another" (Epstein 1988: 99). These constraints, rather than women's preferences or skills, explain most of the ways that women's behavior differs from that of men or why, in the words of Professor Higgins, "a woman can't be more like a man." If, for example, more women than men are found in the "nurturing" or "helping professions" (such as nursing), the explanation probably derives from the career options open to women who were asked to combine training for a career with the expectation that they would eventually engage in full-time parenthood. The explanation is not necessarily in women's biologically more "nurturant" temperaments. Or, if women are less likely to assert themselves in decision-making groups, this behavior can probably be attributed to women's being less frequently located high enough in the organizational structure to make such assertive behavior appropriate. As Kanter (1977a: 159) demonstrated, in *Men and Women of the Corporation*, much of what is frequently cited as evidence of female limitations or inferiorities "can more profitably be viewed as more universal human responses to blocked opportunities . . . opportunity does indeed shape behavior"; or, to put it another way, it is important to keep in mind when "assessing sex differences [that] a distinction must be made between what men and women *can* do . . . , and what they *do* do in situations that provide greater choice among options" (Deaux 1987: 295). To fail to examine how social structures, including the opportunity structure, directly or indirectly constrain people's choices and thereby affect their sense of themselves and their self-worth is to ignore the realities of the male and female experience.[17] In other words, gender relations have to be conceptualized as institutionally defined power relations and, in most cases, they constitute relations among unequals.

These days we are living in a transitional period (at least in some parts of the world) in which gender relationships seem to be in the process of undergoing major changes and where the value of some of the traditional norms governing these relationships has come into question. But it is also a period of uneven change where old patterns of thought and habit persist alongside newer, less traditional ones. This state of affairs invariably gives rise to doubts and ambivalence if not outright anxiety, particularly among those who stand to lose from changes. Even those who stand to gain from it, however, cannot escape the heavy heritage of the past. As the following chapters show, the New Jersey women we interviewed, though welcoming many changes in the gender system, at times questioned the costs most changes exact of them. The male participants seemed even more dubious. Much may seem different today in the world of gender relations than it was twenty-five years ago; "substantial political, social, and economic transformations have certainly taken place in the period between 1964 and the present, [yet] it is possible to exaggerate their depth and to believe that they have eradicated all inequities. The truth, in fact, is more complex" (Graubard 1987: v).

To summarize: Gender relations are here conceptualized as institutionally defined—they represent ongoing relations among unequals because gender is not exclusively an attribute of individuals but constitutes a relation of power. Two facets of this relation call for systematic analysis: (1) how men and women *perceive* the relationship, and (2) how they go about *enacting* it.

Gender and Feelings of Relative Deprivation

All societies are and probably always have been inegalitarian, although they differ from one another in the degree to which this is the case and in which groups are disadvantaged and advantaged. We know of no society of the past in which women have had political power equal to that of men, and in all of them women's economic and social power was also arguably less than that of men. Today, too, in every society of which we

17. Sapiro and Farah's (1981) study of female delegates to the national party conventions showed that, although they were deeply concerned about politics and policy issues, they usually could not see themselves as running for political office. Rather, they saw their role as helping the right men getting elected.

know, women are disadvantaged in these realms when compared with men. Stating that women as a group are disadvantaged, however, does not mean that the women involved necessarily *view themselves* as disadvantaged. Disadvantage is in the eyes of the beholder. What the observer may designate as deprivation may not be so conceived by the person herself and vice versa. Much of any actor's perception is probably also influenced by her expectations for the self and by the person or group she chooses for comparison. The sense of deprivation is relative, not absolute. "People's attitudes toward social inequalities seldom correlate strictly with the facts of their own position. Dissatisfaction with the system of privileges and rewards in a society is never felt in even proportion to the degree of inequality to which various members are subject" (Runciman 1966: 3).

Prior to the 1960s, dissatisfaction "with the system of privileges and rewards" did not characterize the vast majority of American women. Among the women of the 1940s and 1950s, with some exceptions to be sure, it was not customary to think of themselves as belonging to a relatively disadvantaged group. Among the exceptions was Helen Hacker who, in a by-now classic article, maintained that compared with men, women had to be characterized as members of a minority, analogous to other disadvantaged minorities. But she also noted (1951: 516) that other women did not share her assessment; that they harbored no resentment and were willing to "accept the dominant group's conception of them"; so much so that "[m]any 'sophisticated' women are retreating from emancipation" (1951: 516). And so long as many women did not compare their rewards with those claimed by men because they believed men and women were differentially endowed, with women less suited for typically male pursuits, including the exercise of power, unequal treatment seemed justified, and they were not inclined to consider themselves to be relatively deprived or the object of discrimination. Some even welcomed unequal treatment because they attached great importance to the support, especially the financial support, of male partners and valued it above gaining equal status with men.[18] And, as Hacker so pointedly concluded, when a "woman does not wish

18. Kathleen Gerson (1985) documents that women whose chances of earning an adequate income on their own were slim showed the least inclination to resent male privileges and showed the most apprehension of divorce. Some commentators have gone so far as to attribute antifeminism to this sense of insecurity and apprehension. Some commentators, for example, attributed the defeat of the ERA, among other reasons, to women's fear of losing the financial support they currently receive, such as alimony, child support, etc.

for the rights and duties of men . . . the person does not regard [herself] as an object of discrimination" (1951: 506).

By the 1960s, however, the number of women "retreating from emancipation" began to decline steadily, and the number of women who regarded themselves "as an object of discrimination" grew substantially. Many reasons accounted for this attitudinal change. Women's massive entrance into the labor force afforded them the opportunity to compare the privileges and rewards granted men with those accorded themselves and caused many to conclude, in the words of one of the participants in our study, that they were being "shortchanged." The second American Women's Movement, founded during this same period, further enhanced women's sense of being shortchanged and, even more important, helped raise their consciousness to the point that they became aware of the fundamental injustice of the current gender arrangements. Consequently, many women's notions of themselves and the rights to which they felt entitled underwent profound transformations. By the time our study was begun, the transformation was nearly complete in that a majority of women no longer was willing to accept "the dominant group's conception of themselves" as a group inferior to and less competent than men.

Theories of relative deprivation are well suited to explain the nature of such transformations. They address the issue of feeling "shortchanged," the conditions under which such feelings are most likely to arise, and the different forms they are apt to take. For that reason, the analysis which follows will lean heavily on these theories. The concept of relative deprivation, especially as it has been developed by Runciman (1966), denotes a subjective feeling state and not necessarily a person's objective state of deprivation. It involves a process of comparison, people feel disadvantaged in relation to others; they compare the rewards they or their group receive to those received by others they deem no more deserving.[19] If they come up short in this comparison process, they feel relatively deprived. To reach that conclusion, at least three preconditions have to be met: (1) the individual has to be in a position to make the comparison; (2) the individual has to feel entitled to receive the same rewards as the comparison other and to have no cause to blame herself for not obtaining them, and (3) the rewards have to be

19. People may compare the treatment they receive with that received by others in the same group, or it may be a comparison of one's own group treatment with that received by other groups. Not all comparisons need involve others. The comparison can refer to oneself, perhaps to a time at which one felt more advantaged. T. Robert Gurr (1970) lists conditions which may elicit feelings of relative deprivation that do not necessarily involve comparisons with other people or other groups.

desired by the individual, what F. J. Crosby (1982) labeled the attractiveness factor.[20] When these three preconditions have been met, the person feels relatively deprived. Because theories of relative deprivation focus on issues of entitlement or, rather, issues of the subjective sense of entitlement, they help explain why women had been relatively quiescent for so long and, second, why over the last few decades they have begun to reframe issues of male/female relations in terms of equity and entitlement. Women's earlier absence from the public sphere afforded them too few opportunities to compare their situation with that of men and to discover whether they were entitled to receive the same rewards as men and to determine whether they desired such rewards. The preconditions for feeling relatively deprived thus were not met. Once, however, women did make these comparisons, which frequently came along with their entrance into the labor market, and decided they desired and were entitled to the same opportunities, privileges, and rewards men were said to enjoy, the preconditions for feeling relatively deprived were met.

Feelings of relative deprivation, the theory suggests, are not without consequences. No one who *believes* to have been deprived and/or discriminated against, argues Runciman (1966), is likely to feel indifferent about it. Feelings of unfair deprivation thus have the potential to give rise to anger and can even lead to overt acts of protest. In the eyes of some theorists, the very feeling of deprivation is a form of anger. But theorists also maintain that it does not follow automatically that anger will be expressed openly, especially under conditions where expressing anger may incur heavy costs, disapproval, or even retaliation. Expressing anger is particularly problematic for women since they have long operated under the impression that society considers venting anger to be unbecoming to women's "gentler nature." In the case of women, it is, therefore, particularly difficult to decide whether silence represents a genuine absence of anger or just reluctance to acknowledge it openly, and perhaps even to oneself.[21]

20. These three preconditions by no means exhaust the nature of the theoretical contribution and reconceptualization Crosby has brought to discussions of relative deprivation. I stress them here because—as will become clear later—they are particularly heuristic for understanding women's reactions. More recently (1986), Crosby, Muehrer, and Loewenstein have sought to document that a two-factor model (composed of wanting x and feeling entitled to it) performs just about as well as most of the more elaborate models.

21. Even that private or internal sense of grievance gets inhibited at times, as when people acknowledge their group's disadvantaged status but assert never to have been personally discriminated against, perhaps in order to escape the hurt of feeling victimized (Crosby 1982; Sigel and Burnbauer 1989).

Other considerations also enter into the willingness to express anger or act upon it, among them one's estimate of the likelihood that demands for redress can be met. As Runciman cautions us: "The impossibility of remedy can inhibit action without inhibiting a sense of grievance. We must beware of confusing acquiescence with contentment" (1966: 26). Conversely, the likelihood that remedies are attainable might enhance impatience with deprivation and encourage voicing resentment over demands not yet met. Several theorists (Folger 1986; Morris et al. 1989; Pettigrew 1964 and 1967; Runciman 1966) have paid particular attention to the possibility for amelioration and argue that the likelihood that anger will come to the fore is greatest precisely at the moment when the situation has begun to improve, or when the individual is of the opinion that future amelioration is possible. Anger without prospect of redress may be too costly to the self/and or to the group.[22] For example, Morris et al. (1989), in a study of the Civil Rights Movement, commented how with urbanization and diminished public resistance to civil rights, the prospects for success for the Civil Rights Movement brightened; with that, black expressions of resentment over discrimination became more overt, widespread, and forceful. Some would maintain, as de Tocqueville had already noted over two hundred years ago, that long tolerated deprivations become subjectively intolerable once the prospects for improvement brighten.

Runciman's and Crosby's conceptualizations about relative deprivation—discussed here only sketchily—are, of course, but two approaches to a by now well-developed school of thought—variously labeled relative deprivation theory, equity theory, or theories of social comparisons (Stouffer et al 1949; Davis 1959; Pettigrew 1964 and 1967; Gurr 1970; Folger 1986).[23] Although scholars in these fields vary among themselves in focus and emphasis, they agree on the centrality of entitlement. If a person feels entitled to certain values denied to him or her but which another, allegedly no more worthy than himself or

22. T. Robert Gurr (1970), however, held to an opposite opinion, namely, that anger would erupt when no improvement seemed likely. But Gurr's work deals less with individual discontent and more with national, macro phenomena. R. G. Folger (1986), on the other hand, asserted that anger will diminish or disappear when the prospects for amelioration seem bright.

23. For example, the 4th Ontario Symposium was entitled *Relative Deprivation and Social Comparison* and began with the following three sentences: "This book is about relative deprivation. It is also about social comparison. Although these topics have distinct histories in social psychology, they are conceptually similar in many important ways" (Olson, Herman, and Zanna 1986: 1).

herself, does possess, the person will feel deprived relative to the other and become angered or resentful. Unfair allocations, some maintain, become particularly grievous when they derive not from individual merit but from group membership. Denying equal treatment to equals simply on the basis of their membership in a group probably provokes more anger than any other form of discrimination. Individual-oriented cultures, such as ours, are particularly scornful of group-based discrimination because they subscribe (or at least pay lip service) to the notion of meritocracy.

Theories of relative deprivation distinguish between a sense of individual or personal deprivation (that one does not receive one's due compared with what others in the group receive—a sentiment categorized as "egoistical" relative deprivation) and the sense that one's group is not receiving its fair share ("collective" deprivation), even though the individual group member may be personally exempt from the general deprivation. This distinction is particularly useful when studying gender relations because it permits the individual woman not to feel personally disadvantaged and yet to recognize the group's disadvantaged status, to attribute it to systematic, group-directed deprivation, and to be angered over it. Runciman held that such a sense of collective deprivation is far more politically significant than individual deprivation because of its potential for leading to political action and that it plays "the largest part in the transformation of an existing structure of social inequalities" Runciman (1966: 34).

However, the willingness to become politically engaged in order to ameliorate one's group's relative deprivation is not independent of the strength of one's identification with the deprived group, a point less stressed in theories of relative deprivation but of vital importance when considering women. One objective of our inquiry is to discover what impact women's recognition of their deprived status has on their identification with women as a group. As we know, so far only a minority of women has shown much interest in actively working to bring about the above "transformation of the existing structure of social inequalities," much as they may resent the existence of these very inequalities. My aim in observing the New Jersey women is to discover what importance their membership in the gender group has for them. Is it true, as some have suggested (Gurin, Miller, and Gurin 1980; Gurin 1985 and 1987), that women as a group lack the sense of identification with their group so characteristic of other disadvantaged groups, or does group identification, as I will suggest, take on a different contour and priority for them than it does for minorities, but is present, nevertheless? Rather than establish my own or any other researcher's standards on how to define identification with the group, I shall let the participants themselves describe the ways in which they identify and feel close to women as a group. Only this way, I believe, can we come close to comprehending how women's views of themselves and their status in society have changed over the past decades.

2

METHODOLOGY

It is more important to ask the right questions than to find the right answers.
—Kathleen Gerson

To a large extent, the kind of questions social scientists seek to answer dictate the type of method they must use. Often that choice is a difficult one, forcing them to choose between depth of insight into the lives and minds of the few versus generalizability about the minds and lives of the many. Ideally, social scientists would like to accomplish both goals; they want to know what the population-at-large (or a given segment of the population) thinks about an important issue, but they also want to know a great deal about each individual and how she or he comes to hold these thoughts or sentiments. Understanding individuals becomes particularly crucial when the issue is a relatively novel, perhaps controversial, one on which people's reactions and how they arrived at those reactions is not yet well known. Women's liberation is a case in point in that it confronts people with novel formulations of an age-old issue.

In these circumstances, the political scientist invariably faces a dilemma: which goals must be sacrificed or must take second place—generalizability or depth of insight? What method, what strategy of investigation is likely to yield the most illuminating and valid results? Shall one emulate anthropologists, go into the field and observe what men and women actually say and do as they interact with each other? Or should one perhaps conduct lengthy, in-depth interviews with just a few persons in order to reach a fuller, richer understanding of the ways in which they frame vital issues?

If the researcher is less concerned with generalizability and more with understanding the complexity and depth of subjects' feelings and cognition, some type of qualitative research will probably be her or his method of choice.[1] If, on the other hand, the goal is to discover what a

1. Yet another possibility for gaining much information about relatively few people would be to conduct an experiment with college students in order to learn how young

24

representative sample of the public thinks, other strategies have to be adopted; strategies which may force the investigator to forsake depth of insight and richness of detail for the sake of generalizability. For decades now, the method of choice for those desiring to make statements about the population-at-large has been the sample survey, most recently the telephone sample survey. Needless to say, whatever method is selected, a trade-off is always involved. "Anything that a technique does notably well is done, at least partially, at the expense of other things that can only be done poorly" (Morgan 1988: 20).

CHOICE OF INVESTIGATIVE TECHNIQUES

This study employs both strategies, qualitative and quantitative, hoping thereby to enhance our understanding of this relatively unexplored topic. Since our goal was to discover how American adults, especially American women, perceive the current status of gender relations and how they feel about those relations, collecting opinions from a large sample had to be the primary consideration. Consequently, the decision was made by the principal investigators to collect part of our information from a sample survey, which we designed and which was conducted by telephone with a representative population.[2] The enterprise, however, does differ from the usual survey in one significant aspect. The telephone survey was preceded by observations of discussions in a series of moderated focus groups.[3] The focus groups were held before the telephone sample survey so that group discussions could provide insights into people's feelings, which are difficult to access in standard telephone interviews and which, in addition, could guide the questionnaire construction. The need to gain this type of insight was particularly urgent for our project because thoughts and feelings about gender relations tend to be highly personal, complex, and often ambiguous. People at times are unsure or ambivalent about their own feelings, especially during these periods of transition when many once-familiar norms and customs are being questioned. Moreover, people may be hesitant to reveal over the phone to an unknown person (the interviewer) the deeper realities of their experiences and the meanings they attach to those ex-

---

men and women will act under conditions controlled by the experimenting scientist. Here the underlying assumption is that generalization from this sample is warranted because of the imposed controls.

2. Selection was not completely random. For criteria, see Appendix B.

3. To the best of my knowledge, focus groups in conjunction with sample surveys had not been used in strictly academic research prior to our 1985 survey. In the meantime, they seem to have come into wider use (see Conover, Crewe, and Searing [1991] and Delli Carpini and Williams [1991]).

periences. Hence our decision to use focus groups prior to conducting a telephone survey.

SURVEYS PROBLEMS AND OUR RESEARCH

Recently, sample surveys have encountered considerable criticism (Biemer et al. 1991; Tanur 1992; S. Traugott 1993), some of which have particular relevance for our research and, therefore, deserve reiteration here. Interviews, and not only telephone interviews, can be intimidating, especially when the respondent feels called upon to report on feelings she or he would rather not reveal, especially to a stranger. The constraining format of sample surveys with their highly structured questions (as is the custom in most telephone surveys) poses additional problems for researchers and respondents alike. D. W. Stewart and P. N. Shamdasoui (1990: 263), for example, assert that the "processed or packaged version" of sample surveys frequently impedes understanding "the meanings of women's experience." Choices made by a respondent from a list of alternatives proffered by an interviewer may offer, at best, only limited insight into her thoughts and, at worst, may actually be misleading.[4] Moreover, because the choices are defined for the interviewee by the researcher rather than by the interviewee herself, they may not represent any of the options she might ever have contemplated on her own. Even the longest, most inclusive list of choices is bound to omit some the respondent would have wanted to adopt. In addition, "studies which rely exclusively on close-ended questions . . . cannot tap the underlying structure of these attitudes as well as studies which employ a more diverse measurement strategy" (Feldman and Zaller 1988: 25).

Another limitation of the survey method is that, for a variety of reasons, among them considerations of time and expense, telephone surveys usually do not probe the meaning behind a respondent's answer.[5] When the nature of our research objective concerns a set of relatively new, changing and contested beliefs, such as the adoption or rejection of a gender perspective on male/female relations, this restriction constitutes a serious limitation. We are interested not in an interviewee's

4. Jennifer Hochschild, who rejected large-scale sample surveys in favor of intensive interviewing of a few respondents, explained her choice in the following manner: "It is easy to describe simple statements, even if not at all easy to analyze or explain them; survey researchers do an excellent job at this task. But given the opportunity, people do not make simple statements; they shade, modulate, deny, retract, or just grind to a halt in frustration. These manifestations of uncertainty are just as meaningful and interesting as the clear, definitive statements of a belief system" (1981: 238).

5. This, of course, need not be the case, and many excellent surveys do provide ample probes. But, for the reasons indicated above, it has become fairly standard in major national political surveys to feature no or relatively few probes.

words, but in the meaning she seeks to convey with them. Yet, in many standard interviews, the interviewer accepts a respondent's answer as it is offered and rarely is instructed to explore its meaning. Subsequently, when analyzing the data, the researcher has access only to a set of answers whose meaning is opaque.[6] Nor does a researcher know whether an opinion quickly expressed over the phone represents an opinion long held by the respondent or just an unreflective response manufactured on the spot in order to oblige the interviewer. Consequently, researchers must guard against the tendency to equate quickly tossed off answers with stable, meaningful convictions (Delli Carpini and Williams 1991; Zaller and Feldman 1992). A survey response, though truthful at the moment it is given, does not necessarily constitute an opinion.[7] As the literature on attitude stability has shown, verbal statements on a survey may represent nothing so much as a fleeting thought quite unrelated to a respondent's other, more deeply anchored values. Delli Carpini and Williams were cognizant of this hazard when they wrote that researchers, in the process of retrieving opinions, must guard that they do not "create the opinion, alter the fixed opinion, or create the illusion of an opinion" (1991: 3). Finally, researchers have to face the perennial problem in communications, that is, what is the meaning the interviewee attributes to the question. Santa Traugott comments on this phenomenon: "We instruct survey interviewers not to deviate from what is on the printed page. We train interviewers in excruciating detail how to answer requests from the respondent for clarification of question meaning. Often, interviewers are only allowed to say, 'Whatever it means to you.' We do this in hopes that we are thereby providing a standard stimulus" (1993: 223). But what do the answers mean when the interviewer's identical question provides different stimuli for different people?[8]

Although these issues constitute serious limitations if one wants to

6. In subsequent chapters, especially chapter 4, I will illustrate this point with examples from our telephone survey. On several occasions, the telephone answers to some of our structured questions would have left us uninformed, or misinformed, had we not had the focus group discussions on the same subject to fall back on.

7. To guard against that contingency, we introduced a few open-ended questions in order to hear how a respondent framed some of the issues with which we were most concerned. The desire to cover a great variety of topics prevented us from introducing a greater number of such open-ended questions.

8. I am vividly reminded of one interview I monitored. The interviewer read to a female respondent a question from the Michigan National Election Study regarding closeness to women as a group. As I listened, I realized that what the respondent understood by that question was not "women as a group" but "lesbians." (The exact wording of the question can be found in Appendix A and refers to five different groups to which a woman might feel close.)

understand how a respondent relates to a topic, if one wishes to generalize one's findings (even with caution) to the population-at-large, one probably has no choice but to conduct an opinion survey with an appropriately large and representative sample of the population.[9] In contrast to focus group discussions where participants on occasion tend to persevere on one rather narrow aspect of a given topic because it might be of particular interest to the group,[10] sample surveys have the important advantage of affording the investigator the opportunity to inquire into many different aspects of the topic crucial to the research objective under consideration, thereby casting a much wider informational net than focus group participants might be inclined to cast. For example, the female focus group participants in our study hardly ever discussed their ideas about the relationship between politics and women's status. Yet that was a topic of great interest to the researchers since we are political scientists. The telephone survey permitted us to include questions aimed specifically at politics and political participation. The survey method also gives each respondent an equal chance to be heard, whereas in a group setting one or a few individuals may dominate the discussion. One additional great asset of sample surveys is that they have the capacity to collect much detailed factual information about each individual respondent, which then allows the researcher to analyze how each respondent's various opinions "hang together" with his or her other opinions. In this way, one can judge how constrained the belief system which guides a respondent's attitudes and behaviors actually is. Such analysis becomes especially crucial when dealing with a subject which is still sufficiently novel and/or controversial, so that it has not yet become part of the mainstream research enterprise. Finally, sample surveys routinely collect much demographic information on each individual (such as income and age) that are not suitable to raise in focus group discussions but which may be vital for understanding the context from which attitudes and opinions arise.

THE PROS AND CONS OF FOCUS GROUPS

Once we had made the decision to supplement the survey with qualitative data, focus group observations became a parsimonious choice, per-

9. One cannot generalize what men and women think about today's gender relations from a conversation with a taxi driver; nor can one generalize from the rich and vibrant depth-interviews some political scientists have conducted with a few respondents (J. Hochschild 1981; Lane 1962). Some social scientists suggest reaching the generalizability objective by combining many small studies into a meta-analysis (Unger 1990).

10. This perseverance is, of course, significant in and of itself, but it does restrict the scope of information accessible to the researcher.

mitting us to observe how a fairly large number of people went about discussing the topics of concern to us. Focus groups' observations have in common with other qualitative techniques that they offer "insights which go beyond the surface. The qualitative research approach provides 'feel,' 'texture,' a sense of intensity, and a degree of nuance" (Center for Public Interest Polling 1990: 1). Observing focus group discussions is by now a fairly standard practice in many phases of market research. The mass media also increasingly rely on them in order to supplement their news reportage and as "a technique for humanizing a political story" (M. Traugott 1992: 1). By the end of the 1992 presidential campaign, excerpts from focus group conversations had become so commonplace that the media featured them almost as prominently as poll results. But the practice has as yet not gained wide acceptance in political science research, even among "academic people who make a serious study of research methodology" (Center for Public Interest Polling 1990: iii). Because they are still a relatively unfamiliar tool, we will discuss here at some length their nature, strengths, and weaknesses.

What Is a Focus Group?

"Focus group is one of those elusive terms everyone has heard, but nobody defines quite the same way" (Lydecker 1986). The term generally refers to a small group of people (eight to twelve individuals) led through an open-ended, in-depth discussion of a given topic by a group moderator who, in a more or less nondirective manner, seeks to elicit responses from as many participants as possible but carefully avoids being judgmental, hoping thereby to elicit a variety of opinions and attitudes. The main topic to be discussed has usually been decided beforehand by the investigator, but the group itself decides what aspects of the topic will be discussed and in what ways. Group members interact with each other instead of with the interviewer, and it is the group, not the researcher, which defines the agenda and frames it to its own tastes. This method "effectively removes the researcher's perspective" (Morgan 1988: 18) and therefore reduces the researcher's opportunity to specify the parameters of the discussion.

Focus groups provide face-to-face encounters which, when congenial, lend themselves to disclosing feelings about shared experiences that women might not ordinarily reveal to a stranger. In several of our focus groups, participants spontaneously commented on this phenomenon, saying how easy they found it to talk to each other about common experiences. The discovery that other individuals have similar experiences or reactions probably frees individuals from inhibitions they might feel when interviewed by a stranger whether over the phone or in person. The setting thus may facilitate the expression of emotions, such as anger, which under other circumstances women are known to be very reluctant to voice. One of the strengths of well conducted focus groups is precisely that they make such attitudes accessible. I was, for example, quite unprepared for the anger many women in our groups expressed over certain allegedly typical male characteristics. Our telephone interviewees also revealed some anger, but nothing like the amount unleashed in the focus groups. I doubt that even a telephone interview structured precisely to trigger the kind of issues women found most upsetting in our focus groups would generate the kinds of emotions that emerged in the groups.

In addition, group discussions may have brought to the fore in one or the other participant thoughts and feelings about experiences she might have forgotten or even repressed deliberately because they had proven painful. In that situation, focus groups are more appropriate for gaining insight into sensitive topics, such as gender relations, than are structured interviews, especially telephone surveys. The highly nondirective type of focus group we conducted may have, quite inadvertently, had an effect not too different from so-called consciousness-raising groups which have served to "validate the new experience of anger and its expression" (Tavris 1982: 246).

Krueger describes how and why a focus group works:

> The focus group interview works because it taps into human tendencies. Attitudes and perceptions . . . are developed in part by interaction with other people. We are a product of our environment and are influenced by people around us. A deficiency of mail and telephone surveys and even face-to-face interviews is that those methods assume that individuals really do know how they feel. A further assumption is that individuals form opinions in isolation. Both of these assumptions have presented problems for the researchers. People may need to listen to opinions of others before they form their own personal viewpoints. (1988: 23)

A successful focus group constitutes a dynamic interaction among individuals (who probably have never met before) which stimulates in-depth discussion of a topic of mutual interest to them and may provoke a variety of viewpoints and perspectives. "The emphasis is on a summary way of representing the perceived world . . . From this point of view, what focus groups do is treat these perceptions and their representations as the basis for a discussion among a set of participants whose schema and perspectives may be either subtly or wildly different . . . [and their] cognitive processes are revealed through interaction in ways that it would not be possible to observe otherwise" (Morgan 1988: 27).

Same-gender focus groups may be particularly useful for studying gender-related sentiments since women tend to behave differently in mixed-gender than in all-female groups. Various studies have shown that women behave in more stereotypic ways, that is, in ways they consider to be sex-role appropriate, when men are present in the group than they do in an all-female group (Ashmore and Del Boca 1986). "Many, perhaps most, sex-related differences emerge in some environments but not in others. The presence of other people seems to have an important effect" (Unger 1990: 115–16). Mixed-gender groups may, therefore, inhibit revealing feelings and thoughts, especially when the participant thinks her thoughts are not sex-role appropriate. All-female and nondirective focus groups, on the other hand, may provide an opportunity to reveal such feelings and thereby offer good insights into what about today's gender relations most bothers women, what makes them angry, and why they frequently are reluctant to let their male colleagues, friends, or even their husbands know that they are angry or hurt.[11]

Finally, focus groups conducted before questionnaire construction offer several other advantages. First, the observer learns of participants' experiences and reactions which may never have occurred to him or her, and such vital information, therefore, would never have found its way into an interview schedule the researcher might have designed. Unlike the sample survey with its rigid schedule, which both interviewer and interviewee are expected to follow, focus group discussions can linger on a given topic which matters to participants. Such a topic may have great relevance for the participant's everyday life experiences but they may not have occurred to the researcher, or the researcher may have misjudged their importance in respondent's lives. In short, freed of the constraints of a prestructured interview schedule, group members can set the agenda and redirect, whenever necessary, the thrust of the researcher's initial perspective. In a successfully directed exploratory group discussion, the topic under discussion will have been stipulated by the researcher but the approach to it—how it is conceptualized—will emerge from the group. The group, rather than the researcher, shapes the agenda. The research thereby comes closer to the reality as it is experienced by the subjects. This is one of the major advantages of focus groups. As one well-known focus group expert summarizes it: "One reason to prefer experiences is that even self-reported behavior is more useful as data than are opinions

---

11. The same dynamic applies to men. R. D. Ashmore and F. K. Del Boca (1986) offer numerous instances where men act differently in all-male groups than in mixed ones.

that have an unknown basis in behavior. I also prefer experiences because a discussion of them produces a livelier group dynamic—people are more than happy to compare their different experiences. Focus groups are useful when it comes to investigating *what* participants think, but they excel at uncovering *why* participants think as they do" (Morgan 1988: 25).

The focus group format yields additional benefits beyond learning how participants frame a topic. First, it sensitizes the researcher (frequently by observing the group behind a one-way mirror) to the words and phrases citizens use when talking about the topic. Second, if the subsequent telephone survey succeeds in capturing the vernacular and situations with which many interviewees are apt to be familiar, the validity of the survey instrument should be greatly enhanced. The third advantage to be derived from focus groups is that they can also serve other research objectives, such as generating hypotheses. The hypotheses can be developed based on careful scrutiny of the content and feeling tone of the discussions and can then be tested by means of quantitative data, usually in the form of sample surveys.

But focus groups also have their drawbacks. The most obvious is the inability to generalize from them to the population at large. No matter how carefully members may have been recruited and how many groups one may have organized, focus groups can never represent the rich variety of people and opinions that a more extensive telephone interview can tap. Focus group members can never be considered a surrogate for the general public, no matter how carefully and randomly the researcher selected the groups. "Using focus groups to learn about the full range of experiences and perspectives in a broad population can be a fool's errand" (Morgan 1988: 44).

The great potential of focus groups, namely the very gain in frankness that can be achieved nonetheless is also fraught with hazards. At times such emotionally charged small group meetings can create an atmosphere in which a certain mutual outbidding—an "I can top this" phenomenon—takes place. Each woman, wanting to identify with other participants, may try to recall that she also had been exposed previously to injustices similar to those someone else just recounted. Perhaps her recollection may exaggerate just how angry she felt at the time or still feels. Rather than constituting a conscious effort at deception, this dynamic more often indicates a contagion effect which might have taken place in a group of this nature. This is not meant to imply that these women invented their anger, but to suggest that conversations on topics which bear a certain emotional freight may within a group session cause participants to attach more significance to the topic than they ordinarily do in the course of their everyday lives. Group contagion is a possible, though by no means inevitable, side-effect in focus group interviewing. It deserves further scrutiny.

Very nondirective focus groups, such as ours, have another potential liability that merits attention. The female participants were quite willing to disclose a specific situation or experience which had brought forth their resentment. But because of the nondirective nature of our enterprise, in which the participants rather than the moderator chose the situations they wished to discuss, the researcher cannot know whether the situations that emerge in the group discussion are those most likely to provoke anger, whether they reflect a representative range of experiences with which participants have to cope or whether they occur frequently or only occasionally. Hence it is difficult, for example, to draw firm conclusions from a focus group as to the role that the experience of discrimination plays in a woman's everyday life.

Another problem arises in the researcher's selection of cases for analysis. "In writing up their results, researchers seem to gravitate toward individuals who have more interesting things to say" (Feldman and Zaller 1988: 8). Consequently, they must exercise utmost caution and self-control not to be misled by the opinion of the most vocal or the most sophisticated informants. Caution also must be exercised to avoid overemphasizing the stories of those who illustrate the points the researcher wishes to make. In reporting on group conversations, one is well advised to exercise the same caution Unger (1990: 133–4) urges on psychologists: "Whose story should be told? This problem has been ignored by psychologists who tell stories about people who exemplify a point the narrator wishes to make. Such story telling leaves the reader at the mercy of the selection criteria (often unspecified and even unrecognized) of the narrator."

Because one objective in forming a focus group is to let the groups rather than the interviewer raise the topics for discussion, the group will usually ignore many topics of interest to the researcher.[12] I have already mentioned that the female focus groups yielded very little political information. Inattention to research-related topics has to be considered a major limitation of the technique. Nor can a researcher gain as much demographic information (such as income, education, religion, ethnicity, family background, and the like) about each *individual* member as is considered important for the investigation—information which is routinely and easily ascertained in a sample survey or even can

---

12. These caveats need not apply to market research, where group sessions are assembled for the purpose of giving the client detailed information about a topic or product.

be obtained during an in-depth interview.[13] Such information often is vital for exploring certain facets of a topic.

It is also important to bear in mind that the dynamics of the group process have the potential to affect and even to alter participants' initial opinions, thereby shaping them in ways that would not have occurred in "real life" situations (that is outside the confines of the focus group) and may not last much beyond the group meeting itself. Later chapters deal with that possibility, as well as with the danger that the interaction which incurs in such groups may stimulate some members to recall happenings or reactions that may have lost their relevance for the person but which in the course of the discussion acquire renewed though only temporary and hence misleading significance. Thus, what I earlier characterized as a special focus group advantage, namely the potential for recalling forgotten or repressed events, also can prove to be a detriment. This is one more reason for using this technique with proper caution.

Notwithstanding their limitations, our focus group observations greatly enriched our understanding of men's and women's perceptions of gender relations. In fact, we found them to "deliver" much more than we had anticipated. Conceived of originally mainly as guides to questionnaire construction, it soon became obvious that they had an independent contribution to make. By choosing two different "measurement strategies"—one quantitative and one qualitative—we were able to capitalize on the respective strengths of each and to compensate somewhat for the weaknesses of either. "Each . . . reflects a choice between defensible alternatives" (Stewart and Shamdasoui 1990: 263). And, as stated earlier, no one methodology is perfect; each constitutes a trade-off. But combining more than one methodology in the same research design can at least partially compensate for each method's shortcomings. Many researchers actually "believe that combining focus groups with mail or telephone surveys covers all the bases: The focus group offers depth of insight, while the quantitative research ensures that those insights can reasonably be projected to the whole membership" (Lydecker 1986: 3). Although we certainly do not believe that we were able to cover "all the bases," we do believe the combination of techniques greatly facilitated the conduct and interpretation of our telephone survey. Our focus group observations thus served two main purposes: (1) before going into the field with a sample survey, we used

13. It is possible, of course, to collect such information before or even during the group session, but there are problems connected with that strategy. We were fortunate in that respect because the women from the focus groups had previously participated in a statewide sample survey for the Eagleton Institute of Politics. Consequently, we had a good deal of information on each focus group member.

them to assist us with item development, and (2) after the surveys were completed, we used the focus group observations for interpretative purposes when analyzing ambiguous survey responses. During questionnaire construction, we relied on them to alert us to include issues which we otherwise might have paid scant attention. For example, often enough group discussions focused on the lack of respect men accorded women's opinions. This lead us to include in the interview schedule a few questions dealing with respect. Another way in which group observation proved helpful was in suggesting to us both the language people used when talking about gender and the mental framework from which they approached the topic. While it may not have helped us to get completely into the heads of our respondents, it certainly made the process easier than if we had had to rely on telephone responses alone. After completing the telephone survey, we drew on what we had learned from focus group observations whenever the telephone respondents' answers perplexed us.

The focus groups did not, however, serve only an auxiliary function to the telephone survey. Although that was our original intention, the richness of information and insights the groups provided soon convinced me to assign them a far more prominent place in the total enterprise. Listening to men and women in the groups actually helped shape my sensitivity to the role the topic played in the daily lives of the public. I felt as though I became privy to some of their frustrations as well as gratifications, and, most of all, I learned what mattered to them and what did not when they thought about gender. Consequently, as I analyzed and reanalyzed the data, and began writing the book, the focus groups began to receive equal billing with the telephone survey. By now, the book is as much about the focus group members, whose faces, voices, and gestures I still recall, as it is about the voices of the many interviewees to whom I listened on the telephone.

To summarize the rationale for our choice of research methodologies: We used focus groups "as an idea generating method, as a preliminary step in developing a quantitative study, and as a follow-up step to help understand the findings of a quantitative study" (The Center for Public Interest Polling 1990: 1).[14] Above all, we used them to get a better "feel" for male and female reactions than survey results can provide. As Santa Traugott (1993: 224) so tellingly comments: "We

14. The administration of the selection procedure as well as the write-up of the procedure which we adopted was carried out by Nancy V. Whelchel. Many of the details mentioned in the following pages were adapted from Whelchel's (1992) doctoral dissertation "Feminist Consciousness and Sympathetic Feminism: Sex Differences in Origin and Effects." I wish to thank Dr. Whelchel for permitting me to paraphrase some of her descriptions.

know survey respondents only in summary statistical fashion; . . . It is all too easy to forget that the quantities plugged into equations result from complex human interactions." We were determined not to forget these human interactions. But we also wanted to learn about a wider range of relevant topics than the focus groups had chosen to discuss, and we wanted to learn it from a genuinely representative sample. To meet that objective, we resorted to the telephone survey. It permitted us to learn what the adult population of the state thinks and feels about a wide variety of topics related to the change in women's status in particular and about the nature of gender relations in general.

CONDUCTING THE INVESTIGATION: FORMAT FOR THE FOCUS GROUPS

In the fall and winter of 1985, our team of researchers solicited the opinions of 650 New Jersey residents on gender relations, 600 through a telephone survey and 50 through focus groups. First, fifty individuals were observed in six focus groups as they explored the past and present state of gender relations. Group size varied from seven to twelve participants. These groups were recruited several months prior to questionnaire construction. Each group was either all-male (two groups) or all-female. Consultation with focus-group professionals urged adoption of this strategy in order to encourage the frankest possible discussion. The experimental social psychological literature on small groups lent additional weight to that decision in that it documented that women tended to hold back more and to talk less in mixed groups than in single-sex ones (Eagly 1987). Also men and women are known to talk about different topics as well as to speak more openly in a same-gender group than in mixed-gender ones. A major consideration guiding our selection of participants was the desire to reach as wide a spectrum of participants as possible, especially among the women, in order to obtain a panorama of views, experiences, and reactions. In this we were relatively successful in that we ended up with good distributions of working-class as well as middle-class participants.[15] The groups we recruited were rather mainstream in their thinking on this explosive topic; not one of the female focus groups can be characterized as reflecting extreme views of either the Right or the Left. Their political views also reflected this tendency. Ideologically, most participants considered themselves to be fairly middle-of-the road, slightly more identified them-

---

15. Although some of our participants had very low incomes, we are not sure that we were able to recruit the very poor. Even though we offered monetary compensation for participation—as well as transportation when requested—we don't believe we reached that stratum. We also probably missed the very upper-middle-class stratum.

selves as "liberals" than as "conservatives." As is customary, women were more likely to identify as Democrats than as Republicans.[16]

Recruitment was handled by the Center for Public Interest Polling of the Eagleton Institute of Politics at Rutgers University, which periodically polls the public on a great variety of public issues. Our focus group participants were drawn from the Center's list of previously polled respondents.[17] When respondents were contacted, they were not informed that the group discussion would emphasize issues related to gender relations.[18] Most, we have reason to believe, assumed it would involve inquiries into a host of public issues, similar to those to which they had reacted in previous telephone interviews. The first female group we recruited was a large (twelve members) and heterogenous one whose members varied greatly in age. Our observation of that group lead us to conclude that very young women (that is, those under thirty-five years of age) who had come of age when the message of the Women's Movement had become quite widely accepted varied sufficiently from the rest of the female population to suggest the advisability of constituting them into a separate group. As a consequence, we designed the remaining female groups to vary in age from over thirty-five to sixty. Within these groups, we took care to achieve as much diversity as possible with regard to occupation, marital status, education, religion, political party identification, and ideology.[19] For

16. In the telephone survey, 21 percent of the women considered themselves to be liberal; 21 percent conservative; 2 percent were undecided; and 57 percent considered themselves to be moderates or in-between. When this last group was asked which way they leaned, 38 percent opted for the liberal label, and 46 percent for the conservative; the rest refused to commit themselves. Thirty-six percent identified with the Democratic party; and 30 percent with the Republican. Among men, 28 percent identified as liberal and the same percentage identified as conservative. Thirty-nine percent are Republicans and 30 percent are Democrats. The political identifications of the focus group participants are almost identical to those of the telephone respondents.

17. This procedure was adopted in part to increase respondents' confidence in the sponsorship of the project—since the Center's polls tend to be well received by the public—and thereby reduce as much as possible the refusal rate. In addition, it facilitated selecting the type of respondents we needed for our enterprise. Our criterion for selection was to achieve as much variety in points-of-view as possible. Since we had their protocols from earlier interviews, we were able to make that determination, something which would have been difficult to accomplish had we engaged in completely random telephone contacts.

18. It would have been interesting to see if more or fewer people would have participated had we told them upon initial contact that the groups would focus on gender relations.

19. A comparison of the survey and focus group populations showed great similarity with respect to age and income, but focus-group participants had a higher proportion of women who had more than a high school education. However, the proportion of those who had completed college was similar.

the two all-male groups, the criterion for selection was primarily their occupational status. Because blue-collar males, especially those with less education, tend to be more traditional in their social outlook (Lane 1962; Lipset 1960; Nie, Verba, and Petrocik 1976; Terkel 1972), we chose one group composed of men in blue-collar occupations and another with men in white-collar and professional fields. The men within these groups, however, represented a diversity of ages, educational backgrounds, marital status, ideologies, etc.

All focus groups met in the evening on the Rutgers University campus in a conference room equipped with a one-way mirror and an adjoining room for observation and audio-video recording. All the groups were videotaped. The principal investigators and their staff observed each of the sessions. In addition to the audio-video records, the sessions were afterwards transcribed by professional stenographers in order to facilitate analysis.

Each of the sessions was chaired by a trained moderator of the same gender as the group. The moderator was given a brief outline of the topics we hoped the group would cover. We urged her or him to be as nondirective as possible, even if it meant that some topics on the outline would not be covered. We informed moderators to avoid obliging the group to discuss topics of interest to us but which participants found either uninteresting or irrelevant.[20] The meeting (after introductions) was opened with some discussion (suggested by the moderator) of a topic which had recently been in the news but did not deal with gender questions. Only after a brief "warm-up" period did the moderator introduce the topic of gender relations. In the female groups, the moderator never had to bring up the topic; it arose spontaneously. In the male groups, the moderator was always the one to bring it up; nor did men show much inclination to linger over this topic.

INSTRUMENT DEVELOPMENT

Prior to constructing the interview schedule for the telephone surveys, the investigators analyzed the videos from each focus group session. After repeated replays, the researchers isolated frequently recurring comments and themes. This systematic search yielded a rather unexpected finding: The themes which had struck the observers forcefully

20. We do not wish to suggest that this is the only way to conduct such groups. Depending on the purposes for which they are conducted, some moderators are asked to be considerably more directive and to follow a discussion outline more assiduously. Since our main objective was to gain insight into how people thought about the topic spontaneously, we preferred a more nondirective approach.

during the actual sessions in the observation room were not always the ones which, upon closer examination, dominated the discussions. I recall, for example, how my initial reaction to one male group was that a member with an agenda of his own had dominated the conversation and caused others to focus on that private agenda. Repeated replays and especially careful scrutiny of the transcripts disabused me of my initial impression. He neither talked as much as I had recalled nor was his theme taken up by the rest. Frequency, of course, is not the only way by which to judge a group's sentiments.[21] A frequency count, nonetheless, can serve as a useful check against first impressions. Our experience corroborates Feldman and Zaller's (1988) warning not to attribute too much representativeness to the comments of the more articulate individuals.

The themes elicited from the videos were used to develop a substantial number of the questions on the interview schedule. To these questions, we added many questions about all of those topics which had driven our research enterprise in the first place, notably those having political implications. We took care, whenever possible, to phrase the questions in language used by the focus-group participants themselves.

Two illustrations demonstrate how useful the focus group proved in this phase of survey construction. Because we were interested in questions of legitimacy, we had intended initially simply to ask those survey respondents who reported that men tended to denigrate women whether they considered this to be legally and morally illegitimate. Focus-group observations, however, convinced us that women took "such denigration" or "the unfairness of any denigration" so much for granted that they did not necessarily conceptualize the issue in terms of legitimacy, and we kept this in mind as we developed the questionnaire items. Similarly, while we initially had thought of discrimination primarily within the public context (such as in the workplace or in the political arena), the women in our groups applied the concept to a much wider and more private range of behaviors, causing us to include in the interview schedule other instances which touched on those aspects of gender relations. Without including those questions, many deeply felt reactions to discrimination would not have come to the fore and would thereby have masked the true nature of women's attitudes on the subject.[22]

21. Watching the videotapes, it became clear to me how much additional information could be gained from body language.

22. By contrast, sexual harassment—a topic which we had anticipated would come up frequently—was hardly ever mentioned. Consequently, we devoted only one direct question to it during the telephone interview.

THE SURVEY SAMPLE

In December, 600 adult New Jersey residents were interviewed over the telephone. Four hundred of these interviewees were women, 200 were men. We chose to interview twice as many women as men because our main interest lay in discovering how women visualized their role as it had evolved over the last few decades. Notwithstanding this overriding interest, we decided against an all-female sample because women's roles (new or old) do not occur in a vacuum; roles involve reciprocal relationships. Consequently, women's role perceptions and enactments must, to a large extent, depend on how men visualize them, and/or how women *believe* men visualize them. Studying women without studying men does not make sense, either from a pragmatic or a theoretical perspective.

The universe from which the sample was drawn were all adult residents in New Jersey with a telephone, listed or unlisted, who had previously participated in a survey. The sample was in keeping with the usual sampling procedure adopted for all Eagleton Institute polls (with the exception that it oversampled women) and was designed to make sure that each of the state's twenty-one counties was proportionally represented.[23] Although we make no claim that New Jersey is an exact replica of the United States, previous investigations (Zukin and Carter 1982: 216) found that "observations of New Jerseyans [are] generalizable to the nation as a whole." The *New York Times* (New Jersey section, 14 March 1993: 6) reported that "in general . . . New Jersey's demographics mirror the nation's." No claim is made that our sample constitutes an exact replica of the United States population or even of New Jersey's.

THE INTERVIEW SCHEDULE

For our purposes, obtaining a perfect replica of the New Jersey population was not nearly as important as exploring the topic in detail.[24] In order to conduct such an intensive exploration, Cliff Zukin and I, with the collaboration of Nancy Whelchel, constructed a long interview

23. "The three digit telephone exchanges serving the state were used to match telephone numbers and geographic areas. After choosing a systematic random sample of 600 exchanges, the remaining four digits were randomly selected. This procedure insures that those with unlisted or new telephone numbers were included in the target population" (Whelchel 1992).

24. Conover and Sapiro (1992), in their report to the Board of Overseer of the National Election Studies, document insightfully and incisively how much understanding of gender-related issues can be gained with the addition of a few carefully chosen questions to the standard two or three customarily asked on such surveys.

schedule dealing almost exclusively with questions of gender. All told, we asked 80 such questions of women, and 74 of men.[25] In addition, both genders were asked a dozen questions about their political orientations (the interview schedule is reproduced in Appendix A). The questionnaire was pilot-tested at the Eagleton Institute, but the final instrument was administered by a professional survey research organization firm with wide experience in conducting polls on social and sensitive issues. All but a few questions were of the structured and multiple choice variety. The few open-ended questions focused specifically on gender-related matters. The average interview lasted about thirty minutes. Given the public's growing inclination to be suspicious of interviewer's motives and even to refuse altogether to participate in surveys, we were pleasantly surprised to find most interviewees very cooperative and ready to answer even those questions on which we had anticipated encountering resistance.

We present the results from the telephone survey in the customary manner. Unless otherwise indicated, tables and text always refer to the total sample of 400 women when referring to women in general and 200 when referring to men. Because my main goal, as stated in the Introduction, was to present a profile of men's and women's views of gender relations, I have refrained from encumbering the narrative with an excess of statistical analyses, but where necessary and appropriate, tests of significance are indicated on the tables. Quantification, however, is not appropriate for reporting our focus-group findings. While I would not go so far as Axelrod (1975: 7) in asserting that "numbers do not belong in a qualitative study at any time," I think it would be particularly inappropriate in our case for two reasons: first, our focus group format was nondirective and not every member had or did express an opinion on every given topic that someone brought up. What if, for instance, we reported that three women in a group of ten expressed themselves in favor of comparable pay, and the remaining women did not participate in that discussion? Does a report of that number imply that the seven agreed, disagreed, or had no opinion on the subject? What does such a count really tell us? Second, rigorous quantification, as is done in the case of systematic content analysis, might be appropriate after investigators have observed many groups and have gained information on the prevalence of certain ideas in the public so that they can develop an observational code; however, it would have been premature in our case because we approached the topic with no preconceived

25. The discrepancy is due to several questions which were being asked of women only (such as if they had ever been denied employment because of their gender) and some of which were asked of men only. Most questions were asked of both genders.

notions, that is, we had no firm ideas concerning the topics focus group participants would choose to raise or how they would frame them. Although working from a precoded observational schedule was inadvisable, we did attempt to discover and stress the themes most emphasized by the participants and sought to describe them, whenever possible, in the participants' own words. Recurring themes were often introduced by adjectives such as "many" or "most" or "frequently" to indicate that a particular quote did not suggest just one woman's opinions but was echoed by others in the group as well.

When focus group members are quoted, they are quoted verbatim, including their grammatical or linguistic errors and without the customary *sic* added. To protect the privacy of the participants, different names, occupations, and other identifying marks were assigned to each participant. However, we attempted to allocate to each individual an occupation similar in status and nature to his or her own. Although much has happened in the world since this study was begun, a comparison of our findings with more recent ones conducted by the major survey organization shows that sentiments about gender relations have not changed a great deal in the interim.[26]

26. Good sources on the topic are the polls conducted by the Roper and Gallup organizations. The latter quite regularly features questions identical or similar to those we raised. Polls conducted as recently as 1993 and 1994 demonstrate that women continue to be of the opinion that men are treated far better than women. The gap in male/female opinions on that subject continues to be substantial (see, for example, the Gallup Poll conducted in October 1993). A startling demonstration of gender-based differences in reaction can be seen in a Gallup Poll (January 1994) that inquired as to the respondents' sympathy for Lorena Bobbitt (the wife who cut off her abusive husband's penis): 75 percent of the women expressed sympathy for her in contrast with 49 percent of the men (source: *The Gallup Poll: Public Opinion Annual Series* [Wilmington, DE: Scholarly Resources, Inc.]). As this book goes to press, the 1995 results from the Virginia Slims Survey have been made public. They mirror to a remarkable degree our findings of ten years ago, at times down to the same percentage point. Women continue to believe that "regardless of the changes that may have occurred, women still face more restrictions in life than men do" (*New York Times*, 12 September 1995, D5).

3

PERCEPTIONS OF DISCRIMINATION

Gender bias is alive and well; it has gone underground.
—*New York Times*, 7 August 1992

K. T. Poole and L. H. Ziegler (1987: 105) have noted that a sense of gender discrimination characterizes the attitudes of a majority of today's American women of widely differing political persuasions. A "reasonable conclusion is that . . . women have gotten the message: Discrimination is not just a myth cooked to radicalize them. It is real." This chapter will examine whether the New Jersey women we observed "have gotten the message," namely, whether they perceive of themselves as belonging to a discriminated group. The chapter will begin with a brief sketch of the role that thoughts about equality and discrimination play in the context of the American political culture. The special emphasis here is on mainstream thoughts about gender equality as they developed during the Second World War and the period immediately afterwards and may help explain why it was not until several decades after World War II that women "got the message." That background information is followed by a data analysis examining the extent to which women of all ages and walks of life perceive gender-based inequalities and where they notice these inequalities. The chapter next directs attention to a phenomenon I have labeled the "not-me" syndrome, by which I understand the tendency to assert that one is not personally the victim of an evil one believes affects most other members of one's group. Here it refers to a woman's tendency to perceive gender-based discrimination in the society-at-large but to perceive herself as exempt from it. The chapter concludes with women's perception of how much women's position has changed over the past decades and how satisfied they are with what has been accomplished so far. The chapter focuses exclusively on women's perception of gender-based *discrimination*, its practice, frequency, and severity. The broader topic of the gendered nature of society, of which discrimination is but one manifestation, will be discussed in subsequent chapters. This chapter asks one basic question: Do the women in our study think of themselves as being treated in a categorical rather than an individual manner? That is, do they believe they are discriminated against simply because they are women?

GENDER AND EQUALITY

It is not possible to talk about gender discrimination without talking about equality. In theory, the two are antithetical concepts. Yet for centuries even the most egalitarian societies have found ways of reconciling the practice of gender discrimination with a moral commitment to equality, notwithstanding vigorous protests of a few brave women and a very few brave men. The public at large often found nothing incompatible with professing devotion to equality but practicing discrimination, maintaining that discriminatory practices did not violate principles of equality. Maintaining that fiction was of the utmost importance to Americans because the devotion to equality forms part of the central core of the political identity of most Americans. Few would be comfortable admitting to others or even to themselves that they lend but limited credence to the Declaration of Independence's famous words that "all men are created equal."[1] Milton Rokeach's famous study of values (1973) offered empirical evidence to that effect. He found that equality along with liberty are the two values that rank foremost in the political belief systems of Americans.[2] School children, when asked to define what it means to be an American, invariably mention equality (along with liberty) as the defining mark (Sigel and Hoskin 1981).

Such apparent devotion to equality, however, is not to be equated with a desire for all people to be equal in possessions, prestige, or power. "Americans have never striven to ensure that all people live alike. Rather, they have always followed the ideal of an equal start in the race so that those with greater ability and drive are allowed, and encouraged, to come out ahead" (Verba and Orren 1985: 71). In other words, by equality, Americans understand equality of opportunity, not equality of results.[3] The just society is an equitable one in that it

1. The sections on democracy in this chapter are offered merely as a brief description of the tenor of the popular debate on the topic. They are not intended as a discussion of the many different interpretations of the concept itself, something that would be well beyond the scope of this book.

2. Different Americans assigned different priorities to liberty and equality depending largely on their ideological self-identifications (Rokeach 1973).

3. A minority of Americans do subscribe to the notion of equality of results. For a

gives every individual the same start, but it is not necessarily an egalitarian one.[4]

In the United States, periods of social conflict often are triggered when a group believes its members are not given the same start as are members of other groups. Given the right circumstances and realizing that they have been denied equality, members of a disadvantaged group begin to demand equality. "In the United States, equality is a recurring theme. It has flared into a fervent moral issue at crucial stages of American history. . . . The periods of fervor in American politics—the moments of creedal passion, in Samuel Huntington's words—have usually been outbursts of egalitarianism" (Verba and Orren 1985: 246). The Civil Rights Movement of the 1960s was one such period, and that was soon followed by women's demand for full equality with males. A recurrent theme in women's demands for equality is the assertion that current practices violate two basic tenets of the American definition of equality: first, that persons should be judged on the basis of their individual merits and not by their group membership and, second, that each person must be given the same opportunity as any other to succeed and lead a fulfilled life. So long as these conditions are not met, some would argue, women do not enjoy genuine, meaningful equality but are second-class citizens, similar to other disadvantaged minorities, notwithstanding their numerical superiority and possibly other advantages.

Conferring or denying rewards based solely on group membership, a practice we usually call discrimination,[5] is of course a patent violation of the principle of equality. Denying a person equal opportunity on the grounds that she is a member of the female species not only constitutes a blatant and deliberate form of externally imposed inequality but violates the very principle underlying equity, namely, that each person deserves to be judged and rewarded on the basis of her individual merit. To practice discrimination based on gender hence cannot be justified either by its practitioners or its victims. Yet people have had no trouble finding reasons for justifying such discrimination; in part because the practice has been of such long standing (as in the case of gender) that it is not even questioned, let alone conceptualized in terms of justice or

---

fine discussion of the complex nature of people's beliefs on the subject, see Jennifer L. Hochschild (1981) *What's Fair?*

4. Some have gone so far as to suggest that Americans value equality of opportunity so much precisely because it offers them the opportunity to become unequal, that is, better than their neighbor.

5. That is the association we make to the word when we talk about social practices. In itself, the word discrimination has no such connotation but rather refers to making meaningful distinctions.

injustice. It is simply seen as the natural order of things. Only when the justice of that so-called natural order is challenged (usually by the group which feels discriminated against) must the practitioners of discrimination face the question of injustice. Quite understandably, the desire to continue the practice remains strong, especially among those who benefit from the inequitable allocations. Under these conditions, the beneficiaries, in this case men, have to find justifications for continuing the practice. Because they like to think of themselves as fair and just, they are likely to resort to elaborate rationalizations and morally couched explanations to the effect that the practice is just and does not really constitute discrimination and why it, therefore, must be continued.[6]

THE "WOMEN ARE DIFFERENT" IDEOLOGY

Justifications for gender-based discrimination are no exception to the above rule. Although, objectively speaking, gendered inequality is as old as the Republic itself, society, women as well as men, until recently did not conceive of this as inequality, let alone discrimination, and hence had no trouble justifying it. The manner in which people justified the continuation of women being denied equal treatment had much to do with the manner in which society viewed women. Women were visualized either as superior to the rough, competitive world of the male or as inferior to that world. In the first instance, they were judged to be too noble, pure, and kindhearted to engage in many of the activities so rewarding to men; in the second instance, they were seen as too weak physically and mentally, too emotional and too lacking in intellect to assume important, male-dominated forms of labor and other responsibilities. The nurture of home and hearth were considered the responsibilities best suited to women's temperaments and endowments. "Both women and blacks have been portrayed as the hero, more courageous and noble than the ordinary, unoppressed mortal, and as the sambo, more childlike and stupid" (Hochschild 1973: 1018). Whatever the description, the net result amounts to the same: Women are different from men, and, implicitly, they are inferior to them in the areas which count for society, that is, for men. Consequently, denying women access to positions and privileges valued by men cannot by any stretch of the imagination, so the argument ran, be classified as discrimination. And so long as women bought that argument, they were unlikely to perceive of themselves as a discriminated group. This has

6. Of course, ego-defensive motivations also contribute to the adoption of this stance, as I shall demonstrate in the last chapter.

been the case for most of American history. Fifty years ago, Gunnar Myrdal pointed to the social consequences of this dual vision of women when he wrote that "most men have accepted as self-evident . . . the doctrine that women had inferior endowments in most of those respects which carry prestige, power, and advantages in society, but that they were, at the same time, superior in some other respects. . . . As in the case of the Negro, women themselves have often been brought to believe in their inferiority of endowment. As the Negro was awarded his 'place' in society, so there was a 'women's place.' In both cases the rationalization was strongly believed that men, in confining them to this place, did not act against the true interest of the subordinate groups" (1944: 1073). To put it another way, because of these alleged differences, no principle of equity was violated by denying women equal status.[7] Once that rationalization was recognized as a rationalization, those adversely affected by it—in this case women—began first to question and eventually to challenge it. The seeds for that challenge were sown after the United States' entrance into the Second World War, but they did not germinate until the 1960s with the rebirth of the American Women's Liberation Movement. Women's wartime experiences did not immediately result in female challenges to the prevailing gender system. It took the rebirth of feminism to give voice and moral justification to the challenge. Though at first the message was heard primarily by middle- and upper middle-class women, by the late 1970s, it had found a receptive, albeit not an activated, audience among a broad spectrum of the female population.

ROSIE THE RIVETER

To understand how century-old gender beliefs could change over the period of a few decades, it is useful to recount once more the often-told tale of women and the war effort. With the advent of World War II, women entered the industrial labor force en masse for the first time.[8] That entrance was portrayed—by the government as well as by the women themselves—as the fulfillment of a patriotic duty rather than a desire for self-fulfillment (even though that may well have been in-

7. Even today, quite a few women as well as men still subscribe to the old line of thinking. The 1994 Republican candidate for the governorship of Minnesota contended, according to the *New York Times* of 3 June 1994 (p. 1), that there is a "genetic predisposition" for men to be heads of household.

8. Which is not to say that many women had not been gainfully employed well before then. As A. Kessler-Harris (1982) pointed out, women have always left home to seek employment, but these instances were usually dictated by financial necessity (as during the Great Depression) and hence more likely to be class and race-based.

volved in an individual's decision to seek outside employment). Employment had two important consequences: In the first place, women began to modify their exclusive preoccupation with homemaking and their perception of the proper role for women or, rather, their perception that women were suited exclusively for the home. In the second place, and perhaps even more important, women began to work in occupations formerly restricted to men; occupations for which they previously had been considered unsuitable. From all accounts, they managed these new tasks competently while simultaneously discharging their homemaking responsibilities much as they had always done. Most important, they enjoyed their new-found skills and opportunities. In retrospect, what is remarkable about the period is how little these experiences initially changed anything either in society's outlook on women or in the women themselves. Notwithstanding their wartime experiences, women continued to subscribe to the traditional sex-role definition of the prewar period in which the woman's role was defined as that of the guardian of home and hearth and the men's as that of the breadwinner. In this respect, the women did not differ at all from their male counterparts of the period or, for that matter, from their mothers and grandmothers, all of whom subscribed to very traditional sex-role definitions.

To be sure, not all women subscribed to this traditional view. A good number of women—many of them college-educated and/or active in women's organizations—began, even in those days, to reevaluate the traditional female role definition, to reject it, and to voice demands for gender equality (or, as it was then called, equality of the sexes). They understood equality of the sexes to mean a basic restructuring of gender relations, extending well beyond the workplace. The vast majority of employed women, however, did not share in this vision; demands for restructuring society and/or doing away with patriarchy were not on their agenda. Instead they wanted pay equality and wider access to the labor market.[9] With the exception of these two demands, the war period and the immediate postwar period witnessed no widespread set of demands for female equality or a rethinking of woman's "natural" role. Despite that "[i]n the years during and after World War II, millions of women had left the home to take jobs, . . . the expansion of their 'sphere' occurred without fanfare and was not accompanied by any organized effort to challenge traditional definitions of woman's place"

9. The demands for protective labor legislation so frequent during that period can hardly be characterized as demands for gender equality. Nor can some of the other pieces of legislation, usually championed by organized labor, be so characterized. Some of this legislation was designed to prevent women from competing for jobs traditionally held by men.

(Chafe 1972: 226). Consequently, for the first two or three decades after the war, family and public life went on much as it always had, and on the surface, the return to domesticity did not seem to cause major problems for most women. Cynthia Harrison offers the following explanation for why women made the transition from wartime worker to full-time housewife so seemingly smoothly and without any overt resistance: "Because the original exhortations [by government and industry] to women to do war work had never challenged the core of ideas about femininity, because no one had suggested that work was more than a sacrifice women had willingly made for the most motherly of reasons, the [postwar] shift was an easy one. The message was clear: although women *could* do anything, authentic women would choose to be home with their families" (1988: 4, emphasis in the original).

The younger women's desire to get married and establish families quickly, and their wish to make up for time lost during the war years, has often been offered to explain the ease of the transition. This was the generation of men and women who created the "baby boom" and the postwar "cult of motherhood."[10] This analysis overlooks the fact that although the overwhelming majority of the women who had taken their first jobs during the war did desire to establish families, many also had a strong desire to continue working outside of the home. An examination of the literature and the public opinion surveys of the period (Hess and Ferree 1987; Grossman and Chester 1990) offers no evidence that Rosie the Riveter had disliked working outside of the home and could hardly wait to return to full-time mothering. Quite the contrary. From all accounts, most of these women relished their employment experiences, and many were ambivalent and some outright resentful at being once more relegated exclusively to the role of homemaker (Faludi 1991; Harrison 1988).[11]

In short, what makes the immediate postwar period so very different from today is the readiness with which so many women accepted prevailing traditional gender arrangements as normal and natural.[12] H. M. Hacker asserted at the time that "women are retreating from emancipation" (1951: 516).[13] The late Karen Horney suggested that

10. Philip Wylie ferociously castigated this desire in *The Generation of Vipers* (1942), arguing that Americans carried the veneration of motherhood to such extremes that it lead to the cult of "momism," with disastrous results for the offsprings.

11. Materials in the archives of the U.S. Department of Labor's Women's Bureau as well as polls conducted by other organizations indicate that about 80 percent of the women engaged in defense work would have liked to have continued in the labor force after the war.

12. C. K. Fulenwider (1980: 30) attributes it to the fact that women "have come to confuse the order of reality with the order of necessity, not to mention propriety."

13. Consequently, a woman's desire for outside employment was hardly ever couched

women were willing to make the retreat because the prevailing cultural ideology had convinced them not only of their unsuitedness for anything other than a domestic role but had also planted in them the "belief that it represents a fulfillment they crave, or an ideal for which it is commendable and desirable to strive" (1967: 8). Having been socialized in their youth and adult lives to crave that fulfillment (or at least to try convincing themselves that they were fulfilled), they found little justification for drawing unfavorable comparisons between their position and that of men. And so long as they failed to make such comparisons, they, of course, did not give any evidence that they felt relatively deprived or that they conceptualized the treatment they received in terms of sex discrimination. Under these circumstances, neither men nor women could be expected to display any discrimination consciousness, and the question of gender equity consequently did not enter the public debate. Chafe correctly observed that by 1962 (the date of his discussion) women "had not yet developed a sense of collective grievance" (1972: 226). They had not yet developed minority consciousness.

While the issue of racial discrimination took center stage in the public debate of the 1960s, it took much longer for either the public or the government to recognize that the treatment of women also constituted discrimination. Looking back on official endeavors on behalf of women for twenty years after the end of World War II, one cannot help but be surprised at the traditional approach officialdom took to women's needs and problems. The fifties and sixties witnessed a plethora of official and quasi-official activities whose purpose was to protect and improve the status of women, without ever challenging the nature of the prevailing gender arrangements. Prominent among such efforts were the establishment of commissions concerned with the status of women, the convening of major conferences on women, and the enactment of a few "women-friendly" policies. Although the overt purpose of such endeavors was to improve women's lives, these efforts were driven not so much by a desire to assure gender equality as to protect the health and welfare of mothers and their families. Protection was the main goal as exemplified in protective labor legislation. Protection was to benefit the woman herself, but another and perhaps overriding motive was to protect women's health and strength so that they could better meet their obligations to their offsprings and to the nation.[14] Family stability was seen as the main objective; women's rights or gender equality took the

---

in terms of being in her own interest, as being a right to which she was as entitled as any man. Instead, it was justified only when it was seen as an act which helped the family.

14. Organized labor supported most of these efforts as a way of protecting male workers from potential female competition.

backseat to that goal. A telling illustration to that effect was the initial refusal of the Equal Employment Opportunity Commission to apply Title VII of the Civil Rights Act to women. The EEOC justified its reluctance by asserting that sex discrimination did not constitute discrimination in the sense that racial discrimination did. Anyone reading today the reports issued by the various agencies and commissions cannot help but be amazed how very infrequently the issues were framed from an egalitarian perspective, and how terms such as "discrimination" and "equity" were all but absent from the discussion. For example, Ester Peterson, the head of the Women's Bureau, in a 1962 memo to President Kennedy wrote: "Motherhood is the major role of the American woman and her primary responsibility" (cited by Harrison 1988: 139).

SHIFTS IN PUBLIC OPINION

Although Betty Friedan's *The Feminine Mystique* was published in 1963 and became an instantaneous success (at least with middle-class women), and the National Organization of Women was founded in 1966, not until the mid-seventies did sex-role attitudes began to shift and discrimination awareness begin to develop in the population at large. K. O. Mason, J. L. Czajak, and S. Albert (1976), in an important review article on changes in American women's sex-role attitudes, noted that changes began to appear around 1964 but accelerated between 1970 and 1974 (the last year for which she consulted the public opinion polls). Before 1970, the shift was confined primarily to college-educated women, but by the late seventies it had reached a much larger public. "The sex-role attitude changes . . . for the 1970–73 period are, in many instances, as large as those observed between 1964 and 1970, even though the period is half as long" (p. 587). She found that by 1974 women had become "more egalitarian in their sex-role stance" and strongly advocated equal treatment and equal opportunity in the workplace. But, Mason's data also "indicate a continued predominance of support for the basic sex division of labor" (pp. 587–88), with women carrying the primary responsibility for the home and men for the financial support of the family. Although she did notice "that women's attitudes toward their roles in the home have become increasingly related to their attitudes toward their rights in the labor market . . . [nonetheless the] traditional sex role division of labor within the family continues to receive more support than do inequalities in the labor market" (p. 593). Egalitarianism at home, while beginning to develop, was still lagging behind the earlier formulated demands for equality in the workforce. Reading the popular literature of the time, as well as comments by public figures, one is struck by the narrow perception of sex discrimination which prevailed. Discrimination in the workplace, especially in pay and in access to better jobs, was quite readily acknowledged, and so perhaps was access to public office. Rarely, however, was the home viewed from a similar perspective. Feminists drew attention to inequities in the home and challenged them, but the general public at first did not. The public focused instead on daily bread-and-butter issues and took the patriarchal system itself and all of its social and political manifestations more or less for granted.

By the end of the decade, discrimination awareness had grown, and more people began to view society's treatment of women at home and in the public sphere as interrelated issues. A. Thornton and D. Freedman, comparing women's sex-role attitudes in 1977 with those expressed in 1962, found that by "1977 there was a marked increase in consistency among the sex-role attitudes . . . indicating a general and pervasive crystallization of the sex-role attitudes of the sample women between 1962 and 1977" (1979: 5).[15] Sigel and Reynolds (1979/80) noted that young collegiate women had by the mid-seventies all but abandoned any preference for the traditional role model. Sue Tolleson Rinehart (1992), in a secondary analysis of the data collected by M. Kent Jennings and Richard Niemi, noted a general growth in egalitarian sentiments during the interval between 1973 and 1982, and even those women who in 1973 had been traditional in their sex-role attitudes, had begun ten years later to shift to a more egalitarian stance. More significantly, when they reflected on their previous position these formerly traditional respondents recalled their earlier position as having been more egalitarian than it actually had been. Either their sensitivity to gendered inequalities had increased, or they had become more attuned to the prevailing climate of opinion. Other surveys of the period, which included men as well as women (conducted by the Gallup Organization, the National Opinion Research Center, and the Roper Organization), corroborated the finding that the national consensus was moving in a more egalitarian direction.

Probably no one cause could explain this shift, although both the Women's Movement and women's entrance into the labor force are credited with having played major roles (Mason, Czajak, and Albert

---

15. Sidney Verba and G. R. Orren (1985: 98) observed a similar phenomenon among the organization leaders they studied. Performing a factor analysis, they discovered that among all of the factors the gender issue had the most coherence and concluded: "This difference suggests that attitudes toward equality for women have a more distinctive component than do attitudes toward equality for blacks. Gender attitudes are more closely related to each other and less closely related to other attitudes than is the case for racial attitudes."

1976; Simon and Landis 1989; Spitze and Huber 1980). By the 1980s, a widespread shift in an egalitarian direction had taken place, and men and women had begun to view the problem as society-wide, endemic to a whole host of institutions, including the home. Initially, the shift was most visible among younger men and women, especially the better educated ones; by now it cuts across the social spectrum, although class-based differences still remain. And as the perspective from which men and women viewed women's position changed, the general idea that women are entitled to equality became more acceptable. By now the climate of opinion favors gender equality in theory, if not in practice. This seeming consensus, however, masks profound differences of opinion as to what we understand by that equality, what it involves, and where it is applicable. While individuals from all sides of the political spectrum will agree with each other that *political* equality is every American's birthright, they differ profoundly in their interpretation of the concept, and they part ways when it comes to applying the concept to a range of economic, social, and cultural circumstances.[16] Today, the cleavages in society revolve not around the abstract issue of the desirability of equality—that has been settled—but around what constitutes genuine equality, where it should be applicable, whether it has as yet been achieved and if it has not, whether and where it should be pursued further. For example, some who see vestiges of gender-based discrimination may advocate affirmative action to alleviate it, while others, who see as much gender-based discrimination, consider affirmative action only another form of discrimination.

DISCRIMINATION AWARENESS

An analysis of the study's data leaves the inescapable impression that the majority of the participants in the telephone surveys and in the focus sessions firmly believe that women as a group are discriminated against along the whole spectrum of male/female relations. Moreover, such discrimination strikes them as unfair rather than as natural or justified. As far as they are concerned, the picture is clear: "Discrimination is a fact of life. Don't even think otherwise," to quote a focus group member. They see gender discrimination as running through the whole fabric of American life, operating in all spheres. "It is still a man's world" where neither power nor privilege nor recognition are

16. Just how fragile this consensus still is can be seen in the recent battle over the ratification of the Equal Rights Amendment, the controversy over combat duty for female military personnel, and the ordination of female clergy. Opponents of these measures, although defending gender equality as an abstract principle, assert that the principle is not involved in these three issues or is outweighed by other considerations.

shared equally and where women still are considered, in words of some focus group participants, "second-class" citizens. Contrary to what many of these women think, men also share this impression of widespread discrimination, although this opinion is neither as widely nor as strongly held as it is among women (see chapter 7). Among women, this opinion reaches consensus proportions, so much so that many women believe their status in society resembles that of other disadvantaged minorities.

On the telephone survey, we used over thirty questions to inquire into a large variety of situations where respondents might or might not have seen evidence of sex discrimination. These varied from general questions, such as to who gets treated better in society, to specific questions, such as those on the fairness of the division of labor in the home. Irrespective of the arena highlighted in the questions, women almost invariably responded that discrimination continues to be the order of the day. According to them, it not only characterizes the more obvious areas such as pay inequality but in subtle ways affects the total social climate.

Turning first to three rather global, nonspecific gender-related topics, one finds strong evidence that women perceive considerable discrimination still to be operative in today's society (table 3.1). Robust majorities (70 percent) believe that much discrimination continues to prevail, that men get treated better in today's society (69 percent), and that "despite the recent gains of women when all is said and done, it's still a man's world" (82 percent): A high percentage (81 percent) agrees that society gives a man more recognition than it gives a woman for the same accomplishments. Most women do not hesitate to assert that lower pay, poorer job opportunities, and any number of related phe-

TABLE 3.1   WOMEN'S PERCEPTIONS OF SEX DISCRIMINATION IN SOCIETY

Respondents notice unequal treatment in cases where:	Percentage	
A woman seeking a major position is judged more by her sex than her qualifications	86	[54]*
To get ahead, a woman must be much better than a man	85	[64]
Despite recent gains, it is still a man's world	82	[50]
Women get less recognition than men for the same accomplishments	81	[49]
Women get treated as second-class citizens	77	[40]
A great deal of discrimination prevails	70	
Men are treated better in society than women	69	
Women's opinions get less respect than men's	58	
	$n = 400$	

*Figures in square brackets represent those respondents who agree a lot or very much with the statement.

nomena are due to the discriminatory nature of society and/or men and not to any deficiencies in women. Most New Jersey women, both in the focus groups and in the telephone survey, leave no doubt that they would prove themselves every bit as able as members of the opposite sex if only they were given the chance.

A related complaint that respondents take seriously concerns society's failure to evaluate women as individuals and that it instead judges them on the basis of their gender. Eighty-six percent subscribe to the notion that "when a woman seeks public office or a job formerly held by a man, people are more concerned with the fact that she is a woman than with her individual qualifications." A majority concludes that society values male opinions more than women's (58 percent), and that over three-quarters of the women conclude that society often treats women as though they were "second-class citizens" (77 percent). This categorical treatment of women proves to be a particular irritant, and it irritates focus groups members just as much as it does telephone respondents. One focus group member complained that men, encountering a woman of distinction, keep trying to "slot her into being a woman," not giving her a chance to demonstrate her competence or expertise. Women's conviction that they are being treated categorically rather than as individuals emerged, for example, in a discussion about the desirability of a woman becoming president of the United States. A few participants voiced the opinion that becoming president would backfire because the woman would be blamed for everything that goes on. One member put it this way:

> I think men would, I think they would say: "See, you put a woman in the White House and look what she does!" I do, I think that's what they would say. No one says a *man* has been in the White House all of these years and look at the deficit and all these things. But something like that, I think if she made one little slip-up and, of course, you are only human, and you do these things. The same thing if Jesse Jackson had got in, put a black in the White House you know. I just have a feeling that that's the way it would be.

This woman's conjecture reflects the much publicized complaint of women who have entered previously all-male blue-collar occupations and find their male co-workers "broadcasting every mistake that she makes or by acting as though routine performance is a major accomplishment. In both situations the assumption is that a woman cannot do her work as well as men" (Schroedel 1990: 251).[17] Crosby (1991: 188) found that this habit is by no means confined to blue-collar men but can

---

17. According to J. R. Schroedel, 48 percent of the blue-collar women she studied experienced this situation.

be found among men of all classes. A way for men to cling to their sexual stereotypes, she argues, is "to see each competent woman as the exception while maintaining that any mistake made by a female was proof of the inferiority of the entire female gender." The New Jersey women, much like those in Crosby's Newton, Massachusetts, group, have had considerable experience with this practice. When a New Jersey woman compares a fictitious woman president to Jesse Jackson she makes clear her conclusions that blacks and women are treated categorically rather than on the basis of their individual accomplishments.

Another source of frustration stems from their perception that society fails to accord women adequate respect. Here again focus groups and telephone respondents find themselves in substantial agreement (59 percent of the survey respondents believe women's opinions get less respect than men's). Issues such as respect are far subtler and hence much more difficult to document than issues such as pay inequity or women's absence from public office. Focus group discussions offer valuable insights as to just what individuals understand by respect. In one focus group, a thirty-one-year-old, politically conservative woman in a middle-management position complained: "This same man I was in a meeting with—oh I guess it was about a month ago—and every time I started to say something, and he would start talking. I'd ask a question, and he'd start talking about something else. And like I said, it was just as if I wasn't there. If any of the men in the group said something, then they got listened to, and then it was a matter of discussion and all that. But I couldn't even say anything." The "invisible woman" theme crops up more than once and reflects the observation by M. F. Belenky and associates (1986) that "a woman's claim that 'It's my opinion' means that it is just her opinion; a man's identical opinion means he's got a right to his opinion."[18] Again and again, the employed women in our groups voiced their perceptions that men do not accord women the respect they deserve or fail to give them proper credit for their contributions. They spoke of feeling unappreciated and disrespected. Although these complaints may have some self-serving element to them, they nonetheless square rather well with the results of experimental situations. E. A. Blechman's 1984 review of the literature shows that observers of task-oriented experimental groups tended to evaluate women's competence lower than men's even though on all objective measures their performance was identical with that of their

18. S. E. Taylor and H. T. Falcone (undated memo, p. 11) report that the tendency to devalue women's contribution is just as prevalent among college students. In an experimental study of decision-making in male/female groups, women were judged less effective than men. Both genders made few recall errors as to which gender had said what. Gender, in short, is a frequently used cue.

male counterparts. Similarly, in small decision-making groups men's suggestions are accepted with more regularity than women's (Inwold and Bryant 1981).[19]

Complaints about lack of respect extend well beyond work- and task-related situations. It was startling to observe how many women are under the impression that lack of respect for the female sex characterizes gender relations in general. Mary, a widow in her late fifties who had been mostly silent and withdrawn during the group session becomes very animated as she recalled an episode which occurred when she tried to sell some of her deceased husband's expensive personal effects: "Well, one time my sisters and I were having a yard sale. And one of my nephews was there, and he had gone at the time. And we had a television, and my late husband had a fantastic set of tools that he had never used because he bought it and then decided to go into another line of business. Right? So in the meantime he [the nephew] went to the store to buy something or other, and this guy comes up. And he is trying to buy all that stuff for $20. He thinks we are imbeciles." Another person interposed: "Well, I know a lot of people do that at yard sales." Mary was not to be deterred, however. Her voice rose as she continued: "But wait, I was furious. At a yard sale you expect something like a bargain, but this was like . . . " Elaborating on the value of the items, she concluded: "I said I'll take it back in the house first." Note that she began her recitation by mentioning the nephew and his temporary absence, implying that the prospective buyer would not have offered such a ludicrously low price if the nephew had been in the yard since men don't think other men are "imbeciles." Another similarly incensed woman reported going to an automobile showroom to buy a car. The salesman ignored her questions and told her to bring her husband over, though she had told him that her husband does not know how to drive. To her, much more is involved than just a discourteous salesperson. It is just one more sign that men make unwarranted and demeaning snap judgments about an individual woman based on their stereotypic thinking about all women. Petty daily encounters are symptomatic for her of the low regard in which society holds a woman.

One more example shall suffice. Lack of respect for what women are

19. It has been widely observed that in certain groups men tend to make more suggestions. Eagly (1987) points out that this is usually a function of their higher status in the organization. Ironically, men tend to exaggerate the frequency with which women speak up in groups. Epstein (1988: 223) reports a personal anecdote on this point. In a research group in which she participated, the opinion was voiced that the women talked a lot. The women shared the men's opinion of themselves as the more talkative. Yet, a quantitative analysis, however, showed that the women spoke "only about a third as much as the men."

capable of doing infuriates an assistant buyer in a small retail establishment who is single. As she tells it, she had put in an order for storm windows and was about to set up an appointment for installation when "the salesman asks: 'Can your husband be there?' and I said: 'I don't have one.' He said: 'Do you think you could have a man that you know very well come in?' So I said: Forget it! I don't want to see you. And so his answer was: 'I just wanted you to understand what I was discussing.' And I said: 'What makes you think that I don't understand.'" This episode gave rise to an animated group discussion of the condescending if not outright insulting ways in which women routinely get treated.

Yard sales or storm window purchases may not constitute events of world-shaking importance, but to these women they constitute the common, everyday events which symbolize for them what is wrong with gender relations and what makes them angry. What is also important to note is that they don't consciously think about these episodes in ideological, let alone feminist terms. They are angry simply because they feel they are not treated as they deserve to be treated. "Men are 'sexist,'" says one young woman, "and refuse to treat women as equals." These women feel themselves equal to men and wish men would recognize this. To be sure, not all women are willing to confront sexism as head-on as our assistant buyer; many more decide to accept such behavior as "the way the world works," according to a young secretary. Nevertheless, most of the women interviewed resented such treatment. In the groups we observed, lack of respect played a far more central role than we had anticipated, alerting us to the need to "beware of confusing acquiescence with contentment—the impossibility of remedy can inhibit action without inhibiting a sense of grievance" (Runciman 1966: 26). To capture a representative sample of women's attitudes on the subject, we included several respect-related items on our telephone interview schedule (such as asking whether they thought women's opinions were accorded as much respect as men's).

Perceptions of categorical treatment and of lack of respect constitute two important sources of grievance; other grievances surface as women react to more obvious and easier to document aspects of gender-based inequities, such as income and employment opportunities. In spite of recent improvements, women continue to feel seriously disadvantaged when it comes to pay, to the ability to secure or advance in good jobs, and the like (table 3.2). Robust majorities think that men enjoy advantages denied to women. Although today's advertisements are full of pictures of well-groomed, happy-looking young women occupying what seem to be executive suites, women do not think this accurately describes the real world. That world, as they perceive it, still discrimi-

TABLE 3.2   AWARENESS OF DISCRIMINATION IN SPECIFIC ECONOMIC AREAS

Question: "For each of the following, please tell me if you think *men* are treated better, *women* are treated better, or if they are treated the same."	
Percentage of Women Agreeing that:	
Men are treated better in mortgage applications	67
Men are treated better getting jobs in business management	72
Men are treated better with respect to pay	80
Men are treated better getting top jobs in government	83
	$n = 400$

nates against women in not granting them equal access to the opportunities and resources that count. For example, 72 percent believe that women still have a hard time obtaining important positions in business, and 83 percent believe this holds for government careers as well; moreover, many think that even in the less exalted ranks of the corporate structure discrimination still continues to be the rule. It is in these areas of economic opportunity, rather than the subtler, harder to document ones, that men find themselves in substantial agreement with women. They readily agree that men are financially advantaged, and while they may perceive a somewhat smaller gap in advantages than do women, essentially they do agree that the financial world continues to be a man's world.

Women's perception of gender discrimination differs from that of men in that the women consider it to be far more widespread and intense. To their minds, it affects almost every aspect of their daily lives and not just the economic one. In every specific area raised during the phone interviews, a substantial minority—and sometimes a majority —believed they saw discrimination operating in that area. Not one woman, for example, ever exclaimed, "Oh, in this specific situation men and women get treated the same." Of course, women do vary among themselves with respect to the area where they most notice discrimination; some women are particularly sensitive to one type of disadvantage, perhaps in the workplace, while others may focus on another, say the uneven division of labor in the home. Still, the readiness to perceive gender discrimination in so many places is all the more remarkable in that (as I shall demonstrate in subsequent chapters) most of these women do not consider themselves to be feminists. These are women who, as much as they would like to see equality come about are not engaged in an active struggle for gender equality. Instead, they have chosen to accommodate to the world they must face every day, "the real world," in the words of one young woman in our group.

LEVEL OF DISCRIMINATION AWARENESS

To get an overall view of the role discrimination awareness plays in these women's lives, we constructed a twelve-item Index of Discrimination Awareness to measure (1) whether an individual telephone respondent perceives discrimination in the various situations presented to her and (2) how often it shows up or how pronounced it is in any given situation.[20] On the basis of each person's total score (calculated from the answers to the twelve questions) respondents were categorized as being high, medium, or low in "discrimination awareness." The "highly aware" category consists of women who see inequalities in at least eight out of ten presented situations and who tend, in addition, to see discrimination as a frequent occurrence. Thirty-eight percent of the women respondents fall into this group. The rest are divided into those with midlevel awareness and those at the lowest level of awareness (25 percent), who perceive no more than three instances of discrimination out of a possible twelve. In the entire survey, only one woman respondent told us that she saw no discrimination in any of the twelve named instances. We may conclude that some discrimination is a fact of life for almost all of the women.

Demographic characteristics do not affect respondents' level of awareness. Neither age, nor education, employment status, income, or other customary indicators are much related to awareness discrimination. The oldest women (those 65 years and older) are as likely to be aware (28 percent) as women in the other age groups. The youngest group, between 18 and 29 years of age, shows the least awareness. This finding confirms results from other surveys and suggests that the youngest cohort may take the opportunities available to them for granted and lacks the institutional memory to realize that the opportunities available to them are of relatively recent origin and did not come about without considerable struggle.

Even employment status—the arena in which people should have the best chance of noticing overt discrimination—is not related to discrimination awareness (32 percent of the employed and 29 percent of the retired and nonemployed score high). Income and education also fail to relate significantly to awareness, although the trend is such that those who have more resources (especially income and education) are most likely to score high in discrimination awareness.[21] Clearly, discrimination awareness cuts across all segments of the population. It is not a myth propagated by upper middle-class women.

20. For the individual items and the construction of the index, consult Appendix B.
21. Place of residence plays a role only insofar as rural residents are somewhat less likely to be highly aware than either the urban or the suburban populations.

TABLE 3.3   LEVEL OF DISCRIMINATION AWARENESS

Level of Awareness*	Percentage
High	38
Medium	37
Low	25
	$n = 400$

* As measured by the Index of Discrimination Awareness (DA). For details on items and construction of the Index, see Appendix B.

Unlike demographic characteristics, political ideology is related to one's awareness of discrimination. Discrimination awareness and a variety of so-called liberal issues are positively related. For example, women who are supporters of ratifying the ERA also are more likely to score high in discrimination awareness (38 percent) rather than in the low range of the discrimination index (23 percent).[22] The same pattern prevails with respect to support for the Women's Movement. Those who look upon the Movement with disfavor or think it has outlived its usefulness are less likely to score high on discrimination awareness than are the women who think it is still needed. And, much as one would have expected, self-identified conservatives are also less inclined to see discrimination as pervasive as are liberals and twice as likely to consider it a minor problem (40 percent scored low on discrimination awareness in contrast with 19 percent of the liberals). Such findings are in keeping with Rokeach's findings that people for whom equality is the most important value are likely to be liberals. They also constitute clear evidence that the way a person views women's status in society is related to her general set of social values. If she believes in equality and thinks women deserving of equality as much as men, she is more likely to notice instances of discrimination and hence score high in discrimination awareness than a woman who attaches less importance to equality. Is the reverse also possible, namely that her frequent exposure to discrimination has made her receptive to liberal ideologies? The order of causation (another of social science's so-called chicken-and-egg questions) has to remain unanswered. All we can conclude is that (1) where a woman finds herself in the social stratum does not have much to do with her perceptions of gendered inequalities, but where she stands ideologically does play a role, and (2) most women believe discrimination still operates in all or most spheres of life.[23]

22. Conversely and quite logically, 90 percent of those who score high in discrimination awareness also support the ERA.

23. The proportion of women who say they see no discrimination varies from question to question but is quite small; generally fewer than one in five.

THE "NOT-ME" SYNDROME

What the telephone respondents tell us about society's treatment of *other* women, however, does not necessarily relate well to the way they view their own lives. When we seek to find out how much the alleged discrimination has affected these women *personally*, we find that only a minority report having had personal encounters with discrimination and/or having suffered from it. This phenomenon I choose to label the "Not-Me Syndrome." This, of course, is quite different from what we learned during focus group observations, where just about every woman could think of at least one instance where she was discriminated against, an instance she considered typical of the way men treat women. Not so the telephone respondents. As we have seen, they are very aware of discrimination, but when it comes to their own lives, the story changes. For example, a majority (57 percent) tells us (table 3.4) that their opinion is indeed respected on a par with men's, and 51 percent reject the idea that they are treated like second-class citizens.[24] Even instances of sexual harassment are the exception (only 33 percent reported ever having been exposed to it). The notion of having been discriminated against at work was rejected even more emphatically. A robust majority (78 percent) asserts that at work they are not made to feel like outsiders, and a full 71 percent maintain they have never been discriminated at their place of employment in terms of pay or promotions. From their statements, we have to infer that these women think of themselves as exceptions to the general rule they had just proclaimed. They see themselves as having been exempt from a variety of discriminatory experiences or having encountered them but rarely.[25]

This perception of personally privileged status raises the question of whether there is a connection between the frequency of one's own encounters with discrimination and one's sensitivity to other women's experiences. In order to examine that question, we constructed an additive Index of Personal Discrimination Experience, composed of respondents' answers to all of the questions pertaining to their personal experiences with discrimination. The frequency distributions were once again divided into thirds. Only a minority (26 percent) see themselves as having had a considerable number of personal experiences with discrimination and having had them frequently, that is, they score high on the Personal Discrimination Experience Index. Almost half of the women (49 percent) report having had a moderate number of such

24. But only 25 percent believe that most women are respected and all but 12 percent are of the opinion that women are made to feel like second-class citizens.

25. This finding replicates what others have reported in widely differing contexts (Crosby 1982; Grossman and Chester 1990).

TABLE 3.4   WOMEN'S PERSONAL EXPERIENCE
WITH DISCRIMINATION

Respondent's Perception	Percentage
Feels like second-class citizen	
Often	13
Sometimes	35
Doesn't feel that way	51
Don't know	1
Has been discriminated at work	
Yes	26
No	71
Don't know	3
Feels like outsider at work	
Yes	14
No	78
Feels that way sometimes	7
Don't know	1
Has been sexually harassed	
Yes	33
No	67
Respect given to her opinion	
Same as to men's	57
More than men's	12
Less than men's	29
Don't know	3
Was unable to do many things because of gender	
Agrees	46
Disagrees	52
Doesn't know	2
Division of labor	
Husband does fair share	64
Husband does not do fair share	36
Encounters the problem of discrimination	
Every day	5
Often	11
Once in a while	34
Rarely or never	47
Don't know	2

personal discrimination encounters, and 26 percent report few or virtually none (table 3.5, part A). This tells us two things: First, it tells us that most women do not perceive of themselves as steady victims of discrimination, but it also tells us that only a minority believes that discrimination has touched them but rarely.

As anticipated, personal discrimination experience and discrimination awareness are positively related (table 3.5; part B). Women scoring high in personal discrimination experience also are the ones most likely to score high on the Discrimination Awareness Index (59 percent),

TABLE 3.5   WOMEN'S PERSONAL EXPERIENCE
WITH DISCRIMINATION BY DISCRIMINATION
AWARENESS LEVEL

PART A	
LEVEL OF PERSONAL EXPERIENCE WITH DISCRIMINATION (%)*	
High	26
Medium	49
Low	26

PART B				
PERSONAL DISCRIMINATION EXPERIENCE BY LEVEL OF DA†				
	Level of DA			
Level of PDE	High	Medium	Low	
High	59	33	8	100%
Medium	41	44	15	100%
Low	22	49	29	100%

*As measured by the Personal Experience with Discrimination (PDE) Index.
†As measured by the Discrimination Awareness (DA) Index.

while those who have had few encounters with discrimination are also much less likely to perceive a great deal of discrimination (22 percent score high on the Discrimination Awareness Index). This finding lends some weight to my earlier conjecture that personal discrimination experiences might well have contributed to their sensitivity to the presence of societal discrimination.[26] Equally revealing is that even among those women who believe they have had little or no personal discrimination experience most (71 percent) still perceive a good deal of discrimination (they fall in the "high" or "medium" level of discrimination awareness). Whether or not a woman feels she has personally experienced discrimination, her view is that the world treats most women unfairly. The majority of telephone respondents distinguish between their own situation and their perception of how women in general are faring. They consider themselves fortunate in that they never or rarely have been the victims of a discriminatory pattern they believe to be so common in the population at large. In this respect, they resemble the employed women of Newton, Massachusetts, studied by F. J. Crosby, who "express much resentment about the job situation of women but little resentment about their own job situation" (1982: 170). What Crosby found to be true with respect to jobs apparently

26. Of course, we are here once more confronted with the causality dilemma: Do they perceive more discrimination in the society because they personally have been its victim, or do their general feelings about gendered inequalities make them more sensitive to the treatment they receive personally?

holds with equal force for a whole host of female life experiences both private and public.

What might explain the discrepancy between a woman's perception of the treatment to which most females are subjected and her perception of the treatment she receives personally? Individuals are reluctant to think of themselves as victims. Ample evidence in the literature suggests that people will deny victimization, at times even to themselves, in order to protect their self-respect. One can recall, as the focus group members do, a single incident in which one was treated badly, without making oneself appear a loser or victim. The telephone interview, however, did not inquire into isolated, specific incidents of personal victimization—things that could have happened to anyone once in a while—but addressed a range of fairly general issues. To think of oneself as being systematically discriminated against and treated as an inferior in all or most of these situations might be painful, threatening, and humiliating, all feelings against which we generally try to protect ourselves. "To define oneself as a victim is to invite denigration" (Crosby 1982: 164). It threatens our self-esteem and our image of ourselves as being in control of our own fate. That process hurts, and it may hurt most within an American context that emphasizes the individual as the agent of success or failure. In reporting these findings, we do not reject the possibility that even the telephone respondents who might recall past discrimination might not have wanted to admit this to an unknown and unseen stranger, the interviewer, for fear that incidents of victimization might reflect negatively upon themselves.[27] With the data at our disposal it is impossible for us to account convincingly for the difference in responses between focus group and survey participants. Whatever the explanation, the net effect is that the telephone respondents consider themselves to be rather exempt from gender-based discrimination but believe that women as a group are uniformly discriminated against.

The discrepancy between focus group members' views of personal discrimination and that of phone interviewees is one of many instances in which the different inquiry formats may have played a part. Focus group participants are only too eager to admit to having been victims of discrimination. But their admissions should be taken in context. For one thing, as we shall see in subsequent chapters, in their narratives they often present themselves as having overcome discrimination. In addition, the atmosphere in such a group meeting differs greatly from the voice-over-the-wire one in a telephone interview. The women

27. The extreme case which comes to mind are rape victims who often ask themselves if they might not have involuntarily contributed to their own victimization.

can see one another, note their facial expressions, register the other women's reactions to what they have to report, and they gain some sense whether or not their accounts coincide with the experiences of other group members. And if they do more or less coincide, then the group becomes a setting for sharing common experiences; it becomes the occasion for telling how and when they felt discriminated against.[28] Finally, there is what I earlier called the contagion effect, that is, the tendency to report having experiences similar to those of other women in the group, thereby becoming part of the group.

PERCEPTIONS OF CHANGE IN WOMEN'S STATUS

Complaints notwithstanding, most women realized that the social situation for women has improved over the past two or three decades. Focus group and survey participants alike recognize that they are no longer barred from some activities and occupations which previously were reserved for men and that many options are available to them which were inaccessible to their mothers. Focus group members frequently compare their lives to those of their mothers and grandmothers and in that comparison stressed the limited choices and narrow opportunities available to their forbearers. For some members, choice means being able to build a career; for others it means adopting a freer lifestyle, for yet others it means making demands on their spouses their mothers never dreamt of making (such as assistance with childcare), and for a few others it even means questioning the institution of family life. A paralegal in one of the groups represents that last perspective.

> With respect to me, I'm 35 and I'm still finding this thing about having a child, I'm not crazy about marriage . . . I keep thinking I'm going to wake up one day, and people are going to say to me: 'Didn't they live kind of weird back then, you know, everyone had to get married and have children kind of thing.' However, the issue is, today we have a choice. My mother didn't. She had children, and the difference between her and I is she had children, and I didn't. We both had the same goals and aspirations.

She implies that she has the option to pursue her aspirations but her mother had to remain unfulfilled. Although this is perhaps the most extreme statement in any of the groups, the tenor of the discussion in

28. I wondered, for instance, what would have happened if someone in any of these groups had said: "I don't understand your griping; we really have nothing to complain about." Would others, upon reflection, have concurred? Or were there perhaps women in the group who harbored such feelings but did not express them because of the other's prevailing sentiments to the contrary?

all of the women's focus groups was that though it may still be tougher for a woman than a man, life definitely has improved.

If that realization does not always come through unambiguously in the focus groups, it is because the participants spend so much of their time telling one another of their encounters with injustice. But the realization of improvement does come through in the telephone interviews. In those interviews, we included a series of questions about changes in women's status, inspired in part by the many references that group members had made to change. It is clear from respondents' answers that they are well aware of the changes in men's and women's status, that most perceive a lot of change, and that few are of the opinion that nothing has changed as yet (table 3.6). A vast majority (84 percent) shares the focus groups' beliefs that the changes have been for the better. A sizeable segment (42 percent), nonetheless, thinks change is

TABLE 3.6   PERCEPTIONS OF CHANGE
IN WOMEN'S SITUATION

PART A
REFLECTIONS ON PAST CHANGES (%)

Amount of change over the years	
A lot	69
Some or a little	30
None	1
Speed of change viewed	
Too slow	43
Too fast	1
About right	50
No change	6
Change seen as	
Beneficial	84
Made things worse	6
Good and bad	8
No change noted	1
Effect on own life	
Beneficial	50
Made it worse	3
Good and bad	3
Not affected by change	42
Government helped bring it about	
Helped a great deal	11
Helped a little or some	50
Would have happened anyway	34
No opinion	4

(continued)

TABLE 3.6 (*Continued*)

PART B
OUTLOOK FOR FUTURE

Security of gains	
They are secure	71
Could change back	3
Both possible	22
Direction of change desired	
More egalitarian	68
Stay as is today	28
Change back to old ways	3
It depends	1
No opinion	1
Magnitude of desired change	
Favors major change	56
Favors minor change	35
Depends, no opinion	9
Government	
Should become more active	49
Should become less active	8
Continue as is	42
No opinion	1

coming about too slowly, and a majority (68 percent) is quite sure that more change has yet to be effected before real improvement will have been achieved. On the other hand, few women worry that the tide may be reversed in the future, and 71 percent believe the progress made so far is quite secure. This group is pleased that change has come about but believes that much needs yet to be done. As one might expect, compared with men, they see less progress and desire more change, a possibility which men, as we shall see later, view with a good deal of apprehension.

The picture which emanates from these two different methods of inquiry is curiously mixed. On the one hand, there is strong agreement that much gender-based discrimination continues to be practiced in almost all spheres of life. On the other hand, there is strong agreement that the last two or three decades have seen an improvement in women's situation. The picture is neither rosy nor gloomy. Given this mixture of satisfaction and dissatisfaction, we must now ask, what are the women's emotional reactions to this state of affairs? That is the question the next chapter will seek to answer.

4

ANGER OVER DISCRIMINATION

I don't think there has ever been a man who treated a woman as an equal, and that's all
I would have asked, for I know I'm worth as much as they.
—Berthe Morisot (1890)

With so many women so sure that they still are treated as second-class citizens, should we not expect them to be very angry over the treatment? This chapter explores that question. It asks: What part does the knowledge of group-directed unfairness play in the emotional reactions of the women in this study? Do they accept the perceived unfairness as a fact of life, as something normal, or does it lead them to become angry and resentful? The chapter will begin by briefly recapitulating some tenets of the relative deprivation theories that address this question. Next, it will explore whether women react in the manner anticipated by these theories, starting with the findings from the telephone survey, after which the focus group discussions will be described. The findings reveal considerable concurrence between the two groups but also pronounced differences. The chapter will conclude by reflecting on the differences between the two settings and on what might account for these differences.

RELATIVE DEPRIVATION AND ANGER

Several conditions usually have to be met before anger over group deprivation comes to the fore. Anger is most likely to arise when individuals are in a position to compare themselves directly with a relevant group which is better rewarded but no more deserving than they are. Under those circumstances, they will feel deprived, provided that the individuals concerned desire the rewards and believe they can be obtained at a bearable cost. These conditions have been met in the case of women. Today, women compare their group's pay, access to desirable opportunities, and their current positions with those of men, and since they desire these same benefits and rewards but have not obtained them, they conclude that they are at a relative disadvantage. But women also believe that improvement in their position is possible and has, in fact, already begun. Because the times when improvement has begun are precisely the times when people are most conscious of what they are still lacking and most impatient with the pace of progress, relative deprivation theory predicts that discontent and resentment should surface. Crosby holds that the very recognition of deprivation amounts "to one type of anger. It is a sharper emotion than dissatisfaction. Unlike the person who is simply dissatisfied, the deprived person feels he has been the victim of injustice" (1982: 40). Anger over injustice also suggests that a woman is genuinely troubled by the deprivation. This sense of trouble may affect her outlook on the world in which she lives, producing a sense of frustration and humiliation as a consequence of the general disesteem with which she sees the world treat women.

Categorical treatment as "women" should be particularly offensive to Americans because of Americans' ingrained belief in meritocracy. From early childhood on, parents and teachers tell youngsters that they can expect the appropriate rewards if they try hard and play by the rules; they are taught that "neither race, creed, sex, nor national origin" matter, but talent and hard work do. Preferential treatment based solely on gender violates the meritocracy principle and should be unacceptable to women.[1] Their anger should be most visible today, because recent egalitarian rhetoric has propagated the notion that women now can expect the same rewards and recognition as their male counterparts, provided they are equally qualified and ambitious.

SOCIALIZATION TO ANGER

Persuasive though this line of reasoning might seem, reality is rarely that simple. Anger does not automatically follow in the wake of feeling unfairly deprived. "The sense of injustice is made, not born, and although we think of anger as the handmaiden of justice, it is not its inevitable companion" (Tavris 1982: 227). In the case of women, resentment may be counterproductive. Because practices to which people have become accustomed for generations (such as different treatment for men and women) may appear natural even to those disadvantaged by such practices, encounters with discrimination can lead to confusion and consternation rather than anger. This was Jill K. Conway's reaction when as a young scholar she was denied a position which she desired

---

1. Runciman's line of reasoning would not exempt from the feeling of anger men who consider women's deprivation unwarranted; he referred to this type of reaction as "fraternal relative deprivation."

and for which she felt completely qualified. Here is how she describes her reaction: "It should have made me angry but instead I was profoundly depressed. . . . For the first time, I felt kinship with black people" (1989: 191). C. Tavris (1982) similarly observed that women became baffled and confused when they personally encountered discrimination.

Injustice may also not automatically result in anger because "[r]ecognizing and feeling anger is initially very frightening" (Miller 1976: 123). For almost everyone, anger is a corrosive force and costly to the self. This corrosion particularly affects subordinate and other vulnerable groups, producing a tendency to deny it if at all possible. To women, anger may appear especially threatening because from early childhood on they have been socialized (some might say oversocialized) not to get mad, not to fight, not to lash out against the target of their frustration. Being nice is still a trait admired in a girl. When Carol Gilligan interviewed 100 girls in a private all-girls school (as reported in a news summary), she noted how much these young girls had internalized parents' and teachers' admonitions that it is "not nice" for "good girls" to express anger. The girls (made of "sugar and spice and everything nice") were told to cultivate helpfulness and friendliness rather than assertiveness. That same observation was made recently by comedienne Phyllis Diller as she explains why audiences have trouble accepting female comedians. "Look, comedy is an aggressive, hostile act, and men are *brought up* to be aggressive and hostile. Women are brought up to be gracious and self-effacing" (*New York Times*, 12 July 1992, p. 12, emphasis in original).

By the time they are adults, these young women should have learned either to suppress feelings of anger or not to express those feelings. Arlene Hochschild's 1983 study of airline flight attendants reveals just how uncomfortable women are about displaying anger overtly. Stewardesses, she showed, engaged in much more "emotion management" than did men.[2] "Women are more likely to be presented with the task of mastering anger and aggression in the service of 'being nice'" (p. 163). The stewardesses tolerated far more verbal abuse from passengers and "unwarranted aggression against them" (p. 163) than did the stewards. Mastering anger, however, does not always come easily; it must be worked at. Some of Hochschild's subjects described themselves as "talking myself into not caring" (p. 166).

Stewardesses are not the only ones who from time to time consider it circumspect to talk themselves out of their anger. "Even women who now want to be openly assertive can get caught in the fear of being an-

2. The title of her book, most appropriately, is *The Managed Heart*.

gry, which they often don't want to be. . . . Sometimes, too, women are afraid that the degree of their anger is excessive or unjustified" (Miller 1976: 123). Or, as feminist Susi Kaplow wrote in her diary: "You yourself get tired of this anger—it's exhausting to be furious all the time" (quoted in Tavris 1982: 246). Traditionally, suppressing anger has resulted in women accepting their lack of empowerment rather than protesting it. As Tavris (1982: 198) observed, "anger as response to powerlessness is an acquired taste." Many women make a great effort not to care. They "often don't acknowledge anger to themselves" (Miller 1976: 53), believing that their subordinate status leaves them with few other options.[3]

It goes without saying that for a woman to harbor resentment over her own or her group's lack of equality, she must aspire to such equality. If she personally does not aspire to equality, she will find little reason for anger, unless she feels close to women as a group and identifies with their fate. In this case, even though she does not desire equality for herself, she might be angry on behalf of others. We would not expect anger from a woman content with living the traditional female role and believing that this role represents the preferred as well as the morally correct mode for most other women. Such a woman may recognize that men get treated better in many spheres of life, but may believe that they deserve better treatment because they are more capable or have more responsibilities; or she may consider these spheres to be unappealing to women. In that case, no compelling reason exists for comparing the female situation unfavorably with that of the male's. To her way of thinking, the status quo of the past represents the correct way to arrange gender relations.

If, however, our respondents wanted to live in a just world, and believed in America's faith in meritocracy, we would expect anger over the gender-based discrimination of which they are so very cognizant. On the other hand, if cultural tradition and gender socialization had great force in their lives, we would expect them to accept discrimination as a simple matter of life and without much rancor. Since both tendencies are probably at work, we should not be surprised if our respondents reactions reflect considerable uncertainty, ambivalence, and, on occasion, indifference.

3. In a 1986 field study, L. A. Mainero investigated the responses to powerlessness of 98 male and female employees. She found that women were more likely than men to report acceptance and resignation to perceived power imbalances (cited by Ragins and Sundstrom 1989). In a similar vein, a fiftyish woman in one of our focus groups, reflecting on the poor assignments given her when young, comments: "I did not expect to go into the workforce on the same level as a man with similar training."

The task of deciding definitively which reactive pattern best describes our population is complicated in that our conclusions are derived from two different modes of inquiry. We anticipated that the two modes would yield different, though not necessarily conflicting, impressions. After all, we deliberately chose two different modes in the hope that they would complement rather than duplicate each other. Choosing an almost completely open, nondirective format for the focus groups, allowing each group to set its own agenda, had the unintended consequence in the female groups that most of the discussion centered on personal experiences with discrimination. The relevant larger social issues, though brought up now and then, rarely were pursued at any length. In the telephone survey, where the researchers set the agenda, the inquiry concentrated heavily on these broader social and political gender issues. On the basis of our prior group observations, we decided to include some inquiries into personal experiences as well.

Given these different foci, it is not surprising that the two groups' responses also vary—or at least *seem to vary*—from each other. Focus group participants appear genuinely resentful over the persistence of discrimination; they show few signs of indifference and fit rather well into the mold of the resentful woman. Compared with the telephone respondents, they are far more disposed toward anger or at least far readier to give voice to it, although even in the focus groups anger frequently is tinged with acceptance or resignation.[4] With the exception of a few members, they all give the impression of being extremely annoyed that the battle for gender equality still has not been won. Such consensus is lacking in the survey. The telephone respondents' feelings are harder to assess. Many share the focus group participants' feelings of anger but express these feelings mostly when the questioning concerns personal experiences. When the questions turn to the general topic of societal discrimination, the population is divided within itself, and anger does not characterize the group as a whole. Where the telephone respondents express anger, it is highly domain-specific. Closer inspection suggests that the differences between focus group members and telephone respondents may be more apparent than real and may be a function of the difference in topics addressed by the two samples. Focus groups chose to discuss issues that affected them personally, but telephone respondents had to respond to the issues the interviewer presented to them and which may not have had direct relevance for them.

---

4. As we will see in chapter 7, the men in our focus groups react to sex discrimination with considerable equanimity, not to say indifference.

THE TELEPHONE SURVEY: ANGRY, BUT SELECTIVE

Even though telephone interviewees, as we saw in the preceding chapter, share with the focus groups the perception that sex discrimination continues to be operative in all spheres of private and public life, they did not appear to share focus group participants' intense resentment over this perception. The majority of the telephone interviewees seemed relatively unperturbed rather than angry. As we will see, in reply to most questions that deal with the *general* problem of discrimination, the majority professed not being "bothered" or being very little bothered, often stating that they accept this discrimination as a fact of life. Almost all of the telephone questions, however, inquired about discrimination in the larger system or its parts rather than focusing on a person's own experiences. In the few instances where we solicited information about personal experiences, many interviewees become quite ready to voice resentment. It may be "easier, perhaps, to maintain anger against specific individuals you hoped to change; it is harder to keep anger flowing against something so huge and amorphous as 'the system'" (Tavris 1982: 250).

To illustrate the telephone respondents' reaction to societal discrimination, I will first focus on a three-step question sequence designed to elicit respondents' perception of society's treatment of men and women, asking how they felt about observed gender-based inequities. The exact wording for the three questions was: "In general, who would you say gets treated better by society—men, women, or are they treated the same?" One quarter of the women respondents expressed the belief that the genders received the same treatment. Those who said that either men or women were treated better (71 percent) were then asked: "Do you think this is fair, unfair, or isn't this the way you think about it?" (see table 4.1). Only those who declared that men were treated better and considered this practice "unfair,"[5] were then asked, "Is this something that really bothers you, or is this just the way society is?"

Most of the analysis in this chapter will be based on the answers obtained from this subsample because the three-step sequence makes the tightest connection between an individual's perception of discrimination and her feelings about it. The fact that a person recognizes that not all segments of society are equal (the first question) should not by itself give rise to resentment. Societies generally are inegalitarian, and that inequality is usually taken more or less for granted by its citizens. But when the inequality is considered unfair (our second question), re-

5. Since only two respondents maintained that women are treated better, the analysis which follows is based exclusively on those who believe that men are treated better.

sentiment is to be anticipated, especially when the unfairly treated group is one's own. By eliminating from consideration those women who saw no discrimination and those who considered the treatment fair (or at least not unfair), we derive a population which, if it is consistent in its reactions, should have been the group most likely to be resentful (our third question). This sequence, therefore, should provide the clearest test of the extent to which the perception of gender-based injustice results in resentment or anger.[6]

Among the telephone respondents, 25 percent saw the genders treated equally. Among those who perceived unequal treatment, 4 percent thought it fair, 80 percent considered it to be unfair, and 14 percent said this was not "the way I think about it." In the analysis which follows, all of those women who either saw no inequality of treatment or saw it but did not consider it unfair will be omitted.[7] Instead, the analysis will focus exclusively on those women who perceived inequality and judged it to be unfair since the assumption had been that anger would likely occur when a person or group believes themselves to be treated unfairly relative to other individuals or groups they regard as being no more worthy. My assumption had been that this particular subgroup of women would constitute the group most likely to be bothered by the unequal treatment. However, even in this purposefully selected population anger or not being bothered was not the predominant sentiment. Apparently women's agreement that the treatment is unfair did not cause them to react in a uniform manner. A slim majority (52 percent) said they were not bothered by sex discrimination and that they accept it as fact of life (hereafter I will call these the Acceptors). Forty-four percent are bothered (hereafter called Resenters), and 4 percent volunteer the answer "both," indicating that they are bothered by discrimination but, nonetheless, accept it (see table 4.1).

Thus, even among women who condemn the inequitable treatment, a majority is willing to accept that treatment as perhaps inevitable rather than to be discomforted by it. Although, based on relative deprivation theory, the group that thinks it unfair that men are treated better than women has more provocation than others for feeling angry, anger apparently is not the inevitable reaction or at least is not overtly

6. A similar sequence was used in connection with a few other questions, but these dealt with very specific situations (such as the division of housework) or specific populations (such as employed women's reaction to sexual harassment in the workplace) and will be discussed in that context.

7. A detailed analysis of that population yielded no systematic differences between it and the rest of the sample. Moreover many of the Unawares actually were not unaware at all but noted varying degrees of discrimination in reply to most of the other questions.

expressed.[8] Why? The acceptance of unequal treatment that she considers to be unfair may be simply a function of women's reluctance to express anger publicly. It could also be derived from gender differences in expectations for success. Belle Rose Ragins's and Eric Sundstrom's 1989 review of the psychological literature noted that many women simply do not expect to be treated in an equitable manner. Perhaps these women, who are aware of discrimination and find it unfair, are like "females generally [who] suffer from an atrophied sense of deserving (Deaux quoted in Crosby 1982: 8). Finally, the reluctance to be angry may be less a function of gender than of powerlessness. Students of organizational behavior frequently comment that in a hierarchy those commanding less power tend to consider the free expression of anger a cost they can ill afford. For example, Kanter (1977) in her study of one large corporation noted that although sex functions as a major sorting mechanism for the initial distribution of power, all persons, men as well as women, who occupy relatively powerless positions learn to limit their aspirations. It is conceivable that in our sample too a somewhat similar process is involved. Perhaps the discrimination-aware respondents who prefer not to be bothered by the unfairness they perceive also feel powerless to change the unequal power distribution and, hence, consider anger a luxury they cannot afford.[9] However, since we did not probe into the respondents' reasons for accepting discrimination, it is impossible to definitively answer this question.

Yet two more answers to the question of why some are bothered (the Resenters) and others are not suggest themselves. The first answer concerns the Resenters' demographic characteristics. It is often asserted that the better educated and more affluent women constitute the group that is particularly perturbed by gender-based discrimination. In our sample, however, Resenters did not differ from Acceptors in any of the major demographics examined. Neither age, employment, education, occupation, etc. distinguished one group from the other. Even ideological differences were not dramatic, although Resenters were somewhat more liberal but Acceptors were not conservative. The one dimension on which the two groups differed was in their concern for women as a group; Resenters identified significantly more with women than did Acceptors (Sigel and Burnbauer 1989). A second answer could be that the women who are bothered by the unfairness they see (the

8. Given that female reaction, it can hardly be surprising to discover that most men are not bothered either; in actuality, they are virtually unperturbed. Male reactions are discussed in chapter 7.

9. Some support for this explanation can be derived from the fact that the women in our sample are overwhelmingly of the opinion that gender discrimination does not bother men; only 7 percent believe men are bothered by it.

TABLE 4.1   WOMEN'S REACTION TO PERCEIVED
SEX DISCRIMINATION

A. RESPONSES TO QUESTION (%):

In general, who would you say gets treated better by society, men, women, or are they treated the same?

Men	69
Women	2
Treated the same	25
Depends (volunteered)	2
Don't know	2
	$n = 400$

B. RESPONSES TO QUESTION (%):

Do you think it is fair, unfair that men get treated better, or isn't this the way you think about it?*

Unfair	80
Fair	4
Not how I think about it	14
Don't know	1
	$n = 283$

C. RESPONSES TO QUESTION (%):

Is this something that really bothers you, or is this just the way society is?†

Bothered	44
Accepted	52
Both	4
Don't know	1
	$n = 227$

*Asked only of respondents who said men get treated better by society.
†Asked only of respondents who called the practice unfair.

Resenters) simply are more aware of the pervasiveness of discrimination. This can best be seen by comparing their scores on the Discrimination Awareness Index with the scores of those who were not angry (the Acceptors). The Discrimination Awareness Index, the reader will recall, provides an additive measure of a person's responses to twelve discrimination items. High scorers are those who respond that they see discrimination operative in all or almost all of the areas mentioned by the interviewer. Resenters indeed showed more discrimination awareness with 58 percent scoring high, and only 6 percent scoring low on the Discrimination Awareness Index. The Acceptors also score high (43 percent) in discrimination awareness, and even in this group relatively few (13 percent) score low, which causes one to wonder if perhaps they may be not quite as unperturbed as their initial answer would suggest or, conversely, that discrimination awareness is not inevitably accompanied by anger, notwithstanding all of the theorizing to the contrary (see table 4.2).

TABLE 4.2   DISCRIMINATION AWARENESS OF WOMEN
CLASSIFIED AS RESENTERS AND ACCEPTORS*

	Level of Discrimination Awareness (by %)		
	High	Medium	Low
Resenters (n = 100)	58	36	6
Acceptors (n = 125)	43	44	13

*Respondents who volunteered the answer "both" to the question whether they are bothered by unfair discrimination *and* replied that they accept it (4%) are not included.

The impression of a largely unperturbed population changes considerably, however, when, instead of being confronted with a dichotomized choice, respondents are given the opportunity to nuance their reactions, as they are in another question sequence. Instead of asking, as in our first sequence, "In general, who would you say gets treated better by society—men, women, or are they treated the same," this sequence asks explicitly about "discrimination." It is a two-part sequence which begins with the question: "How much sex discrimination would you say there is in American society where women are not treated as equals because of their sex?" In the first sequence, respondents were confronted with a dichotomized choice, whereas in this sequence they could choose from the following options—a lot, a fair amount, some, just a little, or none at all. That question is then followed by a second question: "How do you feel about that *yourself*, does it bother you a lot, some, or not at all?" This sequence differed from the first in yet another way. It was asked of all respondents, including those who during the first sequence expressed the view that the genders are treated equally (the segment we had labeled as Discrimination Unawares or Unawares for short).[10] Given the opportunity to fine-tune their assessment of "discrimination," virtually no one (only 1 percent) rejected the idea that some degree of discrimination continues to be part of American practice (see table 4.3, part A). When next asked to describe *how much* the observed discrimination bothers them, women became more ready to describe themselves as bothered. Very few (15 percent) stated that they are "not at all bothered," and almost one-third (30 percent) said they were "bothered a lot" (table 4.3, part B). The rest expressed varying degrees of discomfort (36 percent are some-

10. A detailed analysis of the discrimination Unawares yield no major demographic differences between that population and the rest of the sample. Moreover, many of the so-called Unawares actually are not unaware but noted varying degrees of discrimination in response to most questions other than the initial three-part one. Hereafter they will be included in the discussion in order to give a more complete picture of how the total sample of women reacted to any of the issues we presented to them.

TABLE 4.3   WOMEN'S ANGER OVER DISCRIMINATION

A. EXTENT OF DISCRIMINATION SEEN BY RESPONDENT

Respondent Sees:	Responses (by %)
A lot	27
A fair amount	43
Some	20
Just a little	7
None	1
Depends	1
Don't know	2
	$n = 400$

B. PERCENTAGE OF SAMPLE BOTHERED BY PERCEIVED DISCRIMINATION*

Bothered a lot	30
Bothered some	36
Bothered a little	19
Not at all bothered	15
Don't know	1
	$n = 384$

C. REACTION BY PERCEPTION OF PERSONAL DISCRIMINATION

	Bothered By Discrimination			
Perception of Extent of Discrimination	A lot	Some	A little	Not at all
A lot of discrimination	65	20	14	1
Fair amount	22	45	18	5
Some	6	48	24	23
Just a little	8	8	35	50
				$n = 384$

*Asked only of those who saw some discrimination.

what bothered and 19 percent a little). It would appear then that very few women are indifferent to discrimination.

As one might expect, the degree of resentment a woman reports is related to the magnitude of discrimination she believes exists in the United States. Those who say they see a lot of discrimination are more apt to be bothered by that discrimination. Conversely, those who perceive just a little discrimination also are not likely to be much bothered (see table 4.3, part C). There is, then, a definite relationship between discrimination awareness and anger; the more discrimination a person perceives, the more likely she is to be angry over it. But the group that sees a lot of discrimination and is bothered by it makes up just a little more than one quarter (27 percent) of the whole sample. Most women recognize some discrimination and are a little or somewhat bothered by it. These choices make a good deal of common sense. Why should someone who does not visualize discrimination as an all-encompassing phenomenon get deeply upset about it? Why pay the high price of anger when in the affected person's opinion the affront is not commensurate? To put it another way, most women are not indifferent to how women are treated by society; in fact, almost all dislike it with varying degrees of intensity but most apparently can live with it (or have learned to live with it).

The above findings suggest that the Acceptors might not be as unbothered as their replies to the dichotomized question had indicated. To test that proposition, we examined their answers to the multiple-choice question since it afforded them the opportunity to make finer distinctions. Under these conditions, the Acceptors show themselves to be far from indifferent (see table 4.4). While relatively few (23 percent) are greatly disturbed by discrimination, most are somewhat bothered and only 10 percent are not bothered at all. As for those who were bothered by unfair treatment, the great majority is clearly very disturbed (64 percent) and virtually none are indifferent. The telephone respondents now show themselves more resentful of discrimination than their answers to the earlier dichotomized question on unfair treatment would have suggested. But pronounced anger over discrimination still does not characterize the majority. Perhaps as Deborah Holmes, a lawyer, recently suggested: "By the time you say 'yes, I'm dissatisfied' on a survey, you've gone through many levels. You have to have felt the discomfort in your stomach, then brought it up into your head, recognized it and labeled it."[11]

So far I have focused exclusively on general reactions to discrimination. What happens when the person herself is a victim of discrimination? My anticipation had been that under those circumstances women would register strong resentment. The findings, however, are far more ambiguous than I anticipated. In some instances, women in this position clearly express strong resentment. When women have to cope with sexual harassment, an experience to which 33 percent have been exposed, 77 percent are very angry about it, and only 9 percent profess to being unaffected. Similarly, when their place of work pays women less than men, 66 percent are very angry. In other instances, however, women are less disturbed. Thirty-four percent of the women in our sample are under the impression that at their place of employment their opinions count for less than do the men's opinions. This state of affairs makes 30 percent of them angry, whereas 35 percent accept it as the way life works, and another 35 percent are both angry and accepting. In reflecting on these distributions, it is important to bear in mind that the personally affected population constitutes a very

---

11. Cited in Laura Mansnerus, "Why We Are Leaving the Law," *Working Women* (April 1993): 67.

TABLE 4.4   HOW BOTHERED ARE THE BOTHERED
WOMEN? A COMPARISON OF THE PERCENTAGES
OF WOMEN'S REPLIES TO QUESTIONS 15 AND 17*

Type of Respondent	Unfair Treatment Bothers Her			
	A lot	Some	A little	Not at all
Resenters	64	28	6	2
Acceptors	23	43	25	10
				$n = 283$

*Both questions were asked only of women who perceived gender-based discrimination, but question 17 asked respondents to state *how* bothered they were; question 15 made no provision for specifying degree of resentment.

small group since, as was shown in the previous chapter, most of the women, in our sample, as in others, feel personally exempt from discrimination.

The observation that women's experience with discrimination or unfair treatment may suggest that discrimination awareness reflects a purely cognitive process, void of deep emotion, which L. Walker and T. F. Pettigrew labeled "cold cognition" (1984: 307). Cold cognition is "a state arrived at through a conscious, rational judgment of the relative positions of self or self's group and some referent on some evaluative dimension(s)" in contrast to the hot cognition, or deep anger felt by deprived groups. Although Walker and Pettigrew consider women one of the deprived groups whom they expect to feel "deep anger," this emotion apparently does not characterize most of the telephone respondents, or at least is not expressed to an unknown interviewer at the other end of a telephone line. Since telephone interviewers cannot easily probe into the meaning interviewees wish to convey (see chapter 2) when, say, they assert they are not bothered, we cannot know how "cold" or "hot" their responses are. Their relative lack of anger may be related to their belief, as we saw in the previous chapter, that much improvement in the status of women has already taken place in the United States. Their perceptions of improvement may prompt them to consider the personal costs of anger to be too high and quite unnecessary. This should be particularly so if they have the expectation that additional improvement is likely to occur soon, a point to which I will return in subsequent chapters.

ANGER IN THE FOCUS GROUPS

The focus groups at first glance seemed to react very differently. Unlike the telephone respondents, focus group members were quite ready, one might even say eager, to tell each other just how angry they felt about their encounters with discrimination. However, most of the instances to which they referred were personal experiences they or their friends had had. They might talk a bit about the general issue of gender-based discrimination, especially when prodded by the moderator, but the bulk of their discussions concerned their own personal experiences. These instances of unfair treatment range widely from the public to the private (see subsequent chapters, especially chapter 5.) The observers never doubted that these women are genuinely resentful; the unfairness of prejudices which they reported really hurt them. As they shared with each other various incidents of denigration, they described their emotions with "hot" words, telling how they were "furious," "livid," "fit to be tied," "mad," or "ready to kill the man."

Conceivably, the all but exclusive emphasis on personal experiences must have been offered primarily as illustrative of the general problem but to the groups' observers it seemed clear that personal hurt rather than societal injustice had provided the initial impetus for members' indignation and resentment (what Runciman labeled "egoistic relative deprivation"). The focus group participants' emphasis on personally experienced injustices, however, did not blind them to gender-based discrimination as a larger social and political problem. They evidently do not look upon their personal experiences with discrimination as isolated, let alone unique, instances in which only they have been treated unfairly, but rather as symptomatic of the general state of affairs. Over and over they referred to their specific instances as typical: "that's the way the world sees a female." The "world" here stands as a synonym for men. In most discussions, it was always men who do the discriminating, who want to dominate women, and who are afraid to grant them equality. Though they may recognize the pervasiveness of the problem, they are much less likely to perceive it as a political one. The women in these groups made relatively few references to social or political institutions that may contribute to gendered inequality. Nor did they discuss in any detail what could be done to improve the situation for women in general. In these brief sessions, the personal anecdote was their preferred way of communicating. It is hard to tell why this was so. Possibly they were deliberately avoiding controversy, much they way some people avoid discussing politics with strangers. Possibly they simply did not think in such larger social or political terms. Finally, they might have thought it pointless to expect that they could change the male world. As a young woman in one of the groups bluntly put it, "Only women will change the roles for women; don't count on the men."

Most members of our focus group shared the young woman's feeling that women have to do it for themselves, that they can't count on men. Consequently, much of the time their tales of unfair treatment do not end with the demands that the victimizer change. Instead, the raconteur not infrequently concluded by saying something to the effect that she had learned how to handle her anger, to minimize the corrosive impact it used to have on her. Instead of relating what she did to the man or men who had caused her problem, she would tell how she learned to cope with the situation, to ignore the males who "tried to trip her" and now "refuses to let the unfairness get me down." "I won't let it get to me and show how much it hurt," says one young woman, or, as a woman in her fifties said, "I try not to let it get me down and miserable."

Three examples from the focus groups shall suffice to illustrate the technique. A young college graduate in a managerial starter position with a big firm was asked to do some typing for her superiors or to bring a "couple of cups of coffee to the conference room." At first, she reported that that "just blew me away," but now "no problem, that does not bother me. It just, you know, I don't care, [they] are paying my salary." A somewhat older woman reported that at first when she started in the business world, she felt angry every day and night because she did not want to be "the thumb of this masculine hierarchy. But these were powerful men and there wasn't much I could do about it." So after a while she decided "to just let it pass"; to accept it because in "those days you didn't expect anything else." Finally, Doris, a middle-aged blue-collar woman, works "for some pretty tough men that pushed you to the edge where they waited for you to say it. And I used to hold it in and hold it in, and do what I had to do. When I said hold it in—I did not scream back. They would try to press a button and get a reaction, and I would just do what I had to do. Okay, fine. And that night I'd go home, and I'm a great person for weeding. I learned what game they were playing, so it made me very strong."[12] This woman *is* angry, no doubt about it, but she has learned to cope with it without letting people know of her anger. How would that woman have answered had we interviewed her over the phone? She too might have said she is "not bothered," because she now has become so "very strong."

Whether through weeding or chopping wood (a technique another woman chooses for letting off steam), *not* letting it bother them is one greatly valued method these women adopt for coping with harassment and discrimination. Very few report that they resort to "blowing up" or

12. Lieutenant Brenda Holdener, a thirty-one-year-old Navy pilot made a similar comment upon returning from the Gulf War. "We're not without the guys who don't want us there, but that just makes women work harder and want to be there" (*New York Times*, 2 August 1992, p. 3).

fighting unfairness outright. Of course, in the focus groups we also encountered the occasional "screamer," the rare "loud mouth" (to use her self-characterization) who parries every offensive comment from male associates with an equally offensive one of her own. But that woman is not typical of the group as a whole. She is a distinct exception. Only a few women in our groups saw male/female relations as a constant struggle over male dominance and were determined not to be dominated. "You have to be better than men. They will come right out if you don't prove a point all the time," says a noncommissioned officer, the thirtyish daughter from a military family. In the same vein, Susan, a pharmacist, told the woman who weeds that she would have refused to hold her feelings in until she got home: "I don't allow it [discrimination] to happen. I'm just very bitchy when it comes to being there. I mean, really, I've been in business for fifteen years, and nobody has ever done that to me." She then cites with considerable self-satisfaction some cutting and even crude comments she has made to males who offended her and concludes her counsel to the other focus group members as follows: "You can't abdicate as a woman and expect to be treated equally . . . ; then you're victimizing yourself and allow that to happen. . . ." This, by the way, was the conclusion she reached after being passed over for promotion in favor of a man whom she had trained. Her way of dealing with her outrage was to quit the job right then and there and open up her own business. She tells the group that to this date—fifteen years later—she receives considerable satisfaction from the fact that the other enterprise did not thrive after she left while hers does. But, she still remembers the hurt after fifteen years as though it had happened yesterday.

Most of the women in our groups demonstrate little taste for confrontation. They avoid it both for self-protection and in the interest of their overall or long-range goals. If they let discrimination bother them, who suffers but themselves, they seem to say. They may recall how it did bother them early on and remember how miserable it made them feel until they ceased caring so much. Listening to these women, one is reminded of the airline stewardesses who told Hochschild how they had taught themselves not to care so much about abusive treatment so that they could continue to do their job. Like the flight attendants, the focus group members too think being bothered interferes with achieving what they want to achieve, especially at work. As long as the world functions as it does, far better not to let it "get to you," as they are apt to say. "If you are serious about your career, don't waste time looking back," ventured a clerical employee in a small municipal system. "Yeah, just keep going; it doesn't pay to see how men got there."

Another way of characterizing these coping techniques might be to say that these women are or have become resigned to living in a world where women are treated as second-class citizens. This was the impression of one focus group member, who exclaimed: "See how resigned we all sound!"[13] The way many women described handling the situation amounts to a form of resignation or perhaps accommodation. But resignation conveys an aura of passivity, of abandoning one's aspirations, of giving up. These women may have adjusted their aspirations, but their anger does not appear to have paralyzed them. A better way to describe their complex reactions would be to say that they are convinced men still look upon them as inferior and resist treating them as equals, especially in work-related situations, and that this will not change in the foreseeable future. Fighting this pattern, therefore, is futile and so is grieving over it ("whining" was what one woman called it). Neither, however, are they willing to return to the lifestyle their mothers and grandmothers had to adopt. Instead they "hold it in" and keep on trying. As a young woman said, "If I went to my boss and said 'Hey, these guys are picking on me,' then I'm being a crybaby [and they will say] 'Aw, you can't take it.' So you don't do that." She agreed when another woman told her "I would not get all that upset about it, that's how life works." To which a young careerist added: "That's what you are going to find out in the real world too."

Perseverance and a certain degree of realism seems to govern these women. Perseverance, they tell each other, can make a difference. Those qualities can get the individual woman much of what she deserves and desires although probably not all that is due her. Comedienne Phyllis Diller (interview, 12 July 1992, *The New York Times*) tellingly describes this dilemma. She urges her female colleagues to keep trying to get bookings in prestigious supper clubs even though there is much bias against comediennes. She tells them that it is definitely possible to succeed, notwithstanding male resistance. But she also insists that "the double standard is just there forever. We have to live with it." Women as a class have to live with the double standard forever, but the individual woman, if she tries hard enough, can begin to transcend it. The focus group members may not aspire to bookings in supper clubs but they, like Diller herself, must learn to live with the double standard without getting emotionally devastated. Our focus groups show, however, that learning not to be bothered is not the same as not being angry.

Of course, in the focus groups too not every woman vented anger

---

13. That is also the impression gained by my two male colleagues as they observed from behind the one-way mirror. What the female graduate assistant and I took for low-key and somewhat repressed anger, they interpreted as resignation.

over personal and/or social discrimination. Those least inclined to anger tended to be older women who had devoted their lives to nurturing their families. Age (possibly leading to resignation) was here compounded with a cohort effect (many women of this generation had never expected equality). Some older women, however, though seemingly less angry, appear a bit regretful that they and women of their generation never had the choice and opportunities women have today. Here is a middle-class woman in her early sixties, who reflected on her life:

> I did stay home. . . . At that time none of the girls, women worked. . . . And we were expected to raise our children and be community volunteers and entertain, and live that kind of life. And I have had a wonderful life. But I kind of *envy* the young gals now that are, that are . . . , you know, I went through college because it was expected of me, not with any goal at all. Instead of being *just* a bookkeeper, I'd be a CPA if I were young today. And I kind of envy the young gals.

Asked by someone: "Do you feel bitter at all," she replied, "Not bitter, just a little envious . . . " She then discussed the type of financial career she would have liked to have pursued and concluded by expressing what seems like bitterness over the low esteem in which housewives are held. She exclaimed, "Do I feel anything about that? I sure do." Although this woman was not overtly or even consciously angry, her retrospection reveals resentment over opportunities denied to her because of gender. This woman is more typical of her age group in our group sessions than the one or two homemakers who harbor no regrets. Even they, however, urge their daughters to pursue careers of their own.

Anger may be what these women feel; not being bothered is how they protect themselves. In short, they are angry, yes, but they cannot be bothered to be bothered! They are probably not so very different from the non-bothered telephone respondents. The focus group participants told each other how angry they felt, but many had also learned to accept discrimination as a given. They believed, as the young woman cited earlier put it so bluntly, "Discrimination is a fact of life. Just forget it."

COMPARING FOCUS GROUPS AND TELEPHONE SURVEYS

Were we to summarize the results from the two samples, we would have to conclude that the focus group sessions give the impression that most women, irrespective of background and age, are resentful of the treatment they receive from men and the discrimination they endure in society. The telephone interviewees' reactions, in contrast, are less unanimous, and resentment is voiced less frequently. On the telephone, the proportion of women who express anger varies from question to question. Although some questions elicit a good deal of anger, this is not the prevailing pattern. Only a quarter of the phone interviewees seem deeply disturbed by discrimination, although most condemn the unequal treatment they see as being grossly unfair to women. Even when they reported that they personally had been victims of discrimination, many telephone interviewees responded that they were only mildly angry about it. Is it possible that some of the non-bothered telephone interviewees reactions are not all that different from those of the focus groups? To be sure, they tell the interviewer that they accept discrimination as a fact of life which does not bother them, but does this necessarily preclude simultaneously feeling resentful? Is it possible that they could be both angry and accepting, accepting in the sense that they are unable to change the situation? Some of the seemingly discrepant results may well be due at least in part to differences in the two methods of eliciting information, including: (1) the different formats adopted for each inquiry; (2) the different dynamics involved in each format; and (3) different question wordings.

We opted for a nondirective format for the group sessions, a decision that no doubt contributed to the participants heavy emphasis on personal experiences. The telephone interviewees were offered fewer opportunities to discuss personal experiences with discrimination and instead were asked to focus on the treatment women in general receive. Other people's misfortunes, as we all know, rarely evoke the sympathy or anger that our own predicaments do. Hence the telephone respondents could afford to be more detached.

In the telephone interviews, many questions were quite abstract, referring to institutions, society in general, or to general practices rather than to the treatment the respondent might have received from *her* foreman or car salesman. But these specific and personal instances are precisely the ones that evoked anger in focus group members. The close-ended, strictly dichotomized questions of the telephone interviews may have inhibited further the expression of anger.

Second, the two formats involved entirely different dynamics. In a telephone interview, the respondent is confronted by an invisible person she does not know and of whose motives for asking her fairly intimate questions she is ignorant. Hence she may well feel on her guard, especially when the interviewer is a man, as was frequently the case.[14] Focus groups, on the other hand, provide face-to-face encoun-

14. Attempts to determine if sex of the interviewer affected the responses were inconclusive. In our survey, it mattered for some questions but not for others. It did matter for some clearly gender-related questions, in which women tended to give more feminist answers to female interviewers than to males (Whelchel 1987). Same-sex interview situ-

ters and, when congenial, lend themselves to disclosing feelings about experiences that women might not ordinarily reveal to a stranger. Like consciousness-raising groups, focus groups validate the participants' resentment over specific experiences and encourage the expression without fear of censure. Realizing that they were not alone, that other women had similar experiences and felt about them as they did may have helped. In several of the focus groups, participants spontaneously commented on this phenomenon, saying how easy they found it to talk to each other about common experiences. The format seems therefore to have facilitated the expression of emotions such as anger which under other circumstances women are frequently reluctant to voice.[15]

Third, question wording probably also contributed to the contrast between telephone and group responses. We had not asked telephone respondents if they were "angry" (we used that term only twice in the interview schedule) but rather if they were "bothered." The choice of the term *bothered* was deliberate, prompted by our knowing that other studies had shown women's reluctance to give vent to anger. We thought that "being bothered" would be a less emotionally charged or threatening term and hence easier to admit to. It is conceivable, however, that the term taps a different reactive mechanism. It may describe how people *cope* with an unpleasant experience over which they have little control rather than how they *feel* about the experience. Someone may be angry but refuse to let it bother them. If that is the meaning some respondents attach to the word "bothered," their reactions would be quite similar to those reported in the focus groups. Not knowing exactly what respondents mean when they answer a question (or even what they understood the question to mean) is a well-known and fre-

---

ations mattered particularly when the question dealt with anger. Women were more willing to express anger when the interviewer was female, and male respondents expressed least anger to a male interviewer. J. Ballou (1990: 3) found gender interaction effects on questions about abortion in about one-third of the items. "In particular, for most of the items where there were effects, it was the case of female respondents being effected by female interviewers to provide more 'feminist' or pro-choice responses and about half of the male respondent effects are in interviews with females." For additional studies, consult E. W. Kane and L. J. Macaulay (1993).

15. The opportunities for frankness and openness were further enhanced by the composition of the groups. To encourage maximum openness, we had decided to organize same-gender rather than mixed-gender groups. It is highly doubtful that most of the women would have been equally eager to admit to their resentment or to make negative comments about men, as they did so readily among themselves, had men been part of the group. For that reason, experienced focus group moderators strongly advised us against conducting mixed-gender groups. The social psychological literature also suggests that women are more reticent in such groups—with men doing more of the talking and women more likely to acquiesce (see Eagly 1987 for a review).

quently commented-on problem in all survey research. It is aggravated when, as in our case, the questions are close-ended and highly structured.[16]

Combining now the impressions gained from both structured phone interviews and focus group discussions, we conclude that most women are by no means indifferent to gender-based discrimination. Quite the contrary; they look upon the treatment they receive as analogous to that of second-class citizens. They think this is unfair. Some are "bothered" by this situation; some are not. Anger at discrimination, in general, seems quite shallow at times and, in the case of the focus groups, seems to be nourished by specific episodes, usually where the person herself was the victim. Only on the telephone survey did we encounter a substantial number of women who professed not being disturbed by discrimination. Using focus group discussions to help interpret the responses of the telephone respondents, one might infer that even among the respondents who profess to not be bothered by discrimination, some may actually be angry but refuse to admit it to the interviewer or perhaps to themselves.[17]

Even in the case of the women who, in both forms of inquiry, acknowledge their anger that anger may well be episodic. It is not likely to structure their daily lives. Nor does one get the impression that their anger is intense or easily translated into appropriate social action.

16. We used several closed-ended questions because we would have been unable to include as many questions on the same topic as we did had we resorted more often to open-ended questions and added many probes.

17. That most women advocate equality for women and greater efforts to bring it about (see chapter 3) lends credence to this interpretation.

RESENTMENT AND
POLITICAL INVOLVEMENT

We can easily see what we have done to ourselves; but we cannot act on what we see.
—Vivian Gornick, *New York Times Magazine*, 15 April 1990

The significance of a given population's collective discontent with the status quo often does not become visible until it finds expression in overt social and political gestures and actions. This chapter explores the degree to which women's resentment over their second-class status affects their political involvement. It will focus on three aspects: first, the spheres in which the second-class treatment is most visible and most painful; second, their readiness to conceive of this treatment as a political problem; and third, their willingness to become involved in efforts designed to better the situation. The chapter begins with observations on the differences between telephone respondents and focus group participants and concludes with the population's perception of the agents of change.

DISCONTENT AND POLITICIZATION

In theory, this should be a propitious time for women to translate their sense of relative deprivations into collective action. Theories of deprivation assert that such collective efforts are most likely to occur in transitional periods when improvements are beginning to occur or when chances for their success seem probable, because in such times the affected people have become most cognizant of what they lack and are most anxious to obtain it. To again quote Tocqueville's famous reflection on the French Revolution: "Thus it was precisely in those parts of France where there had been the most improvement that the popular discontent ran highest. . . . Patiently endured so long as it seemed beyond redress, a grievance becomes intolerable once the possibility of removing it crosses men's minds."[1] This chapter asks whether the

1. See *The Old Regime and the French Revolution* (Garden City: Doubleday, 1955), pp. 176–77.

sense of relative deprivation which clearly crossed the New Jersey women's minds politicized them sufficiently to seek political remedies for their collective problems.

The answer to that question has to be "no." Nothing in the focus groups' discussions or in the telephone respondents' replies to open-ended questions suggests that these women have greatly politicized the discomfort they said they experience over their second-class status. Notwithstanding that many of them looked upon discrimination as a problem affecting and disadvantaging all of them, they generally did not see it as a problem calling for political solution. They were even less inclined to see it as one requiring that they personally become involved in political activity. As much as the modern American women's movement may have tried to raise women's political consciousness, only part of its message seems to have reached these women thus far. They have internalized the part of the message which asserts that they are entitled to equality but that society continues to deny them equality. They apparently have not absorbed the other part of the message, namely that nothing will change in society without women actively seeking to do something to promote change and that for maximum effectiveness they must promote that change collectively.

The apolitical approach of the women interviewed emerges most clearly in the focus groups. It is somewhat less apparent in the telephone conversations. This difference probably is more a function of format than genuine attitudinal differences. The nondirective nature of the focus groups permitted members to overlook or actively avoid political issues whereas telephone respondents had no such option; they had to address the issue because the interviewer confronted them with it and frequently asked them to decide whether or not a given problem should come within the purview of governmental responsibilities. These same telephone respondents may well not have made the connection on their own between a social problem and government intervention had the interviewer not suggested that a link could exist.[2] Nor do we know how focus group members would have reacted when contacted by phone. All that is known for sure is that in the open-ended focus group format the members seldom mentioned that the problems which so troubled them could be solved by political means. Even when one moderator raised that possibility and asked members to react, they refrained from exploring whether resorting to political means might solve the particular problem. Instead, they continued to deal with the

2. On the basis of their responses to open-ended questions, as will be shown presently, we are inclined to conclude that the telephone respondents too have not politicized the issue and that under similar circumstances they would have behaved much as did the focus group members.

problem in a highly personalized, anecdotal mode, reporting on their experiences—the humiliations endured, benefits denied, ambitions thwarted—and how they personally have coped with such experiences.

When participants in either of the two settings sought to allocate blame for their disadvantaged status, they found themselves in complete agreement: Men are the culprits. Men deserve most of the blame. The women were not oblivious to the fact that many of the injustices on which they reported go beyond the personal and are endemic to the society in which they live. They understood that, but they did not look to political solutions. Government, though not absolved of blame for its failure to promote gender equality effectively, tended to be blamed less frequently than were men.[3]

Even when the women in our sample talked about a specific problem related to gender inequity, they rarely focused on government and what it could or should do about it but instead targeted men in general. We heard, for example, frequent complaints about the difficulty of holding a full-time job while taking care of one or more preschool children. Yet only one group began a discussion (and a brief one at that) of the need for affordable day care. And even that group did not approach it as a potentially political issue. They did not discuss, for example, whether or not day care should be a governmental responsibility analogous to public education. This is an issue so relevant and vital for many employed women that the link between private need and political provenance might have suggested itself readily. Yet it did not. It is not a question here whether or not day care is desirable, clearly people can be of different minds about that—and our telephone respondents were divided on the issue—but what is remarkable is that the issue was never couched in political terms. It is this inattention to politics which struck me so forcefully.

Equally striking are the topics that were not raised by the focus groups. Only once did anyone mention abortion (and only then in passing).[4] In only one group did the topic of battered women come up, and in only one group was affirmative action mentioned spontaneously by the group rather than being raised by the moderator. Issues which had received wide publicity—such as family leave, women in the military, mandatory sex education in the public schools—also were never mentioned; nor did the groups discuss sexual harassment.[5] And even

3. When asked why women "have less influence in business and earn less than men," 54 percent of telephone respondents gave governmental policies as the reason why women have not been as successful as men, but even more (73 percent) blamed men.

4. One woman mentioned it within the general context of people telling other people how to live, but no one took up the topic.

5. One group, however, did bring up the subject of rape and there clearly made the

the battered-wife syndrome was mentioned only when a devout Roman Catholic woman wanted to explain (perhaps justify) why she finally divorced her abusive spouse.[6] Once the topic was raised in this fashion, other women had no difficulty relating to the problem.[7] Even in that very animated discussion, no one mentioned public resources available to protect abused women, such as restraining orders, shelters, and other potential remedies. Nor did the group discuss whether or not the problem could be further reduced by enacting appropriate public policies. The women treated violence against women as a personal problem (which, of course, it is in part), but they ignored that it also is a political problem and proceeded to discuss it not in political but in personal terms. The same personalized approach held for other situations as well. When the women in our groups spoke of gender-related grievances, they focused on what has happened to them or someone in their acquaintanceship rather than on what responsibility, if any, the government has for those who are discriminated against or abused.[8]

POLICY PREFERENCES

As for the telephone respondents, once an interviewer inquired into their willingness to seek political solutions for their problems, they were quite willing to entertain the idea that government has a role to play in these matters. There was, however, considerable disagreement as to just how prominent that role should be. Only 49 percent believed that "the government should make every effort to improve the social and economic position of women" and that it should become more active on their behalf; others disagreed, holding that the government should make no further effort because it is already doing enough (42 percent); and 8 percent advocated doing less.[9]

---

political link inasmuch as they objected to the light sentences which male judges tend to mete out to male offenders. And, predictably, the topic of women in the military was mentioned in the group where one woman was still on active duty, but even then it was not discussed as a political issue.

6. Actually, it first arose because of a recent television program on the topic ("The Burning Bed"), but it became personal only when the battered woman pointed to the frequency of the problem.

7. Because individuals often are reluctant to report on painful and embarrassing personal experiences, such as wife abuse, focus groups, given the right setting, may prove a good and relatively inexpensive device to encourage reporting on such long-locked-up experiences.

8. Male focus group members (see chapter 7) are more likely to make the connection with government, but for the opposite purpose, namely, to complain about the adverse effects some policies, such as affirmative action, have for them.

9. See table 3.6.

Once the possibility for a political solution to a specific problem was brought to their attention, however, telephone respondents often found a role for government. This receptivity was most noticeable when it came to policies likely to benefit women in practical and material ways, such as pregnancy leaves or shelters for abused women (see table 5.1, parts A and B) M. C. Molyneux (1985) calls these sorts of policies "practical gender interests." Distinguishing between "practical" and "strategic" gender interests, she sees practical gender interests as originating "from the concrete condition of women's positioning within the gender division of labor" (p. 233), whereas strategic gender interests are concerned with bringing an end to women's subordinate

TABLE 5.1   WOMEN'S POLICY PREFERENCES

A. RESPONDENTS' STANDS ON SPENDING FOR "WOMEN'S ISSUES" (%)

Respondent Favors Spending	More	Less	Keep as Is	DK
Shelters for battered women	69	5	23	4
Day care centers	59	10	28	4
Government needs to help women more	49	8	42	1

$n = 400$

B. RESPONDENTS' VIEWS ON SOCIAL POLICIES FOR WOMEN (%)

Does a woman have the right to return to her job after pregnancy leave?

Favors it	71
Thinks it is up to employer	13
It depends	7
Don't know	9

$n = 400$

How active should the government be in improving women's situation?

Government should be more active	49
Less active	5
Continue as is	42
Don't know	1

$n = 400$

C. RESPONDENTS' STANDS ON SPENDING TAX DOLLARS FOR SOCIAL WELFARE ISSUES (%)

Respondent Favors Spending	More	Less	Keep as Is	DK
College loans to minorities	46	12	40	2
Low-income housing	59	8	31	2
The environment	68	4	25	3
Colleges and universities	51	6	39	2

$n = 400$

status. Customarily, we associate strategic interests with feminism, although feminists are also much concerned with practical gender issues. The opposite does not necessarily follow, as women can be much concerned with certain practical aspects of discrimination and not concerned with the broader, strategic implications of that discrimination. Among the women we interviewed, practical gender interests clearly took precedence. For example, most approved of the idea that the government should build more shelters for battered women, and over two-thirds (69 percent) even declared themselves willing to see their tax burden increased for that purpose. Respondents were somewhat more ambivalent about paying taxes for day care centers, but even there a majority favored government expenditures. Majorities, but not necessarily overwhelming majorities, favor a variety of public policies designed to further women's interests directly or indirectly. This conclusion is based on a "women's issues" index we constructed which consisted of the telephone sample's responses to all questions related to the enactment of policies or public outlays designed to benefit women. (56 percent scored high and only 5 percent obtained low scores.)[10] The focus groups might have made similar political choices had these specific contingencies been raised for them,[11] but what is remarkable is that topics such as building more shelters or paying for them with tax dollars never emerged spontaneously as possible solutions for women's problems. Apparently, the women we observed were not looking for political solutions to problems they considered to be widespread and serious. On other social issues, most women also favored increasing governmental outlays, and very few advocated cutting support (see table 5.1, part C).

Conceivably, the atmosphere of the group settings contributed to the personal, nonpolitical tone of the conversations. The women may have viewed, perhaps even welcomed, such a setting, as nothing more and nothing less than an opportunity to share common experiences and to let off steam. The omission may not therefore necessarily indicate a genuinely apolitical approach to women's issues. (Conversely, the telephone respondents on their own might not have considered finding political solutions to these issues and then would have emerged as equally apolitical.) Another explanation for the apolitical tenor of the focus group discussions could be that participants believed a gathering of strangers not to be the proper setting for political discourse, especially because some of the unmentioned topics, such as abortion, would prob-

10. Males, predictably, scored lower—36:53:5 percent respectively.

11. Ideologically, the focus groups are very similar to the telephone respondents, with most of them identifying themselves as middle-of-the-roaders and slightly more self-identified liberals than conservatives.

ably have turned out to be controversial and might have led to tension in the group. The group members may well have implicitly agreed to dwell on those aspects of gender-related experiences they have reason to believe they share with each other.

SOURCES OF DISCONTENT

The political or apolitical nature of these women's responses to what most of them perceived as an unjust situation becomes more comprehensible when one becomes acquainted with the areas which most seem to trouble them. In analyzing the focus group transcripts, I have focused on the topics cited with the greatest regularity.[12] One topic, housework, commanded an extraordinary amount of their attention. Much of the women's groups' two hours together was devoted to complaining about the unfair division of labor at home, especially the lack of cooperation they receive from their partners.[13] My first inclination had been to bypass those conversations rather than to include them in a chapter on political involvement. I abandoned that idea when I realized what a central role these everyday activities played in the formation of their gendered perspectives.

The household division of labor may well have been the occasion that first made some of these women conscious of their inferior status in the constellation of things, so that they began to consider the situation at home as symptomatic of women's inferior status in society at large. So long as they stayed home while the spouses went out to work, the structure of inequality may not have been apparent to them. But once they too went into the labor market and still were expected to shoulder the main burden of the household, the discrepancy between male and female statuses became obvious and may have provided the spark that ignited their sense of second-class citizenship.

That employed women carry a much heavier burden of domestic responsibilities than their male partners is by now hardly news (among the more recent works on the topic, see Crosby 1991; Gerson 1985; Hertz 1986; Arlene Hochschild 1989). Still I was surprised that the issue of the "second shift" (A. R. Hochschild 1989) dominated the focus group discussions to the extent that it did and to the exclusion of other social problems and their political implications. The groups' concentration on this issue was all the more significant because the groups we

12. For the reason already explained in chapter 2, no frequency distributions can be offered.

13. Those who were without partners complained about the amount of service their fathers expected of their mothers. One young woman, while visiting her parents, quite bluntly told her father: "You know, she could use some help. Why don't you do that?"

assembled were somewhat special. Every participant had previously participated in at least one of the public opinion surveys conducted by the Eagleton Institute of Politics, and these polls concentrate heavily on questions of politics and public policy. Moreover, members were given to understand that the topics raised during their group sessions might suggest questions to be introduced in future telephone surveys. One might, therefore, have anticipated that the participants would have expected the focus group organizers to be interested primarily in their opinions on public policy questions. If that thought occurred to them, it apparently did not shape the direction of their discussions to any appreciable degree.

All of their complaints about the heavy burden of their many and varied domestic responsibilities notwithstanding, only a few of the participants reported having attempted to create a more equitable division of labor at home. Ironically, the one woman who did notice a dramatic change in her blue-collar husband, who "never helped me when the children were small, and I needed it most," and who now helps her "quite a bit, now we are doing pretty good," was a woman in her fifties of a traditional immigrant background. Her tale provoked considerable astonishment in the group, leading one woman to inquire in wonderment: "how did you bring him around?" The storyteller paused briefly and then conceded that it was not she who was able to accomplish this result but her children: "It's just through time because the world changes; the kids changed, the generation and everything changed." She gave major credit to her daughter and then added: "They [the men] see it on TV. They listen to other people. My son grows up, he brings girls, they talk; he listens. And that is how you learn."[14] She did mention, however, that the change came about very gradually. "You can't do it overnight, otherwise you wind up [divorced]." Others reported that their attempts to have husbands share in running the house usually had not met with similar success, and a few did not even make the attempt. In a typical instance, a full-time clerical worker in her early forties felt particularly put upon and complained that she can expect no help with childcare (she has four children) or housework beyond an occasional lawn-mowing. When the moderator asked: "Have you ever chatted about dividing up responsibilities or anything like that?" the woman replied: "Well, he would not even listen to that. He feels like he works hard enough doing his things. So, whatever I do is, you know, you are supposed to do."

Many women of all ages in these groups are dissatisfied with their

---

14. Of course, it is not entirely clear whether she "brought him around" or whether the children and their friends accomplished the feat.

current domestic arrangements. Younger women especially tend to view the "second shift" as a forceful indication that women have not yet achieved true equality. A recently married college graduate, for example, "would not say we have an equal partnership" because her husband, though he helps a good deal, shrinks from certain chores, such as cleaning the bathroom. To her, equality between the genders requires sharing chores equally. Listening to this tale, a woman in her fifties retorted that the young woman really has nothing to complain about. "When I was young and had to go out to work and had children, I got no help. Either you're a mother or you get a divorce. So I said to myself: Hang in there, Mary." Others quickly added that even today things haven't changed all that much for most women. One member summarized it for almost all: "Men want to be treated like a prince, that is the attitude that a lot of men have right now, and they feel entitled to it because their mothers raised them that way, and now it is little wife who takes care of the house and cleans, puts the clean underwear in the drawer and makes sure that he has clean shirts." What most annoyed these handmaidens to princes was that their work is taken for granted and that so little consideration is shown to them at home. Their feelings were very much in keeping with the finding by Crosby, Muehrer, and Loewenstein (1986) that in the domestic realm women are most likely to feel relatively deprived when they are not accorded the consideration they feel they deserve, whereas in the workplace perceptions of monetary discrimination are those most likely to cause feelings of relative deprivation.

Listening to these conversations about the domestic scene, the observers gathered behind the one-way mirror of the recording studio had the collective impression that the women they observed were both hurt and angry but simultaneously resigned to the realization that drastic change in domestic arrangements was not to occur in the immediate future. Some in the focus group apparently shared this perspective. One member put this impression succinctly when she suddenly exclaimed: "See how resigned everyone sounds. We all have a note of resignation." Her comments and those of others suggest that for these women "the gender roles implicit in the marriage relationship basically remained unaltered" (Hertz 1986: 11).

Telephone respondents largely agreed with the focus groups. They too were of the opinion that the domestic demands made of women are inordinate. Sixty percent (60 percent) were of the opinion that "too much is expected of today's women because most work outside the home and still are expected to be good homemakers and parents," so that "young women today have a tougher life than women used to have." They hold that housework should be shared equally when both husband and wife are employed (69 percent) but such sharing, as they see it, is not how it works in reality (83 percent; see table 5.2). They are all but unanimous (90 percent) in their estimate that in most families the wife continues to do most of the work. The employed wife does not reduce, let alone shed, her role of domestic manager. She merely adds a

TABLE 5.2   WOMEN'S PERCEPTION OF THE DIVISION
OF LABOR (%)

What do women think is the desirable division of household labor when men and women are employed outside of the home?	
Man should do most of the chores	1
He should do half	69
He should do some	28
He should do none	1
Don't know	3
What actually happens?	
He does most of the chores	1
He does half	10
He does some	67
He does none	16
Don't know	6
Is that division fair?	
Very unfair	48
A little unfair	24
Doesn't think in terms of fairness	24
Don't know	4
Do you think that too many household obligations is one reason why women are less successful in business than men?	
That is a reason	53
Is not a reason	45
Don't know	3
What do you consider the most important reason for differential success?	
Men have held women back	39
Women have too many household chores	23
Government held them back	19
Women lack ambition and aggressivity	10
Women not as qualified	5
Don't know; can't choose	4
Women's life is tougher today because they have dual duties (home and employment).	
Yes	60
No	35
Depends (volunteered)	3
Don't know	3

$n = 400$

second role to it, that of an income producer.[15] Heavy though that double burden may be, interviewees were no more inclined than the focus groups to want to restrict their role to that of the traditional housewife. Asked what they would prefer for themselves if financial considerations did not require outside employment, robust majorities, notwithstanding their complaints about the heavy burden of housework, opted for outside employment (frequently in combination with family life), and they were convinced that almost all women share their preferences. Only a minority (37 percent) preferred exclusive domesticity.[16]

I have emphasized women's reactions to their domestic situation, a subject not generally covered in political science research, because it is the inequitable distribution of housework that may well have sensitized these women to their relative subordination and powerlessness. The focus groups suggest that this issue above all may have functioned as the lightning rod that led them to the conclusion that gendered discrimination is not confined to the household but pervades society. It may have convinced them that the personal indeed is the political, as feminists are wont to say. Rosanna Hertz, who studied dual-career marriages, reached a somewhat similar conclusion: "The ideology of equality, particularly in marital roles, emerges out of common opportunities and constraints, not out of a prior commitment to a feminist philosophy" (1986: 197).

THE WORKPLACE

When addressing inequities that exist beyond the confines of the domestic arena, the focus group participants continued to use personal anecdotes to convey both their experience of discrimination and their ways of handling it. Here, too, few linked their personal welfare with public policy.

The issue of employment exemplifies the group participants' personalistic, apolitical approach. Notwithstanding that of all areas of gender discrimination, employment is probably the one sphere where government has made the most visible effort to bring about equal opportunity, focus group members usually ignored these efforts. When they did acknowledge government intervention in this area, they considered that intervention insufficient or irrelevant for their own suc-

15. Sociologists call this process "role expansion," as distinct from "role substitution," in which the workload remains constant.

16. Sigel and Sernekos (1992) found that in this minority 63 percent believed that other women shared their view and would prefer the life of full-time homemaker if they could afford it financially; they were apparently unaware that this preference is not shared by most women.

cess or failure in the workplace. As a rule, the participants attributed failure to male resistance, success to women's own determination. The focus group members, and to a somewhat lesser degree the telephone interviewees, believed that discrimination continues to be rampant in the workplace. Both samples attributed women's lack of success to male resistance, vehemently rejecting the notion that women might be less qualified or less ambitious than men and hence less successful. Instead they maintained that it is the male workforce, co-workers as well as managers, who withhold opportunities for women to prove themselves and who deny them the respect they deserve. Lack of respect offended them especially and was cited frequently along with complaints about pay inequities and other aspects of workplace discrimination. Perceptions that men show insufficient respect to women were not restricted, however, to the workplace. Recall, for example, the widow who held a yard sale to sell her late husband's tools and the divorcée who wanted to purchase storm windows. Both encountered a lack of respect in a public context and became increasingly incensed by the men's habit of treating them as helpless and/or ignorant. In the workplace, this lack of respect becomes an even greater source of aggravation. The insulting comments they face at work may only raise their blood pressure, but deliberately withheld job-related information interferes with their getting the job done. Another frequent complaint focused on men's habit of disregarding or belittling the contributions made by women. Several women echoed the plaint of the publisher's assistant whose opinions during a meeting were ignored while a male's were accorded respect. In conversations with activists in the struggle to ratify the ERA and more recently with women on welfare, Jane Mansbridge also noted how much importance these women attached to getting the respect of the men with whom they live. Mansbridge concludes that "respect represents a central but relatively overlooked ingredient of the practice of citizenship."[17] And respect, the focus group members seem to imply, cannot be legislated by government decree.

The focus group conversations offered many anecdotes illustrating why women put so little stock in what has been accomplished so far by governmental fiat and why they approached the problems at work as personal problems that each woman has (or had) to solve for herself rather than political problems. An employee in an advanced technology company had no doubt that policy changes helped her, up to a point, because she "got into a nontraditional field basically when they changed

17. "Citizenship in Everyday Life," talk delivered at Brown University in March 1994 at a conference on "Equal Protection and Its Critics; The Law and Politics of First-Class Citizenship." Cited with permission of the author.

the law and they said: 'You will now let women do this.' " But the law, she pointed out, did not prevent "the guys" from putting all kinds of obstacles in her path and making insulting and obscene comments, which she cited freely. In her opinion, business has found many ways of making antidiscriminatory laws relatively ineffective. Women, she maintained, continue to be treated differently. They constantly "run into blocks. I feel like a lot of the laws that you run into in business, you know, it's because you are a woman . . . but these laws don't carry much weight because [if you complain] they end up getting around it. It's your imagination. We aren't doing that. We don't discriminate."

A few older women, who are no longer in the workforce, had a more sanguine outlook. They thought that matters had improved greatly and attributed the improvement to government-mandated rules and regulations. The younger and middle-aged women did not share this benign view. They were far more guarded, if not outright skeptical. For example, in one group a retired woman with professional training suggested that because of changes in the law the demeaning and unfair practices that she experienced have now ceased. To make her point, she related that fifteen years ago when she wanted to return to work after a pregnancy leave, the personnel officer "sat there and said to me, 'But now that you can stay home and play house, why do you want to come back to work?' And I looked at him and said: 'Because I hate cleaning the doll house.' They can't ask you questions like that anymore." Ruefully, she reflected that she "was too early to really have the advantage of some of the good things that happened afterwards." Immediately other women still in the workforce disabused her of the idea that much has changed. The general consensus in this and the other groups was that, despite the law's best efforts, little has changed. A woman working for a major corporation made this contrast between now and bygone days: "At that point in time, there was a lot of harassment, but it was really open, and I think things are changing to where it appears that you are more easily accepted. It appears that, yeah, we are going to let you do this job and everything is hunky-dory, but [now] the harassment and the prejudices are just extremely covert."

Another exchange shows just how distrustful some of the employed women were of men's readiness to accept them as equals in the workplace. A recently retired computer specialist had entered the field along with other women many years ago when people with such skills were a rarity. She offered her tale of finding employment in a Fortune 500 firm as an example of what women can achieve if they are properly prepared. But the other group members reacted skeptically to this tale of encouragement. The first commentator asked, "Yeah, but did they *stay* equal?"; followed by a second: "So who is up on top now?" A third joins in: "Yeah, that's what I'd like to know!" Finally a fourth: "I'm just saying, did they stay equal while you were there, or did the men get pushed up?" Although the focus group participants encountered discrimination and harassment in spheres other than the workplace, no other sphere of activity, with the exception of the family, occupied an equally important place in the discussions of the focus groups.

These exchanges may help explain why the focus group participants made so few references to politics. They simply had little faith that recourse to laws and other public policy mandates can bring about meaningful redress of the problems that beset them. Their lack of faith did not preclude many of them from welcoming increased governmental efforts to improve women's position—an idea to which men were not nearly so receptive (32 percent). Women approved of such attempts, but as they saw it, these attempts were not likely to meet with much success because males will find ways of circumventing any government action. A leitmotif running throughout the conversations and many of the telephone responses was the belief that men are basically reluctant and even afraid to grant women genuine equality and, consequently, will devise all kinds of tactics to deny it to them. Skepticism of males' readiness to accept women as equals was almost endemic. The women we encountered or, more accurately, those who joined the conversation on this issue, expressed the conviction that they don't get an equal chance in many important male/female interactions because men always need to be in control and feel "threatened by strong women." True gender equality, they believed, will be hard to obtain not because males are misogynous or mean-spirited but because men have for so long been accustomed to playing the dominant role in society that they cannot imagine any other role. Listening to the various conversations, I was struck by the extent to which these women, who come from such different walks of life, all focus on men qua men as the quintessential source of female subjugation. Many among them, however, do recognize at the same time that more than male resistance is involved and that probably the whole social system, including women's complicity in it, accounts for gendered inequity. As one woman asked, referring to the tales of employment woe she had just heard: "Why do we sit for that, though, Sue? Why do we stay there? Do you ever ask yourself why?" Unhesitatingly, Sue replied: "For me it was convenient. I didn't want to upset the boat on that end." This recognition, however, did not prevent most of these women from blaming men as a group and singling out for particular anger special subgroups of males—male physicians, male mechanics, and male car salesmen. Telephone respondents shared that view. They, too, believed men have not changed much in their condescending view of women. They faulted men not only for discriminating against women, as we saw in chapter 3, but for being quite comfortable with a wide array of discriminatory practices, ranging from the domestic and private to the public and commercial. For example, two-thirds of the female population maintained that men are not at all bothered or bothered only a little by the fact that women are discriminated against. This estimate is not far off the mark. Males were less harsh than women when judging their fellow men, but even among them 55 percent were of the opinion that gender-based discrimination did not bother *other* men.[18] Moreover, 80 percent voiced the opinion that men actually promote women's subordinate status, especially when women aspire to positions of power or authority (for example, many of the women believed men deliberately blocked women from achieving influence in business).

POWER AND POWERLESSNESS

The sense of political powerlessness is capsulated in a focus group conversation concerning the 1984 presidential election. Several groups mentioned the vice-presidential candidacy of Geraldine Ferraro and expressed considerable outrage at the insults to which, in their opinion, she was subjected. Several women referred to the episode with the blueberry muffins, expressing their conviction that no male politician has to tolerate such demeaning comments.[19] Others cited the media incident as prima facie evidence that men control the political establishment and seek to keep women from gaining power in it: "But they were trying to manipulate her [Geraldine Ferraro], even maybe just to satisfy their own anxiety. She wasn't equal to them in their eyes," said Belle, the assistant manager of a small ready-wear department. "And we all looked up to her whether we liked her or not," commented a middle-aged clerical worker, who concluded: "I can't think of a woman in the world who could have won that election, starting with Mother Theresa." Telephone respondents expressed similar sentiments of powerlessness and futility. As we saw in chapter 3, they believed that women do not have a good chance to attain top positions in government or business. Like the focus group participants, they too were convinced that women lack political power, with two-thirds asserting that, in politics, women have less influence than do men. This is one of several issues on which both genders agreed: 61 percent of the women and

18. Women, by contrast, did not express similar cynicism about other women's concern; only 12 percent believed that other women were not greatly bothered by gender discrimination.

19. The media reported that on one occasion the candidate was asked by male party officials in the South if she knew how to bake blueberry muffins.

63 percent of the men held that women have less political influence than men. But where powerlessness bothered women, it was, as we will see, a non-issue for men.

BECOMING POLITICALLY INVOLVED

Given their dim view of the male establishment, it is perhaps not surprising that the women in our focus groups showed little enthusiasm for becoming personally involved in the political process. We instructed the moderators to ask participants about the desirability of becoming politically active since, as a rule, the groups failed to address the issue on their own. One moderator pursued the topic persistently. With the exception of one group, the participants did not respond to the suggestion. The one group that resonated at all to the moderator's suggestion was a particularly well-educated group.[20]

Here is an excerpt from this one group's exchange of ideas on the topic of political participation. As the discussion turned to the difficulties women are experiencing when they seek to obtain careers on a par with those held by men, three of the youngest women immediately tied the absence of such opportunities to women's lack of economic and political power. Said 31-year-old Lou, a well-paid woman in a managerial position, "The thing is, there aren't enough of us in powerful enough positions to get women in the job even if the woman is better qualified." Twenty-seven-year-old Doris added: "I think we need to get women into politics." Another echoed these sentiments, declaring that "we need good women who present a good image. As we've infiltrated in the work field, and they are starting to take us seriously, now maybe getting involved in politics . . . " Several other women agreed, but another woman, who used to be active in a variety of social causes and groups,[21] reminded them that it is difficult to get women involved. She talked at length about the difficulties she encountered when seeking to get women to register to vote: "I got a subterranean feeling, 'Oh I don't have to vote 'cause I am a woman.' And I spent a lot of time—I was exhausted. It was a wonderful day, but I was exhausted explaining to women that they were supposed to [vote]." Others agreed, adding that "It involves the way women look at things." Even when the determined moderator kept pressing,[22] asking what women could do collec-

20. In the group of eight, two were college graduates, four had some college education, and two were high school graduates.
21. Incidentally, she is the only woman who ever belonged to any organizations that take a political stand, but she no longer maintains these memberships.
22. The persistence with which she pursued this and other questions related to politics was not planned. We had instructed each moderator to raise certain questions but to

tively to end the injustices about which they had just complained in so much detail, most members refused to follow her lead. When one business woman did follow the lead, suggesting that it would be a good idea if women were to get involved in collective action, another firmly retorted, "I'm sorry. I'm not going to do it. . . . Let stronger females do it." That sentiment was echoed by most of the other women.[23]

So, instead of accepting the moderator's lead and directing their attention to how they might use collective power to improve women's situation, the members dismissed her suggestion and reverted back to recounting how they as individuals have coped with a given problem, have improved their own situation, have succeeded against considerable odds or failed to do so, and how, in either case, few let themselves be bothered by discrimination. The group sessions were replete with personal anecdotes of how many among them overcame sex discrimination, especially at work, but not by lodging complaints or having recourse to politics. They made no claim of having helped eliminate the practice of sex discrimination, but only of how they *personally* succeeded despite that discrimination, because they were able, in the words of a few women, "to prove themselves." They told each other of the particular types of male resistance they encountered, how they dealt with it, and how this experience taught them to stand "on [their] own two feet" without help from anyone. Although few have had the nerve to talk back to their personnel officers about cleaning the doll house, most take comfort from having relied on their own efforts rather than on government intervention.

Under ordinary circumstances, the strong resistance of these women to becoming politically involved would not have surprised us; this is, after all, typical of Americans of both genders, with women participating even less on most measures than men.[24] But given these women's high degree of indignation over the injustice inflicted on them, their resistance to political involvement came as somewhat of a surprise. All the marches on Washington, all the media hype, all the publicity accorded to women's protests, and all the legal challenges not-

drop further inquiry if participants showed no interest or were reluctant to talk about the issues. In retrospect, we are glad that she insisted on raising these questions repeatedly because her insistence revealed just how adamant the women were about not becoming politically involved.

23. The burden of the "second shift" may have contributed to this unwillingness to participate actively. In the case of full-time homemakers, restricted access to and contact with the outside world may have had the same effect (Sapiro 1983).

24. For a review of the latest statistics on political participation in the United States, see Pippa Norris (1994) as well as the many periodic polls conducted by the Roper and Gallup organizations, among others.

withstanding, the women we observed rarely, if ever, considered that they also might want to employ such tactics. The Women's Movement's steady appeal to women to become politically active seems to have fallen on deaf ears.

Because of the focus groups' obvious disinclination to discuss how they might become politically involved, we decided to explore the issue in more detail during the telephone interviews. To that end, we posed two open-ended questions that asked respondents to tell us in their own words what they thought a woman should do if she believed herself to have been discriminated against.[25] Benefitting from our focus group observations, we did not ask respondents what they personally would do, how they might become involved, but instead focused on the advice they might give another woman. By phrasing the question in this way, respondents were given the opportunity to consider the relevance of political involvement for bringing about justice for women, irrespective of their own inclination to get politically involved. But even with this precaution, telephone respondents showed no more enthusiasm for getting politically involved than did the focus groups.

In the analysis which follows, the term "political" is defined very broadly. It will encompass not only direct actions, such as appeals to persons in the government and participating in demonstrations, but also other quasi-political initiatives that might indirectly affect government actions (such as voicing one's complaint on a talk show). Thus it will include all initiatives which have as their purpose to alert (directly or indirectly) some governmental political agent or agency to find a solution to a problem. By including so many diverse activities under the rubric of "political," it should be possible to capture any and all public efforts women might undertake in order not to endure discrimination passively.

Answers that we coded as forms of seeking redress by direct appeals to government and its agencies ranked near the bottom of respondents' preferred choices (preferred by 6 percent; see table 5.3). Among those political means, writing one's representative or contacting an appropriate governmental agency were the most frequently made suggestions. But even those who mentioned an agency were vague about the type or name of the governmental agency that women could contact. Going to the "discrimination board in the community"[26] or "go to a sexual discrimination or harassment place or call" was as specific as many could get. Only a few could name a specific agency.

25. The second question was a follow-up to the first, asking respondents if they could think of actions other than the ones they gave in response to the first question.

26. All quotations in this section are from telephone interviews unless indicated otherwise. All previous quotations were from focus group discussions.

By contrast, the time-honored American practice of seeking legal advice and/or initiating a lawsuit found considerably more favor. These were the suggestions that respondents most favored (19 percent). Suggestions ranged from the succinct one-word answer "sue," through "go see a lawyer," to the graphic, "she should take it to the highest court and fight her ass off." Other somewhat more measured responses ran like this: "If she has good ground that can be documented, she should seek legal recourse," or the rather sober "go to the courts, long battles, cost a lot of money and usually a losing battle because she has a 50:50 chance and has little time for court procedures."[27]

If we add the category of seeking legal help (19 percent) to the 6 percent who make direct political suggestions, we find that one-quarter of our respondents entertained the idea of making direct use of the country's legal and political apparatus. Consulting women's organizations (6 percent) can easily be added to that rubric. "I guess go to a national women's organization that she could talk with, but I wouldn't know the mechanics of it," answered one respondent. Another admonished: "Discrimination is hard to prove. Contact a woman's organization and find out where to go from there." Another 4 percent thought of indirect forms of political action, such as seeking publicity via the media.

Another 5 percent gave answers that might possibly be categorized as potentially political endeavors. These women suggested consulting with someone or some organization that might either give advice or possibly help. Most of these, however, had little idea of who or what such a person or organization might be. Many of their answers were so vague as to be almost unclassifiable, and several were inappropriate, in that they named an agency not involved with matters of discrimination. For example, one woman suggested, "Better Business Bureaus give local help and push the issue." Respondents such as these can best be characterized as having a general but hazy awareness that "out there" some groups or individuals might be able to assist. Many said they would like to see a woman "fight for her rights," but they frankly admit that they lack information on the subject.

Combining all of these political or quasi-political initiatives produces the conclusion that slightly over one-third of the population could be characterized as verging on politicization in that it considers political action a useful way to combat the ill effects of discrimination for a particular person. I say "verging on politicization" rather than "politicized" because not one woman regarded the suggested action as

27. Not all who suggested seeing a lawyer were necessarily thinking of litigation. Some believed a lawyer would be the person to advise them if anything could be done about their complaint or to refer them to an agency that might be able to help them.

anything more than a personal problem requiring a personal solution. Consequently, not one of the telephone respondents who were asked this question ever suggested that women ought to consider collective political action to protect themselves from discrimination. No one, for example, mentioned instituting a class action suit or mobilizing women at their place of employment, to name but two possibilities.

Other women, though they ignored the political route, still did not advocate enduring discrimination silently. They urged the aggrieved woman to seek redress but advocated confining the search for redress to the institution in which she encountered discrimination (16 percent). Those who favored such a relatively narrow action frequently seem to have had discrimination at the workplace in mind. They suggested that the woman should complain to her manager or supervisor or, failing to get satisfaction there, to his superior (it is always a "he" in their examples): "A woman should speak up and tell her supervisor how she feels on the job if she has the same working experience of her male co-worker." Or, as one put it: "She should talk to her boss or someone in higher position, and if that doesn't work, I don't know." If we combine this group with those advocating some form of political action, we can conclude that about six out of every ten women entertained the idea that resources exist somewhere which could help a woman to protect herself from discrimination. In the follow-up question, in which we asked those who had previously made a suggestion what else a woman might do, 72 percent were at a loss to think of anything else. Apparently, most respondents have command over a rather restricted and not particularly political repertoire of remedies for discrimination.

Although a majority of women urged other women to resist sex discrimination, close to four out of ten made no such suggestion. Not all of them, however, believed that women should just endure discrimination

TABLE 5.3   WOMEN'S POLITICAL ENGAGEMENT (%)

Question: "When a woman believes she has been discriminated against . . . what should she do about it, what actions could she take?"

Do nothing	15
Seek redress within the involved institution	16
Seek legal redress	19
Seek redress by political means	6
Seek help from organizations	11*
Miscellaneous	11
Don't know	23
	n = 400

*Six percent named women's organization; five percent named other organizations.

as though it were women's fate. This 40 percent fall into two distinct groups: women who did not know what could be done and women who actually advocated doing nothing about it. In either case, putting up with discrimination would be the result. Close to a quarter of the 400 women (23 percent) said they did not know anything women could do to defend themselves against discrimination. A not infrequent reply was: "I have no idea," and no amount of probing could elicit a response beyond this. Others told us that they didn't know what could be done because they don't keep up with "stuff like that" or are not interested. Still more sobering than the replies of those who had no clue as to what a woman might do are the replies of the 15 percent who believed that fighting discrimination is inadvisable or actually futile. A housewife told us: "Do nothing. A woman never wins." Another concluded: "Do nothing. Nobody is going to listen, so it won't make a difference." Those who had workplace discrimination in mind offered suggestions such as these: "Try harder and if that did not work just to quit." Or, in a similar vein: "Nothing at all, she should just go home." Complaining is possible, "but it will cost her her job" commented another. These two populations (the know-nothing and the do-nothing groups) account for over one-third (38 percent) of the female population. Figures such as these may cause one to wonder just how trenchant an issue sex discrimination really is for many women. Another, more sanguine, way of looking at the findings is to say that a majority is willing to believe it might be worthwhile to attempt to defend oneself against discrimination by a variety of means even though political modes of combat are not the preferred ones.

Whether any of the women who urged their sisters to fight discrimination would do the same if they themselves were the victim is a totally different question. One woman clearly distinguished between herself and the hypothetical victim: "Sue them, I think. Personally I wouldn't do anything." The focus groups also implied in their discussions that women should fight discrimination, but "leave me out of the fight." "Let stronger women do it. I'll instead fight my own battles and do it in my own individual way," as one participant put it.

AFFIRMATIVE ACTION

Our respondents' preference for an individual approach to coping with gender-based inequality expressed itself in other ways as well. It can be seen most clearly in the women's ambivalence about feminism and feminist causes. For example, notwithstanding their recognition that sex discrimination is a problem of society-wide dimensions, the focus group members were ambivalent rather than enthusiastic about recent governmental efforts to reduce discrimination. This was reflected in their attitudes on the Equal Rights Amendment (ERA) and especially on affirmative action ("quotas," as some persisted in dubbing it). Most of the participants supported these efforts just as they supported other actions of the Women's Movement, but very frequently their support was hedged with qualifications of one kind or another. Only a few lent the movement unqualified support. One such supporter, a middle-aged, middle-level executive, had no doubt that the government's affirmative action program has helped her and others like her to get a foothold in a formerly male-dominated field: "That's one reason that maybe I can see it as more important. I probably would not be where I am today if it were not for affirmative action . . . I have seen incompetent women as well as incompetent men, that's not the issue, but I don't think that we would be as far as we are today. So I do think in that way the government did do a good thing for women because I think it is a good thing."[28] Others were not so sure. When they talked about the issue at all (and few raised it on their own), they generally recognized that affirmative action may have been helpful to some women— "maybe it was necessary then . . . now I think people ought to be selected by their qualities." They were divided among themselves as to whether affirmative action is a fair policy that should be continued or whether it is another form of discrimination. A strong sense of uneasiness about the practice ran through the discussion when it was brought up by the moderator, suggesting that some participants consider it to be wrong to give preference to any group, even one's own. One moderator asked a law student how she would have felt if an equally qualified man instead of her had been admitted to law school; the young woman responded, "I would just say, 'well, the better man won.' I mean I really would not look at it like that although I consider myself somewhat of a feminist." The attachment to the principle of meritocracy was strong in this self-proclaimed feminist. Other women also were dubious about the fairness of affirmative action. "For the sake of being fair, let the better person win, not female or male but by testing out; test out . . . I'll always believe that was always the right way to do it. I don't know why." When another participant interjected that women might not test as well as men in certain nontraditional fields because they lack adequate experiences, the other remained quite adamant: "It should be up to the female to go get the knowledge. She should go and acquire the knowledge so she can pass that test." The focus group members seemed torn between the desire to open up opportunities for their gender and

28. This statement came in response to the moderator's question if government could do anything to improve women's situation.

their reluctance to give anyone (even their own group) what might amount to an unfair advantage. In this vein, one woman asked: "What about the dark side [of affirmative action], the quotas? 'cause for every person who gets a leg up, there is someone equally good and deserving who is excluded just because of the same reasons."

FEMINISM

Not surprisingly, therefore, ambivalence also came to the fore in the group participants' discussions of feminism and the Women's Movement. They unanimously subscribed to the notion that the term "feminist" evokes negative reactions in the public, especially in the male public. A middle-aged housewife with grown, career-engaged daughters asserted, "I think in a man's mind it becomes negative." That is also the connotation it had for several other group members. Many of their reactions, of course, were based on misinformation (such as the frequent references to bra-burners) or had more to do with labels and names than with substance. Two of the women in our focus groups (both among the youngest participants), openly declared themselves to be feminists. Others belonged to the by-now proverbial class of females who assert "I am not a feminist but . . . " which is meant to indicate that they endorse some or all feminist goals but distance themselves from the label. Still others were uncertain just how they felt about the issue. As one middle-aged woman answered the moderator's question as to whether or not she would describe herself as a feminist: "I don't really know. I don't think I would. I don't know what word you would choose. But, I don't know, there is a lot of things I think with the feminist movement, I think [girls] would lose some things as well they gain some things."

Reactions to the Women's Movement and its accomplishments reflected similar ambivalence. Agreement was widespread that the movement had been good for women, but some uneasiness about its potential consequences remained, especially with respect to the ways the movement might affect women's relations with men.[29] The women believed the movement had been instrumental in advancing the cause of female equality and gave it much credit for having raised women's consciousness. Focus group and telephone respondents alike shared

29. The question concerning the Women's Movement read: "I'm going to read you three statements about groups trying to change women's status in society. Please tell me which view is closest to your own: First, the Women's Movement has done more harm than good to advance the position of women; second, while the Women's Movement was necessary years ago to advance women, it is no longer necessary today, or, third, the Women's Movement is still necessary if women are to continue to advance."

these generally positive reactions to the movement's struggle for gender equality. In response to the question, one telephone respondent concluded, "Without this [the women's liberation movement] we wouldn't be where we are today." Another agreed, declaring that the movement "had to come somehow so that women could acquire a sense of self and independence or choice where before they had none."[30] A focus group member put it this way: "I think it had to come into existence somehow. I don't know whether it is right or it's wrong the way it is. I just think it had to be." In their minds, the movement's goals and theirs are identical when it comes to the desire to gain access "to the place where they [women] rightfully belong," as one put it, or "they deserve being equal," as another asserted. They credited the movement with having made them conscious of their own subordinate position "because it [the Woman's Movement] pointed out inferior positions and made efforts to change it." Many indicated their belief that without the movement discrimination would have remained unrecognized for what it is. A telephone respondent made that abundantly clear: "Betty Friedan started it all. One woman got up and spoke of their problems. It takes a courageous woman to stand up and say there's something wrong. You have to tell people there is a problem before they can do anything about it."[31]

But many telephone respondents also felt that the women's movement may have "gone too far," that it is too extreme, or at least that it appears that way to men. Few, however, would go so far as did one focus group discussant who argued, "What has happened is it's been so overplayed that it's getting to the point where men are getting sick of women hiding behind it as a defense, on top of which it's going turning into fields that are not necessarily women's causes. It's not of benefit anymore. I mean to hear women talk about Gloria Steinem . . . and all those people, it's not a positive thing anymore. It's turned into—there is a word for it, and I can't think what the word is—it's like an excuse almost for these women to do something outrageous and promote antagonism from the men that are getting the brunt of it. Years ago, when it first started out, it was a nice calm movement. It didn't have much effect but it did eventually snowball into more militant." In the groups, such outright hostility was the exception. A far more common reaction was to list some benefits brought on by the movement but to accompany that positive recognition with some doubts or at least hesitancy.[32]

30. Unless otherwise indicated, all of the quotations dealing with the Women's Movement and with change in women's position come from the telephone interviews.

31. Similarly, a focus group member gave "that Freedman woman" (presumably Betty Friedan) credit.

32. For a perceptive analysis of the ramifications of this ambivalence, see L. Huddy and J. Bracciodieta, "Feminism Under Siege" (1992).

Two considerations were introduced with some regularity: Regret over the movement's alleged stridency and fear that it may "promote antagonism from the men." The fear of male antagonism ran deep. It was not that women believed such antagonism to be warranted but the women showed considerable sensitivity to the fact that some men might be antagonized by the movement, because they believed that its goals, once fully realized, would constitute a threat to men's position of predominance, affording them ample cause for antagonism. The desire to avoid male antagonism runs deep in our sample and may be one additional reason why women expressed some reservations concerning certain "women-friendly" policies, such as affirmative action.

In our focus groups, older women seemed the most appreciative of the changes the Women's Movement helped bring about. They gave it much credit for the changes they saw around them and spoke with approval of the careers their daughters were pursuing. They described how restricted their options had been in comparison with their daughters "because it was before the Woman's Movement." Some seem to divide women's history into the days before and after the birth of the Women's Movement, as, for example, when some spoke of how in their youth it had never even occurred to them to consider any role other than that of housewife. One older woman told how her husband used to be on the road much of the year when her five children were growing up and how she took it for granted that all of the house-hunting, chauffeuring, educating, etc. would be her responsibility. She "never gave the matter any thought" until her daughters refused to make the same accommodations in their own families, thereby raising the mother's consciousness. She still had no regrets but knew she would do it differently now.

Other women credited the movement with increasing women's closeness to other women and an awareness of their common fate: "One of the things I think was important at least in my life was maybe ten years ago I didn't think I had so much in common with women as I have. I think in ten years that's given me a greater understanding and respect for them." Another added: "I don't think ten years ago we could have, all not knowing each other, come into this room [of the focus group meeting] and sit and be as frank to each other as we are tonight." Many women of all ages gave the movement credit for having raised their consciousness to the inequity of their status. They believed that without the movement they might never even have recognized the unfairness, let alone question it.

The telephone respondents were just as convinced, perhaps even more so, that the movement has not outlived its usefulness. Seventy-three percent said the movement is still needed, and only a fraction

TABLE 5.4   SUPPORT FOR EFFORTS TO ENHANCE EQUALITY FOR WOMEN (%)

A. THE EQUAL RIGHTS AMENDMENT	
Another Effort to Ratify the ERA is:	
Important	70
Not important	25
Depends	1
Don't know	1
	n = 400
Personal stand on ERA:	
Favors it strongly	51
Favors it	20
Opposes it strongly	7
Opposes it	6
Depends	7
Don't know, undecided	9
	n = 400
B. THE WOMEN'S MOVEMENT	
It is still needed	73
No longer needed	20
Has done more harm than good	4
No opinion	4
	n = 400

(4 percent) asserted it has done more harm than good (see table 5.4). On the surface, telephone interviewees thus seem less ambivalent than the focus groups, but they were not offered a chance to qualify their judgments. They, too, probably would have expressed reservations or at least would have qualified their responses had they not been presented with narrow choices which allowed for no qualifying statements.

Some support for our speculation can be derived from the attitudes the telephone respondents expressed with respect to the recently defeated Equal Rights Amendment (ERA). We began by asking them if they thought it was important that another effort be made to have the ERA ratified and found that 70 percent believed it to be important. But when we followed up on that question and asked how important the effort was to them personally, the percentage of those who felt strongly about it dropped to 51 percent. Another 20 percent favored it somewhat. The second answer yielded much the same proportion of favorable replies as the first, but the 20 percent who endorsed it without feeling strongly might have qualified their positive responses if given that option[33] and they might have raised some of the same doubts and reservations as were raised in the focus groups.

ALLOCATING CREDIT

In spite of their dissatisfaction with the current state of gender relations, the women we interviewed realized that the situation for women has improved over the last years (see chapter 3). The groups displayed a sense that something approaching a new era for women has begun— one vastly different from the one to which their mothers and grandmothers had adjusted themselves. Their comments were interlaced with frequent references to the generation gap. They saw their mothers as having had no choice but to keep house, raise children, and cater to their husbands, whereas young women today can at least decide what they want to do with their lives.[34] Having a "choice" was a recurring theme. They attached so much importance to it because it permits them to have some control over their own lives rather than being assigned to socially predetermined but not necessarily individually suited roles. Virtually no one, not even among the older women, had any desire for a return to traditional sex-role definitions. Fewer than one-quarter of the telephone respondents (22 percent) professed harboring varying degrees of traditionalism in sex-role orientations (only 5 percent described themselves as "strongly traditional"). A semi-retired focus group member, who opted for a career when still a young girl, was keenly aware that the situation for women has changed for the better: "I think the major change in the last ten years is that everyone started doing what I did twenty years ago and was criticized for."

Who deserves the credit for the change for the better, incomplete though it may be? The answer was loud, clear, and unmistakable: Women themselves have brought on the change. It is they, not government, who brought it about. Respondents were almost unanimous in that attribution. They gave the Women's Movement considerable credit, as just noted, but they extended most credit to the actions of individual women qua women, their determination and their strength in the face of seemingly insurmountable obstacles.

33. By the same line of reasoning, the focus group participants, given similarly restrictive choices, might have endorsed the movement without reservations. Jane Mansbridge (1986: 14) observed that in several states the ERA was defeated in referenda by about the same margin as had endorsed it in public opinion polls.

34. A young and well-educated woman in one group mentioned that older women of her acquaintance "have their family and their cooking and the house, and they would be scared to death to walk out that front door. And you suggest to them to have a job or whatever, they would duck under the spot."

The tendency to give almost exclusive credit to women themselves manifested itself in both samples. After inquiring whether, in their opinion, women's position had changed over the past decades and whether it had changed for the better, we asked telephone respondents to tell us in their own words what they thought was the most important reason for the improvement in women's position in society. "Women" was the all but unanimous answer (91 percent) among those who were able to offer an explanation. Even when those at a loss to account for the change (17 percent) are included in the count, a majority of women (72 percent) still believed that they and they alone have brought on the change. Fifty-nine percent gave most of the credit to women and 13 percent give it to organizations working on women's behalf. "Women have made it happen. They stuck up for their rights," was one interviewee's confident assessment.[35] Men and government, on the other hand, were given very little credit; less than 6 percent asserted that men and society should be given credit, and only 3 percent believed government had made a difference (see table 5.5).

Why, in the opinion of the respondents, have women effected such dramatic change? What has happened to them that they now object to a societal gender arrangement which they had for so long taken for granted? They offered several explanations. The most common was some version of the conclusion that once women had become aware of their inferior status, they reached the conclusion that it was unwarranted. "They became tired of being second-class citizens and began speaking up for themselves." Both focus group members and telephone respondents used the words "second-class citizens" frequently and spontaneously. The phrase had become part of their rhetoric if not their consciousness. Also important to them was the notion that women now "are standing up more for themselves." As one respondent put it, "Women started to speak up for themselves and not accept their lot in life." Both on the telephone and in groups, women showed how important it was to them not to accept their lot in life without question and to make their own decisions as to what they wanted to do with their lives. A strong theme for many was: "I am an individual in my own right." As one woman commented, "Women have finally stood on their own two feet for equality. Women have said that, 'Hey, I have a right to decide what I choose to do with my life. If I want to work, I will work. If I want to take care of my family, I will or both.' " Today, in one woman's words, "women are fighting more, and they have a better view of themselves. They are making changes happen."

35. All of the citations concerning change come from telephone interviews unless indicated otherwise.

TABLE 5.5   CREDIT AND BLAME FOR WOMEN'S
SITUATION (%)

A. CREDIT FOR IMPROVEMENT IN WOMEN'S SITUATION	
Women made it happen	59
Women's organizations did it	13
Men and society did it	6
Government policies did it	2
Miscellaneous	2
Don't know	17
B. REASONS WHY THEY HAVE NOT PROGRESSED MORE*	
Men have held women back	80
Government policy held them back	54
Women have too many household obligations	53
C. WHICH IS THE MOST IMPORTANT REASON?†	
Men have held women back	38
Household obligations	25
Government policy	17
Women are less ambitious	10
Women are less qualified	5
Don't know	4
	$n = 304$

*Respondent could offer more than one reason.
†Respondent was asked to choose the most important reason from the ones she had offered.

These changes, as the quotations suggest, include changes within themselves; "women have changed." "Women are taking more interest now than before about themselves. Women are having more initiative. A lot of women hindered themselves before, now they have more confidence outside the home." Or, as a focus group member in her fifties commented: "Women are beginning to be good to themselves." They are no longer letting themselves get "pushed around by men at work and at home," explained a telephone respondent. Another asserted, "Now they are outspoken and assertive." The consequence is that "women [are] changing the roles for women, not the men" (from a focus group). All of these developments in turn have brought on social changes.

ACCOUNTING FOR CHANGE

When it came to explaining why this refusal to let themselves be pushed around has occurred relatively recently, why women had not rebelled long ago, focus groups and telephone respondents found themselves in agreement with most social scientists that women's entrance in the workforce has made the big difference. Employment was seen as so pivotal because experiences in the workplace brought home to many of them what it means to operate in a "man's world." "More and more women are entering the workforce, and they are finding out what's going on," maintained a telephone respondent. This experience, according to another interviewee, led them to decide: "We didn't want to take it any more—being second-class citizens. If women are qualified for a job or the same pay, we want to be able to have it." In the words of a third, women have begun to ask "to be treated equal in terms of employment and as humans." But these comments, like many others, again refer to individual rather than organizational or governmental efforts to obtain fair treatment. They do not indicate that the interviewees were very politically aware, let alone involved either directly or indirectly, by involvement in relevant organizations, in bringing about the desired results.

Employment, according to our respondents, contributed to change in yet another way. By earning money, women also gained a certain degree of independence, and with it—so they told us—came enhanced self-esteem, which enabled them to refuse to be "pushed around." "More and more women have gone out into the workforce and earned money to give themselves a feeling of importance," said one. Another commented that now "we are going to show men they can't walk all over us." The men in our study shared this impression; they too believed employment has made women more self-confident and independent. They differed from women, however, in their reactions to these developments; they were far less likely to welcome the change, as we will see in chapter 7.

The increase in the level of women's education was seen as another factor contributing to improvement in their situation. Education, our respondents believed, has made women more aware of the world beyond the confines of the home and more knowledgeable and interested in such matters. It has also increased their ambition. Because of education, "women have woken up to the fact that they can do anything a man can do." It has made them "go after traditionally male jobs," among which they cited certified accounting, computer work, and medicine. Education is one reason, they said, why women now refuse "to take it any longer." Education was credited with having made women "smarter" and hence more demanding of equal treatment. Change has come about "because of the fact that women are better educated and more aware, and are better able to stand up for what they want." As one woman said: "Women are more educated and more career-minded than I was in 1950."

Education has also devalued the traditional occupation of housewife. "People are more educated now; once they get an education, they don't sit home." Many stressed how education, combined with economic necessity, has made women career-minded and has "liberated" them from confining their lives to the domestic sphere. Focus group and telephone respondents alike were convinced that education, much like employment outside of the home, is enriching in every sense of the word and that it has contributed greatly to the changes they are currently witnessing. The explanatory weight women attached to education, employment, or other phenomena may vary from woman to woman, but their belief that the change occurred because women brought it about, that "women have made it happen" (a phrase used by more than one woman) was all but uniform.

CONCLUSION

As women assessed their current situation, they were both angry and pleased. Many were angry with the way society and men try to keep them in subordinate positions, especially at work and at home, and they were pleased with the progress they have made so far. They were particularly pleased because they believed that most of their present success was accomplished by their own efforts, often over men's objections. They were angry and "tired of past experiences, what their mothers went through," but before they could throw off the yoke of the past, they had to become aware of their second-class citizen status, and then they had to change "their own way of thinking" before they could "become vocal about their wants." They recognized that the battle has not yet been won and that it is rather futile to expect men to assist them. One "just can't depend on men." "If [women] didn't put the pressure on them [men], there would have been no change in women's position." Nor were they of the opinion that government has done much to help women. Quite the contrary, majorities in both samples actually believed that government has held women back.[36]

Given their dim view of the political establishment, combined with their own individualistic inclinations and the American public's general disdain for politics, it is perhaps not surprising that these women showed little interest in, let alone enthusiasm for, political engagement. Instead, they planned to concentrate on individual efforts, seeing that as the best and most direct way of improving their own situation.

36. This, of course, does not preclude that many women (49 percent) would welcome increased governmental efforts to improve women's position; this is an idea to which men are somewhat less receptive (32 percent).

The Women's Movement may have blazed the trail for them, but now, they imply, it is up to each individual woman to win equity as well as equality for herself. That is, they assert how change came about in the first place and how more progress will be made in the future.

These women's vision of progress, moreover, was much concerned with the problems of everyday living, including job opportunities, equal pay, and a fairer division of labor at home. Almost entirely absent from their discussions was a concern with the strategic goals of feminism and the obligations any individual woman might have to help bring about progress for women collectively. Neither in the focus groups nor among the telephone respondents do we find any indication that participants sensed a collective responsibility for women as a whole. The New Jerseyites are thus much like the professional women characterized by P. Glazer and M. Slater who have "overbought the ideology of merit. They believed that if only one were good enough, worked hard enough, and excelled enough, then one must succeed. They tended to see individual achievement, rather than group political efforts and structural changes as the key to equality" (1986: 238).

MINORITY CONSCIOUSNESS AND POLITICS

The woman who has protested her inequality, her status as an outsider, may expect criticism for having used her voice—an unfeminine, aggressive act.

—Langland and Gove (1981)

A strong sense of collective deprivation is said to be the most fortuitous spark for political mobilization (Martin 1981; Pettigrew 1964 and 1967; Rhodebeck 1981; Runciman 1966). The women we studied possessed that fortuitous spark and displayed a keen sense of collective deprivation, even though many did not feel personally deprived. Yet, as discussed in the last chapter, the sense of collective deprivation did not lead to the predicted mobilization, if by mobilization one means the readiness to become actively involved in promoting gender equality by political and other relevant means. The majority of women rejected that possibility for themselves. This unwillingness to become politically mobilized, far from being unique to women in New Jersey, has been found characteristic of women in the United States generally (Baxter and Lansing 1983; Freeman 1975; Gurin 1985; Gurin, Miller, and Gurin 1980; Miller et al. 1981; Sapiro 1983; Welch 1977). This unwillingness to mobilize politically is frequently interpreted as a sign that women lack commitment to the collectivity of women, that they are deficient in group-consciousness or at least do not have a group consciousness nearly as well-developed as that of other disadvantaged groups, notably blacks (Gurin 1985; Gurin, Miller, and Gurin 1980). The theme of this chapter is that good reasons exist why the rank and file of women—the kind of women we observed—are difficult to mobilize and why they have not developed the kind of group consciousness necessary for mobilization that characterizes committed feminists. They have developed, however, a definite consciousness of being part of a disadvantaged group. I have given this sense of belonging the label, "minority consciousness." I maintain that this form of consciousness has significant political implications.

Before discussing the role played by minority consciousness, I will briefly summarize the explanations that many scholars offer for why women are disinclined to become politically mobilized. I will look first at what is generally understood by the concept "group consciousness." Next, I will discuss why it may well be unwarranted to expect women to show much evidence of genuine group consciousness. I will then describe what I understand minority consciousness to mean and explain why I think it fits the realities of the lives of the women I studied. After that I will detail how the concept was operationalized and examine how it is distributed in the population. I will close with a discussion of how minority consciousness helps us understand women's political attitudes and behaviors.

REASONS FOR NOT BECOMING MOBILIZED

Researchers have advanced several by no means mutually exclusive reasons for why women have not politicized their gender-based dissatisfaction. I shall label the first *the time and tradition explanation.* Virginia Sapiro (1983) advanced the thesis that tradition as well as circumstances militate against mobilization. She held that several factors (only a few of which will be mentioned here) contributed to women's failure fully to integrate into the political life of the nation. She attributes much of this failure to the traditional split between the private and the public world; cultural tradition, buttressed by sex-role socialization, has caused both genders to allocate the private sphere to women and the public one to men. Women thereby come to believe that politics is not for them, that it goes against their own best nature. Women, Sapiro holds, need to begin to realize that the private is political. In addition, she maintains that the relatively isolated life of the housewife deprives her of the contacts that might awaken group consciousness. Sapiro concludes that many women tend to lack the material and psychological resources essential for political integration.

Since her study (covering the period from 1965 to 1972), the purely domestic mode has lost its predominance in the United States.[1] But other contingencies contribute to the continued lack of political integration, including, ironically, women's full-time employment outside of the home. Because most women must combine full-time employment with a "second shift" at home, time has become a precious resource and so has energy; both are essential for political mobilization. The extremely short supply of these resources might help explain why the New Jersey women we observed expressed such unwillingness to

---

1. Her study utilized the data set originally collected by Jennings and Niemi for their longitudinal study.

become politically involved. They are women from all walks of life who work hard all day to make a living and then work hard at night to take care of the house and often young children as well. Political activity, even just sustained political interest, may well appear a luxury to them.

Another factor contributing to their lack of politicization is provided by what I shall call *the sense of powerlessness explanation.* Feeling powerless to affect the current power distribution, women, as shown in the preceding chapter, seem convinced that, at least in the foreseeable future, men will continue to resist any fundamental changes in gender relations. Hence, for women to insist on major changes would, they believe, lead to open conflict with men, something they want to avoid at almost all cost. As one woman declares: "I don't want to see a tug of war between a man and a woman."[2] Nor are they at all sure that the tug of war could be won, at least not while society has so much invested in keeping women in a subordinate position. Being so bereft of power, they cannot fathom how they can bring about genuine change, no matter how desirable it may seem to them. In the focus groups, that lack of empowerment weighed heavily on many participants. "Power issues occupy center stage not because individuals are greedy for more, but because some people are incapacitated without it" (Kanter 1977a: 205). There is no doubt in my mind that many of the members felt incapacitated by their lack of power or, in their words, their "lack of clout."

The "tug of war" metaphor, however, suggests that, in addition to general powerlessness, these women think of their subordination in concrete, personalistic terms. They are aware that many women have similar problems, but the way they conceptualize the problem, the problem ceases being a social one and essentially becomes one between them and "the man." "The man" can be a husband, the boss, or the bank officer. Sometimes "the man" can be men in general, but it is never the sociopolitical system itself that propagates or supports the problem and needs transformation. Instead, the object of attention is almost always a person who is recalcitrant and needs to be either accommodated or subtly manipulated but cannot be confronted openly. One woman in the focus groups came close to making the connection when a young woman told how hard it is to bring up her little boy "to become a good person who treats women the way they want to get treated." Whereupon the somewhat older woman bluntly interjected: "And her son will go to school, and they will call him sissy, and he will come back with his combat uniform on." No one took up the theme, suggesting that maybe the schools, like other parts of the social system, could bring about change. If any change was to come about,

2. This issue will be explored at length in the last chapter.

they suggested, it had to be the result of individual effort rather than social policy. Here is one such typical solution. Another woman told how she works in a wood shop with a man who holds a low opinion of women's woodworking competence. "And just showing him that I could do it is changing his opinion of me, so maybe he will go out and change somebody else's opinion. That's the only way you can do it." This was her answer to the moderator's question about what women could do to bring about social change.

The price of continuing discrimination may seem less steep these days because (as discussed in chapter 3) women are so sure that their situation has improved greatly over the past few decades. This is what I call the *progress explanation*. Most believe that the gains made so far are secure and that the clock will not be turned back. While some theorists (notably Pettigrew 1964 and Runciman 1966) argue that periods of improvement are precisely the times when discontent rises, others maintain that

> a tale of what the future holds in store, can sometimes serve to blunt any resentment . . . In particular, when prospects for change exist and current outcomes represent only a temporary stage in some ongoing process (i.e., these outcomes might soon be replaced by others), then the perceived likelihood of amelioration influences people's reactions. Good prospects for amelioration make it easier for people to tolerate currently poor outcomes. (Folger 1987: 186)

Folger refers to this as the "replacement effect." Judging from the narratives quoted in the last chapter, the women in this study apparently engage in a lot of replacement. They have found individual ways of ameliorating the "poor outcomes" by a variety of techniques. Their efforts have brought about some change and amelioration. The resentment remains, but it becomes tolerable and may eventually become unnecessary.[3] That so many feel personally exempt from deprivation (the "not-me" syndrome) further blunts resentment.

The American *emphasis on individualism* and individual achievement provides yet another explanation for eschewing collective action. The belief remains strong that in our society individuals are judged on the basis of their individual merit rather than their group membership. Indeed, they prefer being judged in that way. "In general Americans do not like to categorize themselves, they prefer to think of themselves merely as individuals" (Gurin 1987: 180). That emphasis, shared by

---

3. Folger (1987) asserts that resentment occurs when the deprivation is seen as unjustified. When good reasons can be mustered for justifying it, the deprivation will yield dissatisfaction but not resentment. The New Jersey women find no justification for denying equality to them.

men and women, offers scant encouragement for relying on collective efforts on behalf of one's group. "These conditions all encourage individualistic thinking and discourage recognition of group disparities or awareness of structural forces that may impede the achievements of certain categories" (Gurin 1987: 181). J. Martin (1986) offers a good example of this practice. She examined how a group of secretaries felt about the injustices intrinsic to their occupations and why, contrary to relative deprivation theories, they do not necessarily engage in collective action. She concluded that although "increases in the magnitude of inequality between groups may cause feelings of injustice, these feelings may make a relatively minor contribution to decisions about participation in collective action" (p. 236). When it is possible for persons "to alleviate their own deprivation without going to the extra effort of alleviating the status of the entire group, this easier alternative will generally be preferred" (p. 239). We may add that it will also seem more congenial, more in keeping with the traditional American ethos.

THE CONCERN FOR PRACTICAL SOLUTIONS

Finally, for many women discontent with current gender arrangements can be traced to the failure of the system to meet some *practical* needs of women, such as affordable day care facilities, adequate child support, and the like. We have seen in previous chapters how resentful the New Jersey women feel about the unfair division of labor at home. Such considerations feature far more prominently in their complaints than inequitable power distributions or the system of patriarchy. With some modifications, what Thomas-Slayter (as cited in Robinson 1993: 13) said about women worldwide has applicability for New Jersey women as well: "For many women in the world, the most urgent issues have more to do with survival than status. They worry about where to get clean water before thinking why only men inherit land."

GROUP CONSCIOUSNESS

The concept of collective or group consciousness is an old one, most frequently associated with Karl Marx's notion of class consciousness. It has come in vogue in recent years in order to increase our understanding of the mobilization or lack of mobilization within certain distinct groups. Most of the time, it has been used to analyze the reactions of disadvantaged groups, especially blacks and women, although it need not be restricted to disadvantaged groups. Miller and his associates (1981: 495), in a seminal article on the topic, define the concept this way: "Group *consciousness* . . . involves identification with a group *and* a political awareness or ideology regarding the group's relative position in society along with commitment to collective action aimed at realizing the group's interests." On the other hand, "group *identification* connotes a perceived self-location within a particular social stratum, along with a psychological feeling of belonging to that particular stratum" (italics in original). Identification thus is considered just the first step; the necessary but not sufficient precondition for developing group consciousness. Conover and Sapiro (1992: 5–6) offer a similar definition of group consciousness. For them, it is a "politicized form of social consciousness; at its core, it is a form of social attachment that incorporates a conscious political component." They distinguish, however, between gender consciousness and feminist consciousness, holding that feminist consciousness includes a commitment to changing women's disadvantaged status. Gurin, in some of her writings, equates that commitment with a willingness to engage in collective action and considers collective action a *sine qua non* of group consciousness. Even though the concept of group consciousness has been variously defined, all definitions contain at least the above three elements: identification with the group, attachment to it, and commitment to action on its behalf. A vital fourth component of consciousness, but one not emphasized in the literature, involves assigning priority (or at least a high priority) to membership in the disadvantaged group over memberships in other groups to which one belongs.

WHY GENDER CONSCIOUSNESS IS HARD TO DEVELOP

It is the absence of that priority assignment which, I believe, explains much of the lack of solidarity (a term I prefer over consciousness) among the women we have interviewed. Many women feel close to women as a group in some respects, yet share far deeper bonds with other groups (perhaps their profession or ethnic group), so that concern for women, though real, is not of paramount interest to them. As Tolleson Rinehart reminds us, "women are not a bounded 'group' in any classical sense" (1992: 37). Because they are not a bounded group, the interests of one group of women may at times sharply conflict with the interests of another group of women even though both may share a common interest in promoting gender equality. The conflict over pornography and protective labor legislations within the women's movement are two such examples.

Nor do I consider appropriate the frequently made comparison with the greater group consciousness of African-Americans. Although African-Americans too are divided among themselves by social class and other highly relevant characteristics, their position vis-à-vis the

dominant society is so very different from that of women. Most important, blacks are far more certain than are women as to whom they have
to blame for their oppression. As Gurin summarizes these differences:
"Solidarity and recognition of group deprivation are fostered when
members of a category interact frequently with each other and only
occasionally with members of the outgroup; when intimate interaction
is restricted to the ingroup; when relations with members of the outgroup are conflictful" (1987: 181).

Finally, there is a vast difference between living one's life as a black
in the United States and living it as a woman. White society constantly
reminds blacks of their disadvantaged status, whereas for women gender becomes irrelevant in many routine daily contacts. We only need to
remind ourselves of the guardedness, not to say suspicion, a well-
dressed black man encounters when entering an expensive store in contrast to the welcome extended to an equally well-dressed white man.
Consequently, blacks know with far more certainty than do women
who is to blame for their oppression. It should come as no surprise,
therefore, that they give evidence of a well-developed sense of group
consciousness.

But there is yet another reason why it is hard for women to develop
a sense of group consciousness. A majority of women live in partnership of one kind or another with men and, hence, in closer association
with members of the dominant group than they do with other women
(the dominated group); because they greatly value their association
with the dominant group (more about that in chapter 8), the fear of
jeopardizing it forms a serious barrier to the development of group
consciousness. In a similar vein, Sapiro considers the woman's fear of
creating "more threats to her personal relationships with men than she
can tolerate" one of the two main barriers which impede the development of group consciousness in women (1991: 15).[4]

In addition, men and women "share economic gains and losses as
members of the family" (Gurin 1987: 181), as business partners, and in
a host of other closely knit activities and associations. All of these forms
of community of interests work against the likelihood that most
women will experience strong feelings of solidarity for women collectively, feelings necessary to engendering in them a sense of responsibility for the group's welfare and a commitment to become active on
its behalf.

Some excerpts from the focus groups and the telephone survey
will give the reader a feel for how the women in this study look upon

---

4. The other barrier she considers is the American emphasis on individual rather
than political solutions.

their obligations to other women. This sense of obligation, after all, must be a crucial stimulus for becoming politically mobilized on behalf of women. When a moderator asks: "Is it up to individual women [to bring about improvements], or should women get together as a group?" their answer is unambiguous: "I think it's up to the individual herself. I think if she cares at all about herself, she'll stick up for herself and do it hopefully in good taste." That comment reflects not only a preference for individual initiative over collective action but also the speaker's detachment from women as a social and political entity. Nor do the other women in the focus groups show much group consciousness or solidarity with women. They give no evidence that they feel an obligation similar to that felt by members of some other minorities to make an effort to improve the lot of women as a group. These women could see that they are part of a common situation (that of "second-class citizens"), but they do not consider themselves part of a common cause. When the moderators suggest that they might help raise the consciousness of a woman who cannot stand up for her rights, they declare that they do not feel such an obligation.[5] The following interchange, initiated by a moderator, illustrates the common reaction. She asks: "Let me pull us back here on something . . . we've been talking about these various problems with women in society and sex discrimination and that sort of thing. What should women do? . . . What steps, is it up to individual women to do these things about it? Should women get together as a group and just collectively [do] these things about it?" Without hesitation, the answer comes: "I think it's up to the individual herself." A young mother and artist is doubtful about the effectiveness of attempting to raise other women's consciousness: "I'm wondering if—I'm wondering if that's something that really the women's movement may have made other people aware of it. I disagree with it. I have a feeling that it is a one-on-one situation. And I have a feeling that each person has to sort of discover her own consciousness or at least her own level of awareness. And that takes a certain amount of self-knowledge." Moderator: "And you think it has to be done on your own? You don't think . . . " Another woman interrupts: "I think that in the final analysis you have to do it for yourself." Another chimes in that other women "have to identify the problem themselves before somehow making their change. A lot of women are just too afraid to be independent and too caught up in having someone else do it for them." Others declare that some women "are just too passive and repressed" to be

5. One woman of the 50 women in our focus groups had once belonged to a woman's group. Another, a social worker, had worked with battered women, but it is not clear in her case whether that was in the line of her professional duties or was volunteer work.

helped. Comments like these come perilously close to "blaming the victim." For all of the anger women voice over the treatment received by men, most of them find the notion of collective responsibility unacceptable. Judging from their own comments, they do not experience the sense of solidarity or of sisterhood so crucial to a grassroots women's liberation movement. If our population is at all typical, not much seems to have changed since Gurin and her collaborators (Gurin, Miller, and Gurin 1980; Miller et. al 1981; Gurin 1985) first commented, based on their observations during the 1970s, that women's group consciousness was much less developed than that of other disadvantaged groups. While this no doubt is the case, I want to advance the thesis that we should not equate the lack of group consciousness with obliviousness to women's disadvantaged status. Many New Jersey women are very aware of that status and deeply disturbed by it.

MINORITY CONSCIOUSNESS: THE CONCEPT[6]

As far back as 1951, Hacker concluded that "common observation would suggest that, consciously at least, few women believe themselves to be members of a minority group the way in which some Negroes, Jews, Italians, etc. may so conceive of themselves. . . . one cannot easily say that the majority of women display minority group consciousness" (p. 508). Forty years later, "common observation" may well reach different conclusions. Women in New Jersey may still lack a sense of solidarity with other women, but many acknowledge that on many occasions and in many situations, they feel as though they belonged to a "minority" although arithmetically constituting a majority. One woman bluntly voices this sentiment: "People put blacks and women in the same sort of category." When the moderator asks what she meant by that, she answers: "incompetent, inadequate, too emotional." The frequent references the women in this study make to their second-class status point in the same direction. For these women, the sense of being treated as though they were a minority, and a minority of lesser worth than the dominant group is not a casual matter but affects them profoundly. It affects their self-concept, their interaction with members of the opposite sex, and their whole fabric of living. Consequently, it is impossible to talk about female attitudes or female behavior without taking that sense of minority status into account. Examining it in detail will offer some indication whether or not much has changed in the four decades since Hacker declared women deficient in minority consciousness.

6. Much of what follows is adopted from Sigel and Whelchel (1986a and 1986b).

DEFINITION OF MINORITY CONSCIOUSNESS

Minority consciousness refers not to objective group membership but rather to a subjective phenomenon. It refers to the perception women have of belonging to a disadvantaged minority and to their feelings about that. Our construct of minority consciousness resembles the construct of group consciousness in that both concepts have cognitive and emotional elements. Minority consciousness differs from group consciousness in deemphasizing the sense of overt commitment to the group, especially with respect to collective action. In spite of this lack of commitment to collective action, however, I believe a sense of minority consciousness has significant political consequences.

MINORITY CONSCIOUSNESS AND POLITICS

Minority consciousness arises from the realization that the treatment a given group receives violates the tenets of equity and equality to which an individual subscribes. Consequently, minority consciousness need not be restricted to people who believe themselves victims of discrimination. Those who are personally not disadvantaged may feel keenly about the injustice suffered by a group, that is, they can demonstrate minority consciousness, regardless of whether or not they are objective members of the group. Defined this way, men also can express minority consciousness, but its source will be different from women's. For men, the source will be their commitment to equality and their concomitant anger over seeing that principle violated. But they lack the personal experience with inequality that shapes and sharpens women's minority consciousness. Both genders may well advocate the same political solutions for bringing about gender equality, but they will have gotten to their policy prescriptions by different routes. Referring to the different routes traversed by men and women, Ethel Klein wrote: "Men were sympathetic to feminist arguments because of their own general concern for issues of justice and equality. The issues, however, did not touch them directly. Men did not feel threatened by the status quo; women did" (1984: 104). Given that sympathy, we expect minority consciousness to have political consequences; we anticipate that the high minority-conscious group, whether male or female, will be the one most likely to lend strong endorsement to policies and practices designed to bring about gender equality.

OPERATIONALIZATION OF MINORITY CONSCIOUSNESS

Minority consciousness is a multidimensional concept consisting of two major components, a cognitive and an affective one, each of which in turn also is multidimensional. The cognitive element in minority consciousness refers to the linked perceptions that, in the eyes of the dominant group, a woman belongs to an inferior group and is denied rights and privileges granted that group (we have labeled these perceptions Discrimination Awareness). The emotional component, or Affective Involvement, encompasses two separate elements, namely, resentment over the categorical treatment of one's group and affinity for the group as a collectivity, expressed in feelings of closeness and concern for its welfare. Resentment indicates the significance the issue of discrimination has for the person, and concern for the group indicates the importance the group has for her.

THE CONSTRUCTION OF THE MINORITY CONSCIOUSNESS INDEX

The cognitive component, captured by the Discrimination Awareness Index, was described in chapter 3, and no additional commentary is necessary.[7] The Index of Affective Involvement consists of six items; four of the items inquire into resentment over specific discriminatory situations. The other two items refer to a woman's affinity or concern for the group as a collectivity. One is the item featured in the National Election Studies since 1972 which inquires into the respondent's sense of closeness to his/her gender.[8] The other item, from the work of F. J. Crosby (1982), seeks to determine how concerned respondents are with the welfare of women as a group.[9] Respondents were categorized as being high, medium, or low in Affective Involvement based on their total scores, which were calculated from their answers to the six items on the Affective Involvement Index. Minority consciousness was measured by combining scores from the Discrimination Awareness and Affective Involvement Indices in such a way as to permit distinguishing respondents who were high on both the cognitive and the affective measures from those whose reactions were more ambiguous and those scoring low on both discrimination awareness and affective involvement measures.[10] Minority consciousness thus reflects a person's feelings about the current gender scene and women's position in it.

7. It is discussed in more detail in Appendix B.

8. The item reads: "Many people share common experiences with or feel close to certain groups. Please tell me whether you feel particularly close to any of the groups I read." The interviewer posed that question with respect to five different groups, among them "other women" (in the case of female respondents) and "other men" in the case of males.

9. The question we adopted was: "How much interest do you have in how women as a whole are getting along in this country? Do you have a great deal of interest, some interest, just a little, or not much?"

10. The above procedure is described more fully in Appendix B.

THE DISTRIBUTION OF MINORITY CONSCIOUSNESS AMONG MEN AND WOMEN

The important role minority consciousness occupies in women's social and political orientations can best be documented by comparing male and female reactions. Distributions on the Minority Consciousness Index demonstrate that men and women are far apart in assessing the seriousness of gender-based inequalities. Far more women than men consider this a serious problem (see table 6.1). Many women in the focus groups were trying to convey that men really do not care when women are treated unfairly. This could also be the reason women are so disinclined to engage in the "tug of war" that might ensue were they to get politically mobilized. Among men, fewer than one in five (19 percent) score high in minority consciousness; 60 percent scored low. A solid majority of males think of sex discrimination as a minor or almost nonexisting problem. Forty-seven percent of women are high scorers but 38 percent scored low. Not surprisingly, men were less likely than women to score high in minority consciousness.[11]

That men and women relate differently to discrimination appears in yet another way. On each of the two indices which compose minority consciousness, the intercorrelations of the items are stronger for women than they are for men, suggesting that women approach the topic with considerably more internal consistency.[12] For men, specific discriminatory practices may constitute exceptions to a general rule of equality; for women these practices are integral to the whole fabric of discriminatory gender relations. The greater internal consistency becomes particularly noticeable in the Affective Involvement Index. There the distributions graphically illustrate how much more salient and troublesome the issue of discrimination is for women than it is for men. For women, the index items are strongly interrelated (13 of the 15 inter-item correlations are significant at the 0.01 level), whereas for men one-third of the inter-item correlations are not significant. Quite understandably, awareness of sex discrimination and bitterness over it are more closely connected for the victims, the women, than they are for men.

Up to this point, the analysis shows that it is quite possible for members of the dominant group to exhibit minority consciousness, but it is more difficult for members of that group to feel the same urgency

11. All correlations are statistically significant at the .01 level or better unless indicated otherwise.

12. Discrimination awareness and affective involvement are positively related (significant at the .001 level both for men and women) but more strongly so for women (*tau* -.48 and .30 for men). For details, see Appendix B.

TABLE 6.1   LEVELS OF MINORITY CONSCIOUSNESS
BY SEX (%)

Level of Consciousness	Male	Female
High	19	47
Medium	21	15
Low	60	38
	$n = 200$	$n = 400$

Kendall's taub = −.24, significant at .000

about the problem that the disadvantaged group feels for itself. The difficulty may be enhanced in that members of the dominant group are the beneficiaries of the minority's problem.

MINORITY CONSCIOUSNESS AND CHANGE

Men and women also feel differently about the recent and projected changes in women's situation and about public policies, sometimes costly policies, designed to benefit women. Theoretically, those who are high in minority consciousness—regardless of gender—should be the ones to endorse those measures that would benefit women. Up to a point, this indeed is the case. The high minority-conscious group is the least satisfied with the magnitude and speed of the improvements effected so far; it advocates more change in an egalitarian direction, and it is not likely to be satisfied with minor change (see table 6.2). Not unexpectedly, the high-scoring women are most intent on bringing about change. The pattern among the two genders is striking. For women, the relationships for seven of the eight change questions are significant at the .01 level. Among men, however, significant relationships between minority consciousness and change attitudes appear only in three instances, and even here they are lower than those observed for women, once more an indication of the greater relevance and urgency the problem has for women than for men. Indeed, why should this be otherwise? Are women not the likely beneficiaries of future change, and do not some men (as we shall see in the next chapter) believe that in the process they might become the losers?[13]

In earlier chapters, I noted that women do not consider themselves defeated by the ubiquitousness of discrimination. Whatever improvement they notice in the status of women, they attribute neither to gov-

13. This interpretation gains some plausibility when we consider that 67 percent of high minority-conscious women and only 37 percent of males say they have been beneficially affected by the changes.

ernment nor to men. In their opinion, it is women who have effected the change for the better. This is one topic on which women with both high- and low-minority consciousness can find themselves in near agreement. Sixty-four percent of the high scorers and 51 percent of the low ones give full credit to women for having found ways to effect

TABLE 6.2   PERCEPTIONS OF CHANGE IN WOMEN'S SITUATION BY LEVEL OF MINORITY CONSCIOUSNESS AND GENDER

	MEN		WOMEN	
	HIGH MC	LOW MC	HIGH MC	LOW MC
A. REFLECTIONS ON PAST CHANGES				
Amount of change	(%)	(%)	(%)	(%)
A lot	75	86	56	79
Some or a little	26	13	43	21
None	0	2	1	0
Total	101 $n = 47$	100 $n = 112$	100 $n = 183$	100 $n = 159$
	(tau$_b$ = .11*)		(tau$_b$ = .21)	
Speed of change				
Too slow	57	25	65	21
About right	39	67	34	67
Too fast	4	6	0	13
No change	0	2	1	0
Total	99 $n = 47$	100 $n = 112$	100 $n = 183$	101 $n = 159$
	(tau$_b$ = .26)		(tau$_b$ = .41)	
Effects of change				
For better	92	81	90	79
For worse	2	10	6	9
Both	6	7	3	13
No change	0	2	1	0
Total	100 $n = 47$	100 $n = 112$	100 $n = 183$	101 $n = 159$
	(tau$_b$ = .11*)		(tau$_b$ = .13)	
Effect on own life				
For better	38	25	67	31
Better and worse	4	8	2	4
Not affected	53	61	29	61
For worse	4	6	2	4
Total	99 $n = 47$	100 $n = 110$	100 $n = 181$	100 $n = 159$
	(tau$_b$ = .09†)		(tau$_b$ = .30)	
Credit to government				
Great deal	24	22	12	12
Some or little	57	42	53	50
Would have happened anyway	20	36	36	38
Total	101 $n = 47$	100 $n = 109$	101 $n = 173$	100 $n = 14$
	(tau$_b$ = .09†)		(tau$_b$ = .04†)	

(continued)

TABLE 6.2 (*continued*)

	MEN		WOMEN	
	HIGH MC	LOW MC	HIGH MC	LOW MC

	B. OUTLOOK ON FUTURE			
Government should become				
More active	55	22	68	29
Continue as it has	43	61	28	58
Less active	2	17	4	13
Total	100 $n = 47$	100 $n = 112$	100 $n = 183$	100 $n = 159$
		(tau$_b$ = .29)		(tau$_b$ = .33)
Security of gains				
Secure	66	80	62	79
Can change back	28	18	33	12
Both	6	3	5	9
Total	100 $n = 47$	101 $n = 112$	100 $n = 183$	100 $n = 159$
		(tau$_b$ = −.08†)		(tau$_b$ = −.18)
Amount and direction of change desired				
Major change back	0	5	0	1
Minor change back	0	3	1	3
No change	17	53	9	53
Minor equal	34	29	28	27
Major equal	49	12	62	16
Total	100 $n = 47$	102 $n = 112$	100 $n = 183$	100 $n = 159$
		(tau$_b$ = −.40)		(tau$_b$ = −.47)

Correlations significant at .01 level unless noted.
Percentages may not total to 100 due to rounding.
*Significant at .05 level.
†Not significant.

improvements in their situation (see table 6.3). Men have a different picture of how these improvements came about. Even among high-scoring males, fewer than one-fourth (23 percent) are as generous in giving women all of the credit; 19 percent actually attribute the changes to male efforts. Men and women may share a similar view of the present, as we found among high-minority-conscious males and females, but they distribute blame and credit differently.

MINORITY CONSCIOUSNESS AND POLITICS

Minority consciousness, as anticipated, relates systematically to political views, especially to political issues that are of particular interest to women and to the role government should play in improving the situa-

TABLE 6.3   CREDIT FOR IMPROVEMENTS IN WOMEN'S
SITUATION BY LEVEL OF MINORITY CONSCIOUSNESS (%)

| | Level of Minority Consciousness | | | |
| | High | | Low | |
Who Made Improvements Happen?	Men	Women	Men	Women
Women	23	64	39	51
Women's organizations	32	15	5	13
Men and society	19	7	23	9
Government policies	6	5	6	2
Miscellaneous (esp. publicity)	4	2	6	1

tion for them.[14] It relates positively not only to practical policies designed to protect women and/or to make their life easier but also to broader issues, such as passage of the ERA or increasing government assistance to women. But here again the relationship between minority consciousness and political preference is stronger for women than for men. Focussing exclusively on issues dealing specifically with women, we note that high scorers of both genders support such issues to a much greater degree than do low scorers. This is only as one would expect, since high minority-conscious people are the ones who most notice and most resent discrimination. Among women, large majorities of the highly conscious (in excess of 60 percent) support all six policies designed to assist women; for example, 68 percent believe government should become more active on behalf of women and 88 percent support the ERA (see table 6.4). Majorities of the male low scorers reject all but one of the policies (pregnancy leave was the exception); low minority-conscious women are ambivalent but not necessarily hostile to many of them.

Supportive though the high scorers of either gender turned out to be, the magnitude of support still is often smaller among men than among women. Even more important, the gender-based difference is generally larger in the high minority-conscious group than in the low one. This signifies that although high minority-conscious males support policies designed to help women, their support lacks the women's enthusiasm. Apparently, even for men of egalitarian dispositions, support for equality of the sexes has its limits. On the other hand, the strong support high minority-conscious women give to all of these policies suggests that for them minority consciousness plays an important role in structuring their political orientations.

14. In earlier work, we found minority consciousness related to negative perceptions of then-President Ronald Reagan and his political agenda (Sigel and Whelchel 1986a).

TABLE 6.4   ISSUE PREFERENCES BY LEVEL
OF MINORITY CONSCIOUSNESS

| | Level of Minority Consciousness | | | |
| | High | | Low | |
Preference for Select Issues (%)	Men	Women	Men	Women
Important to ratify ERA	66	88	48	51
Personally favors ERA	55	69	34	32
Favors more government help for women	66	68	23	30
Favors increased spending for shelters	71	78	47	59
Favors increased spending for daycare	50	67	39	48*
Favors guaranteed pregnancy leave	71	77	67	68*

*A measure of association (taub) is not significant; all others are significant at the .001 level.

In the case of low minority-conscious persons, however, gender does not affect political preferences. Both genders find themselves in close agreement with each other in their reluctance to support some policies. The fact that they attribute less significance to the whole issue of inequality (that is, they are low in minority consciousness) also means that they have less concern for changing the situation for women. Support for the ERA represents a particularly stark example of this. Among low-scoring males and females, support differs by just three percentage points (48:51 respectively), but among high scorers the difference widens to 22 percent (66 percent of males and 88 percent of females support the ERA). Another way of interpreting these results would be to say that the issue of gender equality is remote for low-scoring individuals regardless of their gender, but among proponents women offer far more reliable support than do men. Charity apparently begins at home even when it comes to causes with which one sympathizes.

In short, the most likely supporters for women's rights are high minority-conscious individuals of either gender, and among these women will be the staunchest supporters. The more a woman is convinced that others are treating her not as an individual but as a representative of the category "women" (in other words, the higher her level of minority consciousness) the more likely she will be to advocate policy changes on behalf of women and the more impatient she will be with the progress achieved so far.

However, when it comes to the willingness to engage in political action (that is, to advise a woman who is being discriminated against to take one of the four "political" actions), gender differences all but disappear. Only a minority of the high scorers suggests political action, and slightly more men (45 percent) make that suggestion than women

(31 percent). The last chapter argued that women in general find the activist road unappealing; apparently the same holds true for high minority-conscious women. Of course, "political action" is even more unappealing to low-scoring women; only 16 percent would advocate it. Here too men are more ready to advise political action (31 percent). One might have anticipated that high minority-conscious women, given their strong indignation over the treatment women receive, would support political action more ardently than the rest of the population. Apparently such anticipation is unwarranted.

Four observations follow from the male/female comparisons: (1) Minority consciousness structures gender-related policy preferences regardless of the respondent's own gender. Those who see women treated as a disadvantaged minority share a desire to see women's status improved. (2) The receptivity to changes in women's status and the support for increased resource allocation is considerably larger and firmer for minority-conscious women than for minority-conscious men. (3) Women give women most of the credit for improvements in their position, suggesting they have little faith that either men or government have much desire to help women. (4) Women show no readiness, regardless of their level of minority consciousness, to become politically mobilized in order to improve the situation for *all* women.

MINORITY CONSCIOUSNESS' SIGNIFICANCE FOR WOMEN

Women have come a long way since Helen Hacker's 1951 "common observation" that women do not display minority group consciousness because they either do "not know they are being discriminated against on a group basis [or] . . . acknowledge the propriety of differential treatment on a group basis" and consequently "harbor no resentment" (p. 508). By all of Hacker's criteria—the knowledge of discrimination, recognition of its illegitimacy, and resentment—women have now acquired consciousness of their minority group status. This consciousness, moreover, structures their policy preferences (at least as far as pro-women policies are concerned) in systematic and meaningful ways.

Minority consciousness, however, does not imply "sisterhood" nor should it be confused with group consciousness. Sisterhood implies a close bonding, creating a sense of responsibility for and solidarity with the group. That sense of solidarity was not evident in most of the women we observed, not even among the high minority-conscious women. Apparently, the issue of gender does not have the same centrality for the broad public that it has for feminists. The rank and file of women share with feminists a firm desire for gender equality but part company with them on some other feminist issues. The concept of minority consciousness helps to identify that segment of women who are neither Hacker's unaware and indifferent individuals nor self-identified feminists. Instead, they are women who are highly cognizant of discrimination, are angry over it, and want to see it brought to an end. That, as we have seen, is a very substantial group.

THE MALE PERSPECTIVE

Women may change all they want; unless men undergo corresponding transformations, change will grind to a halt.

—F. J. Crosby (1991)

Women's perceptions of gender relations, our main interest in this study, cannot be understood in a vacuum. Relationships, after all, are two-way streets. To understand women's perceptions of today's gender relations, it is, therefore, absolutely crucial to learn how men view these same relations. Much like women, men have certain notions and harbor certain beliefs and expectations, frequently derived from widely accepted gender stereotypes, concerning the other gender's feelings and behaviors. Many times the perceiver's actions are a direct response to their expectations concerning the motives and expectancies of the other gender; for "[t]he eye of the beholder does not affect perceptions alone, but can affect behavior as well" (Deaux 1984: 114).[1] Whether or not these attributions are correct or incorrect is immaterial in the short run, so long as they guide behavior. Thus how women perceive men frequently affects how they act toward men, and these actions in turn affect how men respond, which then affects women's response, and so forth. This book so far has focused almost exclusively on women's perceptions of male views of women and on their reports of men's behaviors toward women. This chapter explores whether these perceptions represent an accurate picture of men's perceptions of females' motivations and behaviors and of their own response to women's attitudes and behaviors.

The chapter will ask: How similar or dissimilar are men's and

1. K. Deaux (1987: 379), however, maintains that the extent to which expectancies guide behavior depends in part on whether the target (in our case the woman) is more concerned with self-presentation or with self-verification in a given interaction (in this case with a man). She argues that the more a person is concerned with the former, the more the behavior will be shaped by norms and stereotypes which underlie people's expectancies concerning the other.

women's perceptions and what is the impact of these dis/similarities on the character of gender relations? To answer that question, we will focus almost exclusively on the male informants, in order to learn from the men interviewed over the phone or observed during focus groups how men view gender relations and how they feel about the changes they believe are taking place around them.[2] The last chapter gave some indication that men and women do not approach gender discrimination from the same vantage point. Now we will examine in more detail the perceptual screen through which men view gender relations.

In the previous chapters, we listened to women rejoice in the new opportunities currently available to them, but we also heard them complain bitterly about the obstacles men still put in their paths, and about how men hadn't changed all that much from the way their fathers treated women. Here we will ask if the men in our sample share these perceptions, or if they believe instead that they are changing along with their partners at work and at home. Do the two genders share a common perception of recent developments, or do they look at the world through very different lenses? Do they perhaps say to each other—to cite the title of a recent best-seller—"you just don't understand"?[3]

Simple and straightforward though those questions may seem, they do not yield equally simple, unequivocal answers—as the pages which follow will make clear. Put in a nutshell, men's views of today's gender relationships reflect a good deal of ambivalence as well as occasional insensitivity. On the one hand, they are fully cognizant that women's traditional sex roles are in a state of flux. Moreover, most men—some more than others—are sympathetic to women's desire for equality with men. At the same time, many are uncomfortable and a bit alarmed over the changes they see taking place. They worry what the recent developments might mean for their own lives—their family lives, their work lives, and their social relations. A certain sense of regret permeates their recognition that "the good old days" of male dominance might be coming to an end (when, in the words of one focus group member, "a man's word was law"), but they also believe that the change "is only fair" (to cite another) and, besides, there is nothing they can do about it; the clock cannot be turned back. So they are learning to adjust

2. Two hundred men were interviewed over the phone (see chapter 3) and two male focus groups were conducted with a total of sixteen participants.

3. *You Just Don't Understand—Men and Women in Conversation,* by Deborah Tannen. Although her book is an analysis of men's and women's speech interaction patterns and not of gender relations in general, many of her observations have great relevance for that topic as well.

to the inevitable.[4] But whereas gender inequality is a matter of central concern for the New Jersey women, it is not for the men. Not that they are ignorant of women's distress. Quite the contrary; judging from the telephone interviews, they understand that distress, but, as I shall document presently, they consider it a fact of life which does not engage their interest, let alone their commitment.

Nothing illustrates this difference from women better than the men's behavior during the focus group sessions. The two male groups showed none of the sustained interest, let alone the animation or passion, the theme aroused in the women.[5] A fair way of describing male reactions would be to say that they have opinions on the subject and were willing to voice them when specifically asked, but that they showed very little inclination to pursue the topic at some length. Characteristically, it was the moderator who had to raise the topic, and still the groups frequently and quickly shifted the discussion to other topics which presumably interested them more. For example, a moderator's reference to women's lower remuneration was abandoned in favor of a discussion of the steady decrease in men's wages or the loss of union power. Sports, taxes, and traffic congestion were other topics capable of holding their interest; problems in gender relations lacked that holding power. At the end of each session, the moderator asked each group, male and female, for suggestions on how the topic could be pursued in public opinion polls the Institute might want to conduct in the future. Despite the men having talked (or, rather, having been urged to talk) about gender issues for close to two hours, no one suggested a question dealing with these issues. Instead, the state income tax and a few other topics were suggested. In short, gender relations is not an issue that engages these men.[6]

Analyzing men's reaction furnishes one more instance where the impressions gained from focus group observations and telephone surveys offer the observer two complementary and perhaps even some-

4. As one focus group participant, whose wife's employment has become crucial for the family's financial well-being, put it when reflecting on the altered power balance in his home, "I roll with the punches. Nothing fazes me any more."

5. Arlene Hochschild (1989: 6) made similar observations as she interviewed couples for *The Second Shift*, noting that women tended to talk with more animation and at greater length.

6. Whether or not it engaged male telephone respondents is a moot question since, after all, they were not given the option of changing the subject. One way of making a tentative determination is to analyze interviewers' impressions of respondents' interest in the interview. Since all interviewers were asked to record their impressions at the conclusion of the interview, we are currently in the process of beginning such an analysis. Admittedly, interpreting these impressions is by no means a sure guide to respondents' interest.

what contradictory insights into participants' states of mind. Data collected by either method give the impression that *in principle* men, much like women, are strongly in favor of equality for women and cognizant that it has as yet not been achieved. But the focus groups go beyond declarations of principles and provide a fuller understanding of how males define equality, demonstrating how inclusive that definition is for some men and how restrictive it is for others. Focus group observations, moreover, afford an opportunity to note the emotional weight some men attach to the recent changes and, perhaps even more important, to see how men try to navigate between the dictates of principle and the need to protect their prerogatives. They thus give us a real feel for the complexity and ambivalence inherent in the nature of men's reactions.

The format for this chapter parallels that adopted for the early chapters on women (chapters 3 and 4); it will begin with an analysis of men's discrimination awareness, followed by an analysis and description of how the recent changes in women's position have affected various aspects of men's lives, especially their work and family lives. It will conclude with a discussion of men's emotional reaction, including their anger or resentment over gender-based discrimination. Frequent references (both textual and tabular) will be made to women's reactions to the same topic. While these references involve repeating some of the materials covered in previous chapters, they are offered here to facilitate the comparison of male/female reactions.

DISCRIMINATION AWARENESS

Let me first turn to the impressions gained from the telephone survey. Men are by no means oblivious of the persistence of gender-based discrimination. Neither, however, did they see as much of it as the women see. Male recognition of discrimination, though it is substantial, seldom reached majority proportions—clearly a reflection of a major difference in male/female perspectives. This difference in perspective was most pronounced when the questions dealt with gender inequality in general (see table 7.1) In that realm, the differences in male/female estimates never fell below ten percentage points and at times exceeded twenty points. Not only is the proportion of men who saw discrimination considerably smaller than the proportion of women who perceived it, but even in their recognition of discrimination, men's assessment of its nature was less emphatic than was the women's. Thus, they believed that it occurs less frequently, or if it does occur, is less severe. That men believed that discrimination is less pronounced became particularly noticeable when respondents were asked to decide how strongly they

TABLE 7.1   DISCRIMINATION AWARENESS BY GENDER

Percentage Agreeing That	Men	Women
Men are treated better in society	48	69
There is much sex discrimination in U.S. society	57	70
It is still a man's world	34	50*
Women are often treated as second-class citizens	23	50
A woman has to be better than a man to get ahead	43	64*
Even if accomplished, women get less recognition	35	45*
Women's opinions get less respect than men's	44	59

*Only those respondents who agree "a lot."
All correlations significant at the .01 level.

agree or disagree with a given discrimination-related statement. In most of those instances, men perceived discrimination but tended to consider it to be negligible or moderate; women, on the other hand, were inclined to choose the more emphatic option (such as seeing a great deal of it). For example, majorities of males and females (57 and 70 percent, respectively) saw evidence of much discrimination in today's society; among the remaining men, 40 percent recognized the persistence of discrimination but believed it to be of minor proportion, and 4 percent denied its existence. The male/female difference becomes particularly noticeable when respondents were forced to make a simple agree/disagree choice. Here, 69 percent of women believed that males get treated better, but for men the percentage dropped to 48. Outright denial to the effect that no discrimination whatsoever exists, or that women actually are treated better, however, was rare. For example, in response to one question (the first in the three-part series), only 11 percent of the men asserted women get treated better in society, and in response to another question, only 20 percent saw no or virtually no societal discrimination. Men's answers leave no doubt that they do see discrimination operative in many fields. The replies, however, also suggest that for men it constitutes a less serious or rarer phenomenon. In other words, both genders are aware of prevailing gender-based discrepancies in power and resources, but the gulf in assessment which separates the two is substantial. Men are simply less likely than females to note discrimination in all of its pervasiveness and severity.

What makes the gulf in assessment significant is that it is not based on differential reflections about women's qualifications. There is no gulf of any consequence between men and women with respect to that. Men left little doubt that in their opinion women are as qualified in most areas under scrutiny as are their male counterparts. They were even quite sure that what holds women back is not lack of talent or ambition (only 8 subscribed to that explanation); instead, they attributed it to a variety of extrinsic factors, male resistance being the most frequently offered explanation. But that apparently did not prevent them from attributing less significance to the severity of discrimination.

The male/female awareness-gulf narrowed substantially with respect to some largely economic practices (see table 7.2). In fact, in a few of them the two genders find themselves in almost complete agreement. These areas tend to be restricted to practices where women's disadvantages have by now become common knowledge and are easy to document. For example, men and women were in full agreement that women have a harder time gaining pay equity or attaining top managerial positions in business. That agreement probably is not surprising given that the media and public debates and speeches periodically draw attention to the continuing gender-based wage gap and to phenomena such as the Glass Ceiling in the corporate world, and the all-male, all-white composition of the centers of power (a point that was brought up frequently during the Senate Judiciary Committee's confirmation hearings of Judge Clarence Thomas).

That similarity in perspective when dealing with concrete, so-called bread-and-butter issues stands in sharp contrast to reactions to more ephemeral, hard to document signs of bias, such as the lack of respect accorded women's opinions or society's inadequate recognition of their achievements. There men showed themselves to be less sensitive. We already saw in the female focus groups how much women resented the frequency with which their opinions were ignored, and the telephone surveys further corroborated this finding. Men did not seem particularly attuned to this phenomenon. For example, 45 percent believed that equal respect is accorded women's opinions, and 7 percent actually believed women get more respect, although 44 percent did agree with the majority of female respondents (58 percent) that women's opinions are accorded less respect.

The Discrimination Awareness Index gives further evidence that men are less aware than women of the prevalence of gendered inequality (see table 7.3). As might have been predicted, fewer men than women scored high on that index. However, even more important

TABLE 7.2 DISCRIMINATION AWARENESS IN SPECIFIC ECONOMIC AREAS

Percentage Agreeing That	Men	Women
Men are treated better in mortgage applications	56*	67
Men get better jobs in business management	65*	72
Men are treated better with respect to pay	81	80
Men are more likely to get top government jobs	77	83

*All correlations significant at the .01 level.

TABLE 7.3   LEVEL OF DISCRIMINATION AWARENESS
BY GENDER

Level of Awareness*	Men	Women
High	18(%)	38(%)
Medium	42	37
Low	41	38
	$n = 200$	$n = 400$

*As measured on the DA Index.

than the difference itself is the fact, as we saw in the previous chapter, that the intercorrelations among the items on the Discrimination Awareness Index are stronger and more consistently significant for women than they are for men. These lower intercorrelations suggest that men approach the issue of gender discrimination with considerably less internal consistency (see Appendix B and also Sigel and Welchel 1986b: 13).

One important difference—as stated before—is that women see discrimination pervading almost all social interactions and spheres of life, whereas men notice it in a narrower range of life experiences, and even there they consider it to be less frequent and less severe than do women. It would be wrong, however, to declare that most men are either oblivious of or choose to ignore subtle and not-so-subtle manifestations of gender-based inequality. But it is correct to assert that considerably fewer among them are aware of it, and where they are aware, they see it as a less serious issue than do women. To quote an old see-saw, it is as though both genders agree the glass of equality is not completely full, but men judge it to be half full and women to be half empty.

The male focus groups add balance to the picture which emerged from the telephone interviews. Much like the telephone respondents, the group participants acknowledged that gender bias still exists. But the focus group discussions offer yet another insight, namely that awareness of discrimination assumes a peripheral role in most participants' thoughts about gender relations. The moderator must always bring up the topic; the participants never raised it on their own. When confronted with the issue, they invariably viewed it within the context of the workplace and restricted it to questions of pay equity, access to specific occupations, and promotions. Even there, they displayed rather evasive ways of dealing with the problem. At times, even those who appeared most convinced that women are as competent as men found ways to rationalize women's lack of advancement. Charles, a well-educated computer specialist exemplifies this process. He told the group: "I see nothing, personally, that men have that women don't have." But later in the evening, he offered a different interpretation for women's (or at least some women's) lack of success: "I think, watching the TV news, some women protestors are trying to say that it is because they are women that they are not progressing but I get the feeling that they've just been left out of society somehow." James, a corporate representative in his sixties did not deny that his colleagues, who are unenthusiastic about women climbing the corporate ladder, at times give women a hard time. He related a lunch conversation with a woman, a young and rising star in his company, who was upset because the men in the company, especially her boss, were constantly putting her down so that she was considering resigning. He offered her a different slant on the situation by telling her: "Maybe he [the boss] is trying to find out if you have what it takes to stand up under that kind of strain, which is part of the business." He then advised her not to quit but to "stand up in the arena where the bull-fighting has gone on before amongst males." In other words, he advised her to fight like a man, or at least tried to convince her that this was the way all successful men play the corporate game. Charles and James represent two poles of male reaction. Charles maintains that women can achieve what they aim for; if they don't, it's because something is personally wrong with them. James recognizes that men seek to thwart women's ambitions and urges them to keep on fighting. However, he did not offer to help the young woman by putting in a good word with her boss, who is a close friend of his. Between Charles and James lie all the men who believe there is some discrimination "out there" but not in their own place of employment (unless it be "reverse discrimination")—and, anyway, the problem isn't all that serious.

Nor are the male focus groups noticeably more attuned to non-employment related forms of discrimination about which the female group members complained so loudly. They never referred to the subtler, hard-to-pin-down manifestations which trouble women. Our male focus group members, for example, never took note of the lack of respect that so often bothered women in the workplace, in commercial transactions, and in a variety of everyday interactions. This topic, the reader will recall, is one source of serious female discontent and frustration. Women spoke again and again of being "treated like imbeciles" when it comes to negotiating the price of repairs or seeking to sell possessions; of being treated disrespectfully in car dealerships, of being deliberately "tripped up" by male colleagues in blue-collar trades. Yet the focus group males never brought up those topics. One wonders, don't their wives, lovers, sisters, or mothers ever mention to them any incidents of discrimination or embarrassment that they may have experienced? Nor did the male participants make any reference to sexual harassment at the workplace.

Are males really unaware of the frequent and subtle ways in which many features of everyday life remind women of their inferior position? Or do such accounts just not register with them? Is it perhaps more comfortable not to talk about it because one does not want to be called upon to deal with it? Or perhaps, as J. F. Crosby and G. M. Herek suggest, "under certain conditions, bringing the situation of working women to a man's close attention poses such a threat to him that he actually minimizes the extent of gender injustices" (1986: 56). Maybe all of the above motives are involved to varying degrees. The telephone interviews would point in that direction. For example, when telephone interviewers raised the issue of discrimination directly, majorities of men concurred that women's accomplishments tend to get inadequate recognition, and many agreed that a woman has to be better than a man in order to achieve as much. But these opinions were voiced only in response to a direct, close-ended question by the interviewer. That men never raised them spontaneously during focus group discussions leads me to infer that this kind of inequality, if not a nonissue, is at least not a vital one for men, notwithstanding that it is such a burning issue for women. Men may even be aware that women mind this kind of treatment very much, as when 77 percent of the men asserted that women often feel treated like second-class citizens or when 58 percent assert that women are very bothered by discrimination. But it required the stimulus of a direct question to direct their attention to the problem.

Hence my earlier conclusion that the issue of women's equality does not greatly engage men.[7] But then again, their failure to mention discrimination during group discussion may not be so much a sign of emotional distance from the problem but may be, as Crosby and Herek suggest, a sign of feeling troubled or threatened, and that may be the reason why they seek to avoid the topic. Whatever the motivation, it is quite evident that men, when offered the stimulus of a direct question, recognized that discrimination is still a fact of American life—a conclusion on which both genders can agree. But it is also clear that more women than men hold to this tenet and they do so with considerably greater conviction. In no instance did men show more discrimination awareness than did women, and seldom did they reach parity with women in their awareness. That women brought up the issue of discrimination without prompting but men required a direct prompt

7. The contrast in response patterns displayed in focus groups and on the phone offers yet one more example of the usefulness of relying on more than one method of inquiry. It also serves as a caveat, to the effect that both survey responses and qualitative materials must be interpreted with extreme caution.

strongly suggests that the issue is more central for women. Men apparently can disregard it; women cannot.

In the focus groups, a slight generational difference in the levels of sensitivity becomes noticeable. Some young men, especially the better-educated ones, were somewhat more ready to acknowledge *personal* familiarity with the problems women face.[8] Older men were more inclined to profess not having encountered it or to downplay its prevalence. Here is how a professional man in his late fifties viewed it: "If I look at my own situation or the people that I'm aware of, and maybe it's just the companies that I work for, I didn't see the discrimination at the professional level. I guess it's kind of like I haven't seen it firsthand." This statement is all the more astonishing since he works in an occupation notorious for its exclusion of women. Like other middle-aged or older men, he readily conceded that there may be discrimination "out there"; it is just that he believes he has had no personal acquaintance with it. Younger men, by contrast, were readier to state that they had encountered it, especially if they live with employed women who report being hurt by instances of alleged discrimination or maltreatment. A thirtyish blue-collar worker whose wife is a nurse told us: "my wife has called me up in tears countless times, and I was ready to go down there and get hold of that doctor and tell him 'if you are going to talk to my wife like this, you are going to talk to me like this.' " Although this particular conversation began by dealing not with gender discrimination per se but with physicians' arrogant treatment of nurses (all of the physicians his wife dealt with were males), it lead the focus group males to offer a gender-based solution to her problem. "You know you need a couple of strapping male nurses there to give those guys a shot," one young man suggested—a suggestion which met with the group's approval.

THE PRINCIPLE OF GENDER EQUALITY

Perhaps even more revealing than their recognition of the persistence of inequalities is the way in which men deal with that recognition. Here the focus group observations are particularly helpful. For example, when the discussion turned to women in the workforce, males had no trouble agreeing that women are entitled to equal opportunity and treatment, including equal pay for equal work. But some men also had no trouble finding reasons why in their own work situation women ought to be treated differently from men. Either women's work was seen as less difficult, or as performed in more pleasant surroundings,

---

8. Responses to the telephone survey showed no significant age differences.

or performance standards expected of women were lower, or a host of other reasons why the women they encountered at the workplace really did not "deserve" equal status or equal pay. In this way, the men could then avoid having to deal forthrightly with the issue of equal pay and equal opportunity. Their redefinition of the situation permitted them to minimize the issue of pay discrimination without appearing to be unfair or biased against women. For example, a young man in an architectural firm would like to see fewer female architects in the field. He told the group that although the female architects are very good, they are hard to work with because they insist that everything be done their way. "I think they feel insulted when you try to change something. They have given you a detail, and now you want to change it because it is easier to do or it saves money, but they want what *they* drew. They feel very insulted if you want to change." This reaction he attributed to "the female inferiority complex," implying that architectural firms would be better off without so many female architects. Another young man, performing heavy physical labor, believed that physical strength and agility deserve more recognition and pay than "mere" clerical skills and asserted that it "is not fair" for secretaries or other "girls" performing physically nondemanding tasks to demand pay equivalent to his own. "So, I'm for a woman coming out and being a mechanic or climbing a pole and finding out, this is what you have to do to make this salary. If you don't want to do it, then fine. Go back into the office and make the less money." He concluded his case for rewarding physical skill more than clerical skill with the comment: "What's happening now is that these ERA's pushing for this equal pay for equal job, I'm really against that."

This devaluation of their contributions is precisely what women in our focus groups resented so bitterly. They questioned why men seem to make such a fetish of work that requires strong muscles, as though that were the best way to prove one's worth. One female factory worker, frustrated by her male co-workers' deliberate uncooperativeness, found her own way of coping with the problem: she insists on loading the heavy cartons by herself, although the job specifications entitled her to a helper. Then at night she assuages her resentment by weeding furiously in her garden.[9]

Some men justified their objection to women's recent advances by attributing them to quotas, affirmative action, or related government

9. A female truck driver, delivering a package to my house, told me how upset she originally was when the male drivers concluded she must be a lesbian, saying: "Why else would a real woman want to schlep boxes and drive a heavy rig?" Since then, she has decided to concentrate on the good pay and the benefits of the job and to ignore the men since they were "hopeless" (personal communication, July 1992).

policies rather than to women's own ability to handle their new jobs. We noted earlier that the women required a moderator's prompt before addressing the issue of affirmative action. Male participants brought up the issue on their own. Discussing the policy lets them quickly reach the conclusion that women's entrance into and promotion within previously male-dominated occupations and trades is the result of preferential treatment rather than competence. In this way, they can declare, to themselves and others, their support for gender equality in general and yet remain unenthusiastic or opposed within the context of their own work situation. Men in blue-collar jobs were particularly inclined to adopt this strategy. Although women's recent advances appear to have led to some male resentment and to considerable apprehension in both groups, it was expressed most openly in the working-class focus group, especially among those employed in the traditional blue-collar occupations that involve a lot of manual labor.

Nevertheless, it would be unfair to characterize any of these men as hostile to women's progress. They are apprehensive, yes, and at times resentful, but they are rarely, if ever, hostile. Instead, I am inclined to characterize their reaction as primarily one of ambivalence. In principle, they believe in equality, at least equality of opportunity, but they are uncertain what this might mean in practice for them. Affirmative action in particular presents them with a knotty problem and gave rise to some of the livelier discussions in both male groups. A freelance artisan told us that when his wife applied for a position, she had to take an aptitude test. "Well, with the women they [presumably the prospective employers] immediately added ten points to the average figures, to get more women in like that. Now I see a need, a need about this procedure . . . but I'm not sure about that yet. I'm not sure about my feelings on that but then something has got to come at a time probably." A middle-level executive expressed his ambivalence this way: "I've always had a problem with the concept of affirmative action . . . It just seems to be sort of a phony thing. I think in my mind I think it would affect the minority more than it would affect, say, me as a manager . . . because then the person who gets the promotion has to live with the stigma of you got the job because you are a minority. . . . I can't say I have not been in favor of it but I just think it's kind of a hokey concept." We noticed earlier that many women too were somewhat ambivalent about affirmative action but, in contrast to the men, they decided to opt for the policy rather than maintain a "men-only" recruitment procedure.

How do men cope with the tension between their principled beliefs (such as the belief in gender equality) and the natural tendency to hold on to accustomed privileges as they go about their everyday activities? For answers to that question, the next section will examine male attitudes and behaviors in three related realms: employment, family life (especially the impact of wives entering the workforce), and reactions to the recent changes in women's positions. I shall dwell particularly on the workplace and the family because, judging from the groups' discussions, it is in these two sites that the conflict is the most pronounced, or at least most apparent. They are also the sites where social class differences become most visible. The nature of the class differences makes it useful to discuss the two groups' reactions separately, beginning with those voiced in the working-class group. These class differences, it is important to point out again, are noticeable only in the male focus groups but not during the telephone interviews; and no class-based differences were observed in the female population (either during interviews or in group sessions). This finding leads me to question the frequently voiced assertion that women's dissatisfaction with current gender arrangements is largely a middle-class phenomenon. Based on the responses of the women in this study, it would appear that, for women, the issue of discrimination overrides matters of class.

EMPLOYMENT

The conflict between principled beliefs and long-ingrained behavior patterns becomes particularly acute in the case of working-class males. That working-class males should be especially conflicted is not surprising since this is the group most vulnerable to or threatened by current changes. These men see themselves being made obsolete by technological advances, by demands for new skills for which they have not been trained, and by the ever-present threat of losing their jobs. To these technological predicaments is now added the possibility of having to work alongside women in formerly all-male jobs and possibly even be "displaced by women," as one man phrased it. Women's massive entrance into the workforce touches their lives very directly and, judging from their conversations, causes them a good deal of anxiety. It has forced many to cope with novel situations with which they have not yet come to terms.[10]

The situation confronts them on two separate, yet related fronts: at home as their wives take on paid employment and in their own workplace as they have to work side-by-side and perhaps even compete with women on jobs previously characterized as "a man's job"; a designation

10. The anxieties expressed by these men don't seem to be atypical. Judging from the many media reports which appeared soon after the 1994 November election, fear and anxiety over becoming displaced by women, minorities, or machines fueled the resentment of many white males. Much in this vein, Secretary of Labor Reich referred to the election results as "the revolt of the anxious."

meant to imply women would be unable to discharge satisfactorily the duties of the job. For some, proof that women could handle these jobs became a blow to self-esteem they found difficult to tolerate. Thus, one manual laborer categorically announced that women have no business being garbage haulers, police officers, or roofers. Another gleefully commented that when his company introduced a training program for women, "they lost millions of dollars, because they were sending women out, and they would fall down a pole, or couldn't take the weather. Most of them lasted about six months." These men tended to be employed in jobs that involve heavy, tiring manual labor. They have traditionally considered the ability to perform that kind of hard physical labor a mark of masculinity; women's ability to perform it competently diminishes the significance of their labor, if not in the eyes of others, then at least in their own eyes.

   Their anxieties about the impending changes are expressed in a variety of ways. Some, as mentioned before, denigrated their female coworkers' suitability for the job by attributing their employment to affirmative action mandates ("quotas" as they preferred to call it). Others attributed female success to male coworkers' help with the assigned tasks.[11] "Technically, you're a male. But they are women, right? They have to do men's work. And if they can't handle the job, you've got men that will help them do their job. Which I don't think is right," said Luigi, a skilled maintenance worker in an industrial plant. Not that Luigi himself is inclined to help them! In fact, he refused to do so. He almost looks upon such help as a kind of sabotage of the male prerogative to perform certain types of labor. Another technique, also observed by Crosby, is "to see each competent woman as an exception while maintaining that any mistake made by a female was proof of the inferiority of the entire female gender [in the workforce]. Through the use of these and a number of other devices, the men managed to be, simultaneously, supportive and resistant" (1991: 188). In our groups, workers dealt with the problem by devaluing both the difficulty of the task and the skill of the women who perform such labor. They attributed women's suitability to perform previously male-dominated work to the technical revolution which has simplified many tasks and thereby made "real men's work," namely, heavy physical labor, super-

11. That such help seems to be the exception rather than the rule can be seen from the anecdotal evidence cited. While some women, as we have seen, are of the firm conviction that men actually work at making women fail, I found no evidence of that in the focus group. But I also found little evidence that men went out of their way to help women learn the trade as they might do for new male co-workers. A. Kessler-Harris's (1982) pioneering study of working women documents that in some trade unions men actually were fined by their unions if they helped women.

fluous. In their opinion, work that women can handle, just can't be very difficult; anyone can do it, even a robot. Al, a middle-aged man trained as a mechanic, certainly felt that way as he asserted that machines and robots have taken the place of "real" work. "Most of these jobs are set up for women. You don't need a man to sit there and watch four machines when a woman can sit there watch four machines."

Neither this professed disdain nor the implicit fear come through as clearly in the phone survey as they do in the focus groups. That might be because the survey questions touched upon the issue in a more general, abstract manner and did not inquire into a respondent's own work experiences. For example, when the telephone survey respondents were asked to respond to the statement, "some people attribute women's lower pay or absence from top level positions to lack of appropriate qualifications," over two-thirds of the male respondents rejected that explanation. They also left little doubt that they knew whom to blame for the female's lack of progress; 73 percent of the men declared that men themselves are the culprits, that it is they who have held women back (80 percent of the women agreed). Why do the telephone answers reflect a perspective so different from that voiced in the working-class focus group? The telephone survey referred to women in general, not to the women at respondent's place of employment. Nor did the survey inquire if women presently are, or in the future might be, a threat to the phone respondent's job security in his workplace. This is, however, precisely what the focus group men had in mind when they discussed women's entrance in the labor force. They did not dwell on the general situation of employed women. Rather they recalled their own experiences when women began to enter male occupations and what the consequences had been for themselves or their co-workers. Behind these men's efforts to belittle women's labor lies not so much a disrespect for female competencies as an intense fear that they may lose their own jobs, that they may become replaced by women or machines. Over and over, these men returned to the theme that women "are going to take men out of employment." They see that as a real possibility if the economy should restrict further. Ted expressed that fear well: "She has more seniority. The woman bumps him out. He goes on the streets; she stays. She takes his job. It's not right." And along with that fear came anger. The 29 March 1993 issue of *Newsweek* devoted a major section to such fears, especially as they were felt by white males. Focusing on that fear and resentment, Ellis Case (p. 54) wrote: "Even in cases where the grievance is unfounded, it is no less real; for as long as women and minorities get jobs and opportunities (however few) that white men believe (however unjustly) they are not entitled to, those men will feel aggrieved."

Feelings of being "justly aggrieved" form a refrain that is repeated over and over by men in the blue-collar focus group, and this stands in striking contrast to the women's perspective. Dissatisfied though the women may be with the progress they have made so far, they see an expanding opportunity structure; blue-collar males see one that is narrowing for themselves. Women begin to consider entering occupations formerly closed to them; men, in contrast, observe the nation's need for the kind of physical labor they perform disappearing before their very eyes. No wonder that many men in the working-class focus group, especially the older ones, feel threatened by the recent changes. They realize that the change to a service- and information-processing economy threatens their capacity to earn a living in their accustomed way. They are only too painfully aware that, at least in the short run, "there is no escaping the fact that women stand to gain more [from the change] and men less" (Rossi 1965: 248).

In the middle-class male group, the topic of women in the workforce did not arouse the same controversy, let alone anxiety—at least not overtly. The middle-class men gave the impression that the whole issue has no immediate relevance for them. The group seemed disengaged, if not outright bored, throughout the session. Whether the demeanor in this one group accurately reflected how they feel about the topic is hard to determine. What is certain is that the middle-class men certainly gave less *overt* expression to alarm about female co-workers entering their field than did the blue-collar males. Objectively, they also have less cause to be alarmed. Some are in highly technical or related professions, such as engineering, or hold fairly high managerial positions—all places where they are not yet likely to encounter a great deal of competition-from women.[12] Which is not to say that they expressed unvarnished enthusiasm for seeing women enter their place of employment; they too voiced reservations. Their concerns, however, were more likely expressed in terms of reservations about the general principle of affirmative action or other abstract issues. So long as the discussion turned around the abstract topic of equal opportunity, the men were generally approving, but when they recalled personal encounters in their own work situation, they too hedged their seemingly strong approval with a host of qualifying statements. They told one another that women are sometimes hard to work with because they are apt to equate a compliment or a friendly gesture with sexual harassment. They voiced the opinion that when women rise in the hierarchy, they become picky, "very, very over conscientious" or bossy, aggressive, and in the voice of

---

12. The women they are most likely to encounter in their work life are secretaries, clerical workers, and others in positions subordinate to theirs.

Robert, a middle-level corporate manager, "overly assertive because they are so anxious to do a good job, and it makes it very difficult for a male to come in and to try and contend with that because you're always being put on your mettle to prove, and they're trying to prove that they're right. . . ." Should we not, therefore, infer that these men too may be ambivalent about women's ambitions? They may well be sincere in their support of women's desire to enter the workforce on an equal footing with men, but they can muster a host of reasons why in their particular case the female colleague is perhaps not quite equal and, therefore, not quite as deserving as they are. At one point during the conversation, George, a scientist, announced that he has personally hired women for his company and thinks "it's great"; women are a wonderful "untapped resource." But he also insisted that the untapped resource should stay home as long as there are children still at home. Somewhat later he confided with some puzzlement: "My wife tells me I don't like women in the workplace." The focus group women might have been inclined to agree with his wife. While they probably don't doubt that "in principle" he believes that women should be given an equal chance, they, like his wife, may doubt that he really wants to act upon his beliefs. In their own lives, they have encountered too little genuine acceptance and too much male resistance to put much faith in male protestations of egalitarianism. Recall the many instances they cited in which men actually tried to impede and obstruct their work. As we saw earlier (see especially chapter 4 and 5), women are under the impression that the "exodus of women into the economy has not been accompanied by a cultural understanding of marriage and work that would make the transition smooth. The workforce has changed. Women have changed. But not much else has changed" (A. R. Hochschild 1989: 12).

That even middle-class men are not completely reconciled to accepting women as their equals in places of employment becomes clear when the moderator asked them how they would feel if they had to work for a female boss. James, the businessman who had counselled the female executive to tough it out and fight like a man, pondered over that contingency and decided he is not quite sure how he would react. "I guess I'd have to adjust to it. I've never had a woman boss and as a result, why, it would be quite a tremendous change. I don't know whether I could handle it, to be honest with you." Some of the women in the focus groups could have predicted how he might handle it. Here is how the young financial assistant we encountered in one of our focus groups would have explained it to him: " A man—most men are very threatened by having a female boss. I think they just, they think their macho pals are going to say: 'Hey, hey what did your boss say? You let a chick like that boss you around? Something like that."

Younger middle-class men did not express quite the same doubts about having to work under female superiors; they were more accustomed to working with and under female colleagues. Dick, a civil servant and considerably younger than James, maintained that he has no problem when he finds himself in a unit headed by a woman. He is appalled when another unit chief, an ex-military man, suggests that he should look for a transfer to a male-headed unit: "I don't think that is a reasonable attitude, and I think if you feel that way about women, then you are going to have a problem with people in general about other things." Ironically, even though he thinks his colleague's attitude is unreasonable and maintains that personally he has no trouble working for a female supervisor, he is far from enthusiastic about working with a lot of women. "I work in a place where it's mostly women," he relates at another point, "and it drives me crazy. I'll tell you, I can't stand it." Most of the middle-class men, however, have come to expect that women will work where they do and will work in the same capacities.

The telephone interview did not inquire into men's reactions to a female boss or to women holding the same job as they do, but the interview offers indirect evidence that here too respondents' reaction might vary by age. Asked if recent changes in women's position had made any difference in their lives, younger men were more likely than those over fifty to consider themselves to have been affected; moreover, younger men were more likely than older men to believe they have benefitted from the change.[13] It is among the younger middle-class men, those most accustomed to seeing women in the workplace, that we encountered least resistance, overt or covert, to giving women an equal chance. On the whole, though, middle-class men of all ages gave the appearance of being more accepting than blue-collar men of seeing women enter their own fields. What we cannot assess, of course, is just how deeply felt their professed egalitarianism is. Moreover, in commenting on these class-based differences, it must be borne in mind that the well-trained middle-class men in our group are, at least for the time being, less likely to have to face female competition in the workplace than are their blue-collar counterparts.[14]

13. Compared with women, however, men—irrespective of age—had been less affected by the changes (58 percent declared themselves unaffected in contrast with 42 percent of the women).

14. The above finding is consistent with those from many others which have shown education and support for gender equality to be related (Klein 1984; Gilbert 1985; Hertz 1986; Blydenburgh and Sigel 1983).

FAMILY

The recent changes in women's lives have a direct impact on family life, but again the impact varies by social class. Nowhere does the men's ambivalence and the sense of loss become more apparent than when middle-aged and older blue-collar males discussed their wives' employment history. The need to depend in part on income from the wife's employment diminishes their traditional roles as providers and, indirectly, their exclusive authority over the family. Here their anxieties about status and economic security become clearly visible.[15] The focus groups reveal most poignantly what a strong hold traditional definitions of gender relations still have on these men (Crosby 1987; Hertz 1986; Weiss 1987), although many would probably reject the idea that their outlook is traditional. In principle, men and women shared similar sex-role orientations; both rejected the idea that a woman's main role is that of wife and mother. But that is in principle. Observing the focus groups does not yield quite the same picture. There the men appear to be quite traditional in their outlook. In the blue-collar group, almost all of the married men's wives are now employed full-time, many having entered the labor market relatively recently. Economic necessity rather than a need for self-fulfillment dictated the move, at least so the husbands report. Tony is an electrical worker in his mid-forties whose wife, much to his chagrin, now holds a full-time clerical position. "I wouldn't let my wife work. I told her; I said 'Look, you got the kids, you stay home. When the kids go to school all day, then you work.' That's fine, up to a point, I tried to do it on my own. Working 20 hours a day to make everything go. She said 'hey look I gotta go to work.' Well, I was against it, but it had to be done. As far as I was brought up, Pop did the work; Mom stayed home with the kids. Alright? I was raised that way, and that's the way I saw it." That is also pretty much the way the other middle-aged and older blue-collar men saw the situation. The husband as the breadwinner and the wife as the homemaker describes their image of the normal and good life. "But the average income today [doesn't permit it]," according to Bill, a somewhat younger craftsman, "it's really necessary for both unless maybe the husband is a doctor or lawyer, you know, but the average income today, if you just want the normal American dream, you have to have both husband and wife working." And so they "permit" their wives to

15. A great number of studies exist to the effect that men's sense of well-being and even their self-esteem is closely connected to their sense of power and authority over their families, including their wives (Bernard 1972 and 1981; Gilbert 1985; Guttenberg and Secord 1983; Kahn 1984; Pleck 1983 and 1985).

work.[16] I was struck by how often the term "permit" is used, and how often they asserted that initially they "had not allowed" their wives to work. Comments such as these suggest two things. First, by permitting or forbidding, the role of the man as authority figure is maintained, his personal power over the family is not diminished. Second, only economic necessity justifies deviating from the traditional family structure in which the wife's role is exclusively defined as that of homemaker. The wife's employment thus is seen as a means to an end, the end being the family's welfare. The employed wife is the helper; her employment serves family, not personal, needs; it serves essentially the same needs as do her domestic activities, namely, the maintenance of the family. Of course, not all men expressed the same frustrations as the just quoted Tony. But what is equally telling is that only one man, who was much younger, challenged him with a contrasting interpretation.

Moreover, the wife's entrance in the labor market has social as well as personal consequences which some men find hard to take. Her help is necessary,[17] acknowledged, and appreciated, but it is also seen as a sign that the man has lost some status, if not in the eyes of society or his family, then in his own eyes. The very fact that help is needed can sometimes be in itself a severe blow to the man's sense of power and even to his self-esteem. "Men typically look to their breadwinning role . . . to confirm their manliness. Finally, male power, especially power over women, appears central to many men's sense of well-being and self-esteem. . . . This power often takes the form of being the good provider and having a dependent wife and children" (Gilbert 1985: 9). Diminishing the significance of the provider role also diminishes power in the family. In the dual-earner family, as the husbands often discover to their chagrin, the wife is no longer a totally dependent individual. She is alleged to have become more assertive ("bossy," one calls it) and less deferential to her mate. Several focus group members commented on how their word can no longer be law in the family—as their fathers' once was—because they are no longer the sole support of their families. A young man in a service occupation put it this way: "Thirty years ago, if the man said: 'This is what we're going to do and that's it,' the woman would say 'okay.' Nowadays, boy, you've got to argue up and down, to get the point across, to get your way, or try and get half your points across." Asked by the moderator why this is so, he replied

16. Arlene Hochschild (1989: 60) made a similar observation when she wrote that working-class men spoke of "letting my wife work."

17. Rosanna Hertz (1986: 4), moreover, maintains that wives' "employment is viewed as secondary, even when their income is not supplementary or targeted for a specific purpose."

"they're allowed to give their opinion more." Note again the word "allowed." He attributed the alleged change to outside employment and the Women's Movement. "Women are becoming more aware. They have a little more input to their relationship now. I think part of the times women try to get the upper hand." This young man saw women's employment as more than just a reflection on the male as the provider, but also as a threat to his power, his masculinity, and his position of authority in the family. Losing that authority must be doubly painful for those who never possessed it any place else, least of all at work (Rubin 1976). Women understand that only too well. That is why they often give in or create myths in order not to wound their partners' diminishing self-esteem, as we will explore more fully in the next chapter.

In the female focus groups, we noted an occasional reference to the effect that a few men, especially the younger ones, were beginning to change, that they were not quite as "macho" as their fathers. In the male blue-collar focus group, too, the younger men did not subscribe as much to the traditional script. Their relative openness may have been due in part to their realization that one income no longer can sustain the family adequately. Twenty-four-year-old Kevin was quite clear about that. "If I were going to get married, I would take the view that, because I'm younger than most of you gentlemen, I would expect my wife to work, because I know I couldn't make it on my salary . . . So I would enter into a marriage with the idea of my wife working." Their less traditional outlook extended beyond financial considerations. A few men commented how they welcomed women's inclination to meet them on an equal footing, and how that equality facilitates open discussion about a lot of issues men never before could bring up in front of women. Moreover, the younger blue-collar men, especially those with some education beyond high school, also were more sensitized than their elders to the idea that women, and not only men, may have needs for self-fulfillment which extend beyond the confines of hearth and home. This point was never raised by the older men, for whom the wife's work seems to be strictly a means to an end. It struck me as remarkable when replaying the tapes that virtually none of the middle-aged or older men ever commented on what working outside of the home might mean for women. Yet we know that employment is very meaningful for most women—and not just professional ones. "Blue-collar women are proud of their accomplishments on the job . . . Working-class women see their work as something good for them as well as their families . . . and define themselves as breadwinners even when they have husbands who also support the family" (Ferree 1987: 340). One wonders how often these men talk with their partners concerning the meaning employment has for them. Otherwise, they might have known that the women not only have accepted the need to work outside of the home but that they get satisfaction from it and pity their mothers and grandmothers for having missed that opportunity.

While most blue-collar men referred to their wives' employment strictly in terms of family needs, middle-class men were more apt to refer to the fulfillment their partners derive from their work and/or the opportunity to utilize their training. That difference, however, may be deceptive, since even in the middle-class group this opinion did not arise spontaneously in the course of the discussion. Rather, it came up only because in this group the moderator made a strong intervention by commenting that so far all but one man had discussed their wives' employment solely in terms of "sheer economic functions," and then asked the group: "what about the woman [who is] in the workplace because she wants the exact same things; she wants to fulfill herself?" Once the moderator presented the group with that alternative, the middle-class men had no trouble acknowledging that women may indeed seek fulfillment beyond the confines of the home. What are we to make of the fact that they never brought up the topic on their own? Are the focus group women perhaps correct when they insist that "men just don't get it"? Or do the men get it but the need for gender equality isn't very central to their thoughts, that it is so peripheral that it has to be brought to their attention? The attitudes they expressed lend a great deal of credence to Arlene Hochschild's conclusion that "some men seemed to me egalitarian 'on top' but traditional 'underneath' " (1989: 16). Perhaps because of the moderator's intervention, the tenor of their discussion differed considerably from the one in the working-class group. Instead of telling one another that they "permitted" their wives to seek outside employment, they seemed to take it for granted that their wives have a right to choose outside employment if that is what they desire. As one man put it, he has "adjusted to the idea" because he thought employment is good for his wife. Burt, a thirty-four-year-old system analyst (whose wife currently is not working because their children are very young) knows that his wife is "dying to get back [to work] because the children are driving her nuts. I can understand that, so I fully expect her to go back to work at a point of time which we haven't really decided on yet but it may be before the youngest one is in school."

Notwithstanding their professed sensitivity to women's personal needs, for some it was very important that the fulfillment of these needs should not be construed as a diminution of the husband's role as provider. A professional with an employed wife insisted: "I would say that we're lucky enough that financially she doesn't have to go back; it is not a necessity in her case. It would be more of a mental change to get back into the adult world rather than the world of kids and to get into something where she feels a little bit more self-actualized." In this group, acquiescing to a wife's desire to work outside of the home was seen as proof of the man's unselfishness, his concern for her well-being, and of his egalitarianism. Although they did not dwell on it, for some men in the group, the role of chief provider matters as much as it does to the working-class men.

It is best, however, not to exaggerate just how "liberated" middle-class men are. They may not be as outspoken as working-class men in their preferences but essentially they too opted for a fairly traditional family pattern. Although not voicing opposition in principle to their wives seeking employment, they voiced plenty of reservations. The presence of children in the family gave rise to a number of them, and the "latch-key" child became a reason for resisting a wife's entrance in the labor force. As a salesman put it: "I am not saying women don't belong in the workplace. I think there's some sort of balance in there that it has to be struck in some way." In this context, it is interesting to note that the women in our focus groups never raised the question of balance at all. Not one woman ever asserted that she or other women should be obligated to choose between seeking employment or taking care of their children.[18] They seem to have taken for granted that they are entitled to combining outside employment and raising children, just as men have traditionally never questioned whether they could combine being a father and a breadwinner.

Focus group men found yet other reasons beyond child care for their lack of enthusiasm for the two-paycheck family. They spoke of hectic weekends full of chores and errands instead of well-deserved rest and relaxation. Consumerism, they believed, also is due to women's entrance into the labor force. The second paycheck enables the family to cultivate a more comfortable lifestyle, and this in turn leads to an ever-increasing demand for more goods, often well beyond what a single income can provide. Where blue-collar men looked upon their wives' employment as a matter of economic survival, some middle-class men looked upon it as a way of creating a more affluent middle-class life-style but were concerned that the style now is becoming exceedingly elaborate. They thought that women's careers have caused families to demand an ever higher standard-of-living, "what they call frou-frou,

18. Even the few women in our groups who had opted for staying home while the children were still young shared in the general consensus that whether to work outside of the home or not to work is a personal decision and either one is perfectly acceptable, and that there is nothing incompatible between taking care of children and also holding down a job.

things that are luxuries. Today, a lot of things are necessities in the eyes of many Americans that used to be luxuries." They cited, among others items, the need for a second car, a larger home, perhaps even a vacation home. Maybe these husbands do not feel the need to permit or forbid employment to their wives, but to a large extent they also look upon their wives as helping provide for the comfort of the family. And they are quite candid that they have come to enjoy the higher standard-of-living their wives' employment facilitates. So once again it is the utility function of the woman which comes into play.

At times, the middle-class men looked upon the luxuries obtained in this way as a mixed blessing. In and of themselves, the luxuries may be nice but, for some, having to give up the traditional family style seemed a high price to pay. A computer scientist in one of our focus groups reminisced about life in his parents' home and recalled that it was natural for women "to stay home back then. She [his mother] was very, very adamant about being home. It never crossed my mind that she would go out and work when I was younger." To which another wistfully replied: "I always ask myself the question why has society changed?" Although occasionally bewildered, these men are not actively fighting the change any more than are the blue-collar men, but like their blue-collar brothers, they think the earlier days had a lot to commend themselves. One college-educated man worried that the change is "having an adverse effect on society" and that women's desire for a career contributes to the disintegration of the family. He strongly implied that women are making the wrong choice. Another concurred, stating that: "It's a matter of priorities, that people have to choose what comes first, family or career." Again the implication is that women, not men, are the ones who have to make the choice. In principle, the men all advocated gender equality and acknowledged the need for change. In practice, they were somewhat uncomfortable with it. A female executive (quoted in *The Wall Street Journal* of 2 November 1982, p. 31) well captures males' ambivalence when she asserts that many men will say to their wives: " 'I support your career. I think it is wonderful.' But that's not what they mean. They mean 'I support it as long as it does not interfere with what I want to accomplish.' " One of the younger men in our group perfectly illustrated this orientation. His wife has received many promotions in a large corporation, and he is proud of her success. But he is particularly pleased because it permits him to spend much time and money on his hobbies. He is an avid sportsman and because of his wife's busy schedule, he can spend a good deal of time away from home indulging in his hobbies.

The middle-class men's group's reference to the need to make choices stands in stark contrast to the conversation in the women's groups. Among the women, the topic never even came up! Women discussed how it often is difficult to combine care of the family with outside employment, and they frequently complained that they do not get enough assistance from their mates. But they never questioned that they had made the right choice when they decided to join the workforce rather than to restrict themselves exclusively to the care of home and family.[19] Nostalgia for a return to traditional family patterns never entered their discussions and perhaps not even their minds. This is all the more remarkable because we had in the groups a fair number of single women with very limited incomes who are the sole providers for their children. But even these women firmly maintained that they are as much entitled to a life beyond the home as any man. The previous chapters indicated how much employment contributes to their sense of independence and self-esteem, quite apart from the financial comfort derived from it. The focus group men may intellectually recognize this, but many don't seem to have internalized it as yet. The Mom who bakes cookies with the kids while the husband is at work, and who then upon his return greets him with a smiling face and a freshly powdered nose still seems to many men the image of the ideal family or may even be their version of the "normal" family. But it definitely is not the women's version of either normality or the ideal. If the focus group observations have made one thing clear to me, it is that men and women do not share identical visions of what constitutes ideal family life. Men may have come to accept that women's roles are beginning to change but that does not necessarily mean they welcome the change, attitudinally they have changed much less than have the women.

Robert S. Weiss (1985 and 1987) made a similar observation when he studied a group of occupationally successful men in New England. Although the men understood their wives' desire for outside employment and believed themselves to be supportive of it, in reality they did not greatly modify their preferences for the traditional division of marital responsibilities. Weiss maintains that their "understanding of the partnership agreement of marriage is very close to English common-law expectations of marital partners . . . in which the husband is head of the household and responsible for support and the wife is responsible for domestic services and child care" (1987: 110). Moreover, the "traditional understandings seem to hold even when the wife has a career and not just a job" (p. 113).

19. As mentioned in previous chapters, some women in the five groups expressed a personal preference for the role of housewife, and the telephone survey yielded similar results (38 percent professed preferring an exclusively domestic role). But whatever an individual's personal preference, all strongly subscribed to the idea that the choice had to be left to the woman herself.

Most men in the two groups, however, did not consider themselves to be "traditional." They did not think that they were clinging to what Weiss called "traditional understandings." The telephone interviews confirm this self-image: At most, one-quarter thought of themselves as even moderately traditional (only 5 percent classified themselves as unequivocally traditional). Instead, most either described themselves as moderately modern or genuinely modern in their sex-role orientations.[20] When presented with the traditional role definition "with men's place in the workforce and women's in the home," almost all rejected the latter in favor of one where roles are adopted on the basis of individual preference. A plurality (43 percent) strongly preferred that women make their life choice on the basis of what is best for them as individuals and not on a societally dictated "gender-appropriate" basis.

As these men see themselves, they have adopted sex-role definitions that differ from their fathers'. They honestly believe they have changed. A fairly young blue-collar focus group participant expressed this feeling well. Commenting on how he has changed over time, he declared: "It's just the way it happened. And now I find that I'm totally on the other side. Completely opposite from what my parents believed where women were concerned. Anyhow, I surprise myself sometimes. I'm so open-minded." That comment is reminiscent of the observation made by a female focus group member that some men are in the process of changing because they "learn" more modern notions from other young people, from television, and other sources.

One danger in drawing conclusions from self-descriptions is that the climate of an era often influences how people want to see themselves, or at least how they want others to see them. These days, the staunch traditionalist—the man who is not "so open-minded"—may be reluctant to categorize himself that way, lest he be considered a male chauvinist. Given the many focus group comments which began with "I am all for women's equality but . . . ," caution in taking self-definitions at face value may well be appropriate. "I am all for their equality but . . . " may serve the same purpose for men as the "I am not a feminist but . . . " serves for women. Rather than calling these men genuinely traditional in their sex role attitudes, however, I would

---

20. The exact phrasing of the choice offered to them was: "Some people feel there are traditional roles for men and women—with men's place in the work force and women's in the home. Others feel there should not be roles based on sex—that men and women should do whatever they want as individuals. Which of these views is closest to your own, or are you somewhere in the middle?" After the respondent had made a choice, she or he was asked: "Do you feel strongly about this, or not so strongly?" If the respondent had chosen the option "somewhere in the middle," she or he was asked: "Which side do you lean more toward—traditional roles or individual choice?"

characterize them as very ambivalent about the changes they are witnessing. They understand and in principle approve of women's desire for equality but in practice they are hesitant to make the changes in their personal lives necessary to support that equality. Their ambivalence thus indicates "a broader tension—between *faster-changing women and slower-changing men*" (A. R. Hochschild 1989: 205, italics in original).

DIVISION OF LABOR

The inequitable division of labor in the household was one of the major sources for women's complaints. Listening to the focus group men discuss the topic, one suspects that women's complaints have merit. The men we observed were not particularly empathic with the dual responsibility thrust upon wives as they are working two shifts, one at home and one at work. When the male telephone respondents were asked if "too much is demanded of today's young women because they are expected to be good workers as well as good homemakers and parents," 51 percent rejected the notion that too much is demanded while 60 percent of the women believed the demands are excessive.[21] In the focus groups, men simply ignored the subject, as though it were quite natural to expect women to work two shifts, perhaps assuming that they could do it with as much ease as they might add a weekly aerobics class. If they mentioned it at all—as a few blue-collar men did—they did so to complain about demands their working wives are beginning to make on them, especially with respect to help in the house. Our maintenance worker expressed this complaint in his usual colorful way: "My wife works in a bank. She's in air-conditioning all day. I work in a factory. I'm in the heat all day. I come home, and she gets pissed off because I don't have dinner ready." The college student who declared, "It is hard out there. Hard even for girls. It is easier to get married and have a husband who works real hard" is a distinct exception; for most group members the second shift is a nonproblem. In the female focus groups, as we saw earlier, men's lack of cooperation in the domestic sphere carried at least as much, if not more, emotional baggage as any other gender-based inequity about which they complained. Because women related that the uneven division-of-labor was becoming a source of conflict between men and women, I was surprised at the male focus groups' failure to discuss the topic at even a moderate length. Apparently, they either do not notice the uneven division of labor as such, or

21. The male/female difference on this measure of empathy seems to have maintained itself over the years (see the Yankelovich poll of 20 February 1992).

believe it poses no problem, and it only becomes a problem for them when their wives or partners want to alter the division, that is, when it interferes with men's personal comfort or preferences, as when weekends are taken up by chores instead of relaxation, or when they are called upon to help with housework. Male telephone respondents again voiced more egalitarian sentiments than did the focus group participants. Asked how labor should be divided in the household when both partners are employed, over two-thirds believed it should be divided evenly (an opinion held by 90 percent of the women), and virtually no man believed that men should be exempt from domestic responsibilities. F. J. Crosby (1991: 148) cites a national survey conducted in 1978 in which 67 percent of the men expressed the same sentiments. Apparently not much has changed since; good intentions there were aplenty then and still are. However, only a small segment of the males in our study (14 percent) believed that equal sharing actually takes place. Nor do either men or women doubt that the customary arrangement is unfair (68:73 percent respectively). The telephone respondents' expressions of concern, in contrast to the focus group's relative silence on the topic, can probably be explained because interviewees were required to deal with the issue, so they gave the socially desirable response that the current arrangement was not fair. But in the focus groups, where no such stimulus was provided, men rarely raised the issue because for them it was not an issue of any consequence. The middle-class group all but ignored it, whereas in the blue-collar group some fleeting comments are made to the effect that the wife may complain that "I don't uphold my end," as one man puts it, and they may even concede that the complaint is justified. But it is stated matter-of-factly without any discussion that maybe something could be done about it. That the men in the focus groups never addressed the issue seriously may support Jessie Bernard's (1972) argument, namely, that men and women operate under two different marriage contracts. It would seem that in many families even today the husband's contract ("the husband's marriage" as she called it) requires little change in his lifestyle and work responsibilities, whereas "the wife's marriage" requires taking on the additional obligation of functioning as a housewife.

CHANGE ATTITUDES

Telephone respondents' attitudes concerning changes in the social situation for women reflect a fair amount of ambivalence and tension. In the first place, respondents reported having observed considerably more improvement in women's situations than the women themselves have noticed (see table 7.4, part A). Second, men were not nearly as

TABLE 7.4   PERCEPTIONS OF CHANGE IN WOMEN'S POSITION (%)

	MEN	WOMEN
A. Reflections on Recent Improvements		
Amount of change perceived		
A great deal	82	69
Some or little	17	30
None	1	1
Satisfaction with tempo of change		
Too slow	38	43
About right	57	50
Too fast	5†	6
No change	2	1
Change has been		
For the better	86	84
Both for better and worse	7	8
For the worse	6*	6
Don't know	2	1
Effect of change on own life has been		
For the better	29	50
Both for better and worse	6	3
Not personally affected	58	42
For the worse	6	3
Amount of change due to government		
A great deal	20	11
Some or a little	47†	51
Change was inevitable	32	34
Don't know	1	5
B. Outlook on the Future		
To improve position of women government should		
Become more active	32	49
Continue as it has so far	57	42
Become less active	11	8
S/he considers the improvements to be		
Secure	79	71
Secure and not secure	4	3
Not secure	18	22
For the future, respondent favors		
Major change back	3	1
Minor change back	2	2
No change	39	30
Minor change for more equality	33	30
Major change for more equality	24	38

*Significant at .05 level.
†Not significant.
All other correlations significant at .01 level.
Percentages may not total 100 due to rounding.

enthusiastic about the changes as were women, and they were less eager to see major, fundamental change take place. Their reaction had best be described this way: Most favored the recent improvements; turning the clock back to the days of old is not what telephone respondents desire, only 5 percent advocated reversing the changes (see table 7.4, part B). They know that sex-role definitions are in a state of flux, moving in the direction of greater equality for women, and they have come to accept that, but they rarely favor the change to quite the same degree as do women. Two somewhat contradictory stances characterize these men. On the one hand, they subscribe to egalitarian sentiments but, on the other, they are somewhat less enthusiastic about the egalitarian change (current and future) than were the women. In their opinion, women's position has already improved dramatically over the past two decades (82 percent believe that, compared with 69 percent among women), and only 24 percent expressed themselves in favor of major additional changes (though 33 percent favored minor changes). Fewer women believed the change has been all that great and, consequently, they were not nearly as complacent, and more of them (38 percent) expressed the need for major change. In spite of men's smaller appetite for additional change, what is perhaps more significant is that the preponderance of males (85 percent) believed the recent change has been all for the better, and in that they find themselves in perfect agreement with the women (84 percent).

However, men differed considerably from women when seeking to account for the recent changes in women's position. Women, as we saw earlier, gave themselves almost all of the credit (60 percent) for what has been accomplished so far. Men did not share that view. They were far less inclined to give women the lion's share of the credit (38 percent do so). They also liked to think that women had received help from a variety of sources, including government and men, and that, moreover, the change would have come in any case. Why there should be such a gender-based discrepancy in assessments is unclear, but it does conform to what the female focus group women and telephone respondents had to say on the topic, namely, that men often fail to give women the recognition women think is due for their achievements (see table 7.5).

Before attaching too much significance to men's positive feelings about current changes, it is well to keep in mind that a majority (59 percent) of males professed *not* to have been affected at all by the changes, whereas a majority of women believed to have been affected. Cynics might be tempted to declare that this attitude of "life-as-usual" is the very reason why men can afford to be egalitarians. Older men were particularly likely to declare themselves unaffected (72 percent of

TABLE 7.5   CREDIT AND BLAME FOR WOMEN'S
SITUATION (%)

	MEN	WOMEN
A. Credit for Improvement in Women's Situation		
Women made it happen	38	59
Women's organizations did it	15	13
Men did it	19	0
Government policies	5	6
Miscellaneous	7	2
Don't know	17	17
B. Reasons Why Women Have Not Progressed More*		
Men have held women back	73	80
Government policy held them back	43	54
Women have too many household obligations	52	53
Women not as ambitious	22	22
Women less qualified	29	22
C. Which Is the Most Important Reason?†		
Men held them back	50	38
Women have too many household obligations	22	25
Government policy held them back	11	17
Women less qualified	9	5
Women are less ambitious	6	10
Don't know	2	7

*Replies in response to: "I am going to read you a short list of reasons some people have given for why women have less influence in business and earn less than men. Please just tell me if you think each *is* or is *not* a reason why women have less influence and earn less." Respondent could offer more than one reason.

†Respondent was asked to choose the most important reason from the ones she or he had volunteered.

those over 50 believed they have been unaffected),[22] but even among the younger men, a majority, albeit a smaller one (57 percent), declared that the recent changes in gender relations had not touched their lives. Somewhat unexpectedly, neither marital status nor sex-role orientations played a role here. Education, however, did; college graduates and those with some college education were more likely to consider themselves affected by the change, whereas those with the least education were singularly unaffected (74 percent).[23] Apparently then, for most men life continues in much the same fashion as it did for their fathers.

22. Twenty-nine percent declared it had made their life better; 6 percent said it had made it worse; and 6 percent said that it had affected them both positively and negatively.

23. In view of the many complaints expressed in the blue-collar group, that assertion may seem surprising. It does, however, fit in what others (Crosby 1991; Gerson 1985; A. Hochschild 1989; Komarovsky 1976; and Rubin 1976) have had to say about the traditional ways still operative in most blue-collar households.

Are we to conclude, therefore, that women have done most of the changing? Quite a few women might think so, judging from their telephone responses and group discussions. As demonstrated in earlier chapters, wasn't that a chief source of their complaint that men made virtually no accommodations to the changed realities, that for "the prince" life at home goes on pretty much the way it has always gone? Male focus groups' descriptions of life at home lend considerable confirmation to women's perceptions. Given these perceptions of lack of overall change, it is not surprising that the men in the focus groups did not get very involved in discussions of changing gender relations.

ANGER AND EMPATHY

Where men and women really part company is in their emotional reactions to observed discrimination. Males did not give the impression that the persistence of discrimination causes them pain, rather they see it as a fact of life—perhaps not a desirable one, but a fact of life nonetheless. Comparing the discussions in the female focus groups with those in the male ones reveals that stark difference. The women expressed much anger over discrimination; men expressed none. The responses to the telephone survey permit us to explore how men deal with acknowledged discrimination and how they *feel* about it. We asked if it makes them angry and whether their anger varies with the degree of discrimination they perceive. Inasmuch as men are not the victims of discrimination, their reaction to it probably differs from women's, but inasmuch as most people like to think of themselves as fair and just, one would expect that the recognition of injustice's persistence causes discomfort and anger in men. In general, however, our expectation was not confirmed; the men we interviewed were not particularly disturbed by the persistence of women's inferior status, although most acknowledged its existence (see table 7.6). For example, even though most men (70 percent) believed that society treats men better than women and thought that this is unfair, they were not greatly upset by it. Almost two-thirds (62 percent) accepted it as a fact of life, and only 30 percent (compared with 44 percent for women) told the interviewer that it bothers them. Even so, each man thought that he is more bothered by this injustice than are his fellow men. Where 20 percent declared themselves to be bothered "a lot" by societal discrimination, they granted similar concerns to only 6 percent of the rest of the male population. Women share men's assessment of the male population, but think that other women are greatly disturbed by discrimination.

The split between cognition and emotion that characterizes women, we now see, is even more pronounced among men. This split becomes

TABLE 7.6   DIFFERENTIAL REACTIONS TO PERCEIVED
DISCRIMINATION, PERCENTAGE OF RESPONSES BY
GENDER

	MEN	WOMEN
AMONG THOSE WHO CONSIDER TREATMENT OF WOMEN TO BE UNFAIR, PERCENTAGE WHO		
Is bothered by it	30	44
Accepts it	62	51
Both (volunteered)	4	6
No opinion	2	1
AMONG THOSE WHO BELIEVE SOCIETY DISCRIMINATES A LOT, PERCENTAGE WHO		
Is bothered a lot by it	18	30
Is somewhat bothered	33	36
Is not bothered	47	34
AMONG THOSE WHO KNOW WOMEN DON'T GET AN EQUAL CHANCE AT RESPONDENT'S PLACE OF EMPLOYMENT, PERCENTAGE WHO		
Is bothered by it	19	61
Is bothered a little	23	22
Is not bothered	49	16
No opinion	9	1

All correlations significant at the .01 level.

even clearer when we turn once more to the Index of Discrimination
Awareness (see table 7.7) and direct our attention to the reaction of those
men who are the most conscious of gender-based discrimination, that is,
those who score highest on the index. If anger over discrimination were
to surface at all, this group should be the one most likely to experience it.
But that turns out not to be the case. Only one-third of the most
discrimination-aware declared themselves bothered, and over two-
thirds (67) percent are *not* bothered. In fact, that most-aware group of
men was barely more bothered than those who score lower in awareness;
the least-aware group, for example, was only slightly more indifferent
(75 percent) than the most-aware (67 percent). Women, as we saw earlier, also were not uniformly angry over what they perceived to be injustice, but in the highly aware group, many more women (55 percent) than
men *are* "bothered" by the problem, and in the least-aware groups, 31
percent reported themselves "bothered." Men's lesser concern is under-
standable in view of the fact that the changes apparently have not im-
pacted on their own lives as much as they have on women's and in that
they are more satisfied with the change already accomplished than are
women. No wonder gender relations today are fraught with misunder-
standings, if not outright conflict. This has to be expected when one
partner to the interaction changes much faster than the other, what Arlene Hochschild (1989: 12) called "the stalled revolution."

TABLE 7.7   LEVEL OF DISCRIMINATION AWARENESS
AND ANGER BY GENDER (%)

Level of Discrimination Awareness*		Men		Women
High		20		38
Medium		43		37
Low		37		25

	Bothered		Not Bothered	
DA Level and Anger	Men	Women	Men	Women
High	33	55	67	45
Medium	33	38	67	62
Low	25	31	75	69

*As measured by the DA Index.

In certain instances, individual men's lack of concern over discrimination borders on the callous. For example, during the phone survey some men admitted candidly that the women who work in the same place as they do are discriminated against in pay and promotion. That, however, did not bother most of them; rather 49 percent considered it to be a fact of life which they can accept, and 9 percent professed no opinion, compared with only 16 percent of women who accepted it as a fact of life. Lack of concern and empathy manifested themselves in other ways as well. Many men frankly admitted that they did not have a great deal of interest in "how women as a whole are getting along in this country" (29 percent professed considerable interest but 26 percent had none whatsoever). By contrast, 40 percent of women are very concerned. Clearly, concern over discrimination plays a very different role in men's lives than it does in women's.

POLITICS AND POLITICAL ACTION

If, as argued in chapter 5, the women showed no interest in becoming politically active on behalf of gender equality, we certainly would not expect men to display such interest. And, indeed, several men in the focus groups made that point perfectly clear. The scientist who declared that he strongly supported gender equality made a distinction between being an active and a passive supporter of women's rights. He declined becoming "an activist and a supporter of a woman's right to whatever . . . So I suppose you could be a passive supporter in that you do not discriminate." The college-educated civil servant opted out on grounds of gender: "If you are a woman, I would really be impassioned for every single thing that would help me. But I'm not; I'm a man, so I'm for it [for what would help women], but I'm not willing to go out and demonstrate and all that."

Notwithstanding the genders' similarity in political nonactivism, men did differ from women politically. For instance, they showed less willingness than women to spend additional tax dollars for policies designed to help women, such as day care centers (40 percent respectively) or shelters for battered women (57 percent) (see table 7.8).They also were less concerned with granting women the right to return to their job after a pregnancy leave and less inclined to support government spending that would benefit women.[24] Even support for the ERA, previously an issue on which the genders agreed to the same degree, found the New Jersey men less supportive than the women. Once more, issues which loom as issues of concern for women have less urgency for men. Maybe males' acceptance of an unfair status quo is just one more case where sympathy—much like charity—begins at home or, more precisely, begins with the self. As P. J. Conover observed: "When it comes to thinking about social groups it matters enormously whether we are part of that group. Try as hard as we can, the political sympathy that we feel for other groups is never quite the same as that which they feel for themselves or that which we feel for ourselves" (1986: 17). Mustering such sympathy probably is particularly hard when remedying the situation will have to come (or is perceived to come) at the expense of one's own group or one's self.

CONCLUSION

A summary description of the ways in which the changes in women's lives have affected men could profitably begin with the question underlying L. A. Gilbert's study of men in two-career families: "Has the subtle revolution in women's lives wrought large-scale changes in the lives of men?" (1985: 5). If we answered that question not just with respect to men in two-career families but with respect to all of the men in our study, men in two-paycheck families, men whose wives are not gainfully employed, and single men, the answer would have to be that "the subtle revolution" has brought changes in men's lives but the changes, for the most part, have not been substantial. That revolution has changed men's attitudes to some degree, but it has not changed them profoundly.[25]

The conclusion has to be that the men who participated in our study are quite aware of the "subtle revolution" and are aware that many or

24. Of course, men's well-known greater fiscal conservatism is not restricted to spending on behalf of women; except for defense spending, they object to most increases in governmental outlays (see Sigel and Whelchel 1986a).

25. Because marital status does not significantly affect behaviors or attitudes in the sample, I have not distinguished among them on the basis of marital status.

TABLE 7.8   MEN'S POLICY PREFERENCES (%)

A. STANDS ON SPENDING FOR "WOMEN'S ISSUES"				
Respondent Favors Spending	More	Less	Keep as Is	DK
Shelters for battered women	56	7	34	4
Day care centers	40	21	37	4
Government should help women more	32	11	57	1

B. RIGHT TO RETURN TO JOB AFTER PREGNANCY LEAVE	
Favors it	73
It is up to employer	21
It depends	5
Don't know	1

C. THE ERA AND THE WOMEN'S MOVEMENT	
Thinks ERA should be ratified	57
Personally favors it strongly	40
Favors it	28
Opposes it strongly	11
Opposes it	9
Depends	6
Undecided	6
The Women's Movement	
Is no longer needed	25
Is still needed	66
Did more harm than good	8
No opinion	1

most women no longer are willing to accept the subordinate status their mothers took for granted. The men not only understand that desire but support it and support it in a way that I believe to be genuine. However, they support the ideal in an abstract sense, as a principle. The problem for them becomes acute when they reflect on its ramifications and on what gender equality would mean for their own lives. It is then that their ambivalence comes to the fore. As they see it, reorienting their thoughts, feelings, and behaviors in consonance with the professed principle exacts a steep price which most of them never imagined they would have to pay. Judging from their comments, they found it somewhat easier (or possibly necessary) to pay the behavioral price, that is, to change their behavior, rather than to change attitudes developed over a lifetime. Thus, they have learned to live or associate with women who are in the workforce, the military, and a host of other fields. They have also learned to work under female bosses and to consult female authority figures, such as female physicians and members of the clergy. They have even begun to assume some domestic responsibilities, such as help with child care and household chores. Adopting such new behaviors may be hard enough, but it is nothing compared with the cost of assuming a new posture vis-à-vis the other gender, a posture based on equality with, rather than superiority to, women.

The steep price of changing attitudes frightens quite a few. The focus group members (with some exceptions) bear testimony to that, even though they were hesitant to come right out and say so. Still the underlying message came through: they are reluctant to give up—as they know they must eventually—their positions of power or dominance over women. For the New Jersey men, much as for most men in the United States, maleness is associated with being the provider and protector of women, it is that role which entitles them to dominance. With the diminution of their role as the sole provider, they see their power and authority eroded as well. And that is tough to take, especially when they have been socialized, as most of these men have been, to anticipate more traditional roles for themselves. Hence, their nostalgia for the good old days. Just recall the many references the men made to their parental homes where father was "the boss," and a warm dinner was always on the table waiting for him when he returned home from a day's work. That nostalgia, moreover, is reinforced by the very nature of today's social institutions, which have done little to adapt to the new realities. Men as well as women cannot help but "carry with them a history of male dominance, and they live in a society whose customs are an outgrowth of a patriarchal socioeconomic structure" (Gilbert 1985: 11). Equally important, however, is to recognize that the men in this study declared themselves to be in favor of gender equality. Virtually no one among them believed or advocated turning the clock back. This stance comes out more clearly in the telephone interviews, but it is discernible in the focus groups as well.[26] Telephone respondents and focus group males share the belief that women's position in society has improved, that women today are more nearly equal to men, and that this is a development of which they approve. They accepted (although with some reservations) the idea that a woman's role should not be restricted to that of housewife, that she should have the same (or almost the same) freedom to choose as do men.

Women have a drastically different view of men's modernity, as we have already seen. Linda was not the only woman who contended that the male still prefers the woman who caters exclusively to his comfort rather than to her own needs, or, to quote yet another woman, the

26. That the interview focused almost exclusively and at great length on the issue of gender equality may also have contributed to the frequency of egalitarian answers. The typical telephone interview might have induced respondents to give more socially acceptable answers. Thus men in the telephone interviews were more likely to express egalitarian sentiments, and women were perhaps more reluctant to express anger.

trouble is: "that we [women] are still coping with men who were raised by our mommies." That may be how women view men. Yet, neither focus group observations of men nor their telephone replies permit us to reach such sweeping and highly critical conclusions. We can conclude only that men and women differ considerably in their view of current gender relations. As yet, men and women do not share identical views of the meaning and the necessity for women's full emancipation.

COPING WITH CHANGE

Maybe what we are doing is offering up a sacrificial generation—a generation of people who will have to absorb the conflicts until a new generation swings itself ponderously into place.

—A. J. Leavitt

I started the research for this book with two assumptions. My first assumption was that today's men and women are subscribing to a gender perspective greatly different from the beliefs of their forebearers in that most no longer believe in the *nature-ordained* superiority of men and their concomitant right to dominate women. Although remnants of that belief system still remain—more so with respect to some areas than others and more so for some people than for others—people now increasingly tend to attribute women's disadvantages to societal arrangements rather than to inborn deficiencies. Judging from the prevailing rhetoric, the notion that gender is a social rather than a natural construct is beginning to gain increasing credence in the population, just as it has among social scientists. Rhetoric, however, frequently has not been translated into practice. Much of public and private life continues to be male-dominated.

My second assumption, therefore, was that the contrast between changed rhetoric (reinforced by the changes in women's lifestyles and the consciousness-raising of the Women's Movement) and lagging practice (both in the private and public worlds) would have been felt quite keenly by women, leading them to experience an acute sense of relative deprivation. Women, I assumed, are beginning to compare the rewards and privileges society bestowed on them with those bestowed on men and would find their own rewards inadequate. They would, I expected, attribute this deficiency to nothing other than society's general devaluation of women, a devaluation based on stereotypes rather than on the consideration of individual merit. I thus assumed that the revised gender perspective, though affecting both genders, would be most pronounced for women. I consequently made them the main focus of my investigation.

As the previous chapters have demonstrated, in general my expectations proved well founded. Almost all of the men and women to whom we spoke believe that men and women essentially are equal and, therefore, following the American credo, should be treated as equals. Both genders, however, also realize that such equality is rarely practiced, although men and women differed somewhat as in their assessment of the frequency with which the principle is violated (with women seeing more violations than men). The two genders differ most in their emotional reaction to this perceived inequality. Though both genders profess believing in equal treatment, few men were disturbed by gendered inequality, whereas women were disturbed, as might have been expected from theories of relative deprivation.

Notwithstanding that the genders' emotional reactions differ, few men or women can escape the feeling of living in a transitional period where gender relations are undergoing major changes at the same time that many other old patterns continue to persist. For example, we have seen that most men and women have come to accept, whether grudgingly or cordially, that women are about to enter most fields of employment, but far fewer seem to have accepted the notion that such changes in employment may have to be accompanied by adjustments in the domestic sphere. In the typical nuclear family—which itself is beginning to become an endangered species—the division of labor has remained remarkably unchanged, notwithstanding women's massive entrance into the labor market. Other aspects of gender relations, among them changes in sexual mores and family constellations, are also undergoing rapid transformations. Change, hence, has been uneven but, more important, it is perceived as inevitable; few, women or men, really believe that the clock can be turned back.

It would, however, be perilous to ignore just how threatening change can be for the individual, even when such change might seem morally correct or beneficial. A change in gender relations may well be particularly threatening because "it challenges deeply held, often sacred beliefs . . . [and] uproots perspectives which are familiar, and, because familiar, comfortable" (Langland and Gove 1981: 3). This challenge is particularly hard for those who believe they might stand to lose from change. Hence it is not hard to understand why the men in our sample, the alleged beneficiaries of the current system, are reluctant to forsake their dominant status and the benefits it bestows and feel ambivalent if not actually threatened by further change.[1] Some of the younger men

1. It can, of course, be argued that men do not really benefit from current arrangements because the cultural imperative of male superiority is as restrictive for them as the imperative of female submissiveness is for women and that genuine equality would be liberating for both genders.

are not unmindful that in the long run they might actually benefit from the change, but even they tend to express the opinion that, at least in the short run, the change involves a diminution of males' customary powers and privileges. A diminution that seems all the more disturbing since from childhood on men of all ages have been socialized to the idea that being a male implies superior endowment, that male dominance constitutes the natural order of things. These deeply held, "almost sacred" beliefs nowadays have to contend with the belief in gender equality. To the extent that more and more men are beginning to subscribe to the more recent trend, it becomes difficult for them to oppose gender equality outright. To think of oneself as a fair and principled person precludes such opposition. The dilemma then is: How can they protect their traditional image of maleness and yet not appear to be unfair to the opposite sex?

Women, on the other hand, who are the potential beneficiaries of these changes, also experience ambivalence and possible anxiety.[2] True, in the long run the changes will benefit them, but in the short run, some women may feel unprepared to make the emotional and behavioral adaptations implied by genuinely equal status. Like men, they may feel that they are being asked to navigate unchartered waters without the aid of a compass. They too have to part with long-held "sacred beliefs" about what it means to be and act like a woman. Societal definitions of "the modern woman" create a double bind for them, especially in the world of work. To succeed, they are asked to practice some allegedly typical male behaviors, such as competitiveness and leadership, but when they do, they are described as lacking in femininity. Some ambivalence, some fear of change, thus has to be anticipated on the part of both genders, notwithstanding their generalized commitment to equal treatment for both. Both genders, as we have seen, are learning to cope with change, but, in doing so, each gender is in the process of devising a different set of coping strategies in order to minimize the potential costs or maximize the benefits of change. This chapter will explore the strategies the men and women in our study adopt when they encounter inequalities for which they can find no moral justification. More specifically, what strategies are chosen by those who are the beneficiaries of current inequalities and what strategies are adopted by those who hope to benefit from future changes? Two considerations will govern that choice: The strategy must meet her or his self-interest (to protect an advantage or conversely to gain

---

2. Several of the sections which follow are derived from my 1991 presidential address published in *Political Psychology* 13, no. 3 (1992): 337–52 under the title "How Men and Women Cope When Gender Role Orientations Change."

one) and must also not interfere with the person's positive self-image. An intrinsic part of a positive self-image includes the perception that she or he is a fair and just person who deals fairly with others (Reis 1987: 149). Fairness, within the American context, implies treating equals as equals. To maintain their self-image as fair people, those who, usually for self-serving reasons, violate this traditional precept, will go to considerable lengths to justify such violations. These justifications and the behaviors that accompany them, I call "coping strategies."[3] Both the disadvantaged (the so-called underrewarded) who can be expected to experience discomfort over inequitable treatment and the advantaged (the so-called overrewarded) adopt such coping strategies. "Presumably, both the perception of underreward and overreward results in feelings of distress, in the form of anger in the former and guilt in the latter case" (Major and Deaux 1982: 44). To assuage either anger or guilt and to avoid perceiving of oneself as either victim (the disadvantaged) or victimizer (the beneficiary), people resort to a variety of coping strategies which permit them to deal with contemplated changes.

MALE COPING STRATEGIES

Men, as we saw in the previous chapter, concede that women are entitled to equality, which in turn would require of them that they support women's quest for equality and manifest it in their own behavior. On the other hand, having to live with equality poses a real problem for them since, as the beneficiaries of traditional gender arrangements, they enjoy many advantages they would have to forsake were genuine gender equality come to pass. They are understandably reluctant to embrace that contingency. If they want to retain their privileged status and yet think of themselves as fair and just human beings, they, consequently, are fazed with the task of finding morally acceptable justifications for maintaining their advantages. This they find relatively easy to do. As C. F. Epstein so pointedly remarks, "The privileged do not seem to require much persuasion that their gifts are inevitable or deserved" (1988: 234).

In reviewing male responses, I was able to distinguish six types of

3. The exposition which follows rests on the assumptions developed by equity theorists that people subscribe to the notion that a just society is an equitable one and that equity requires that the rewards people receive are commensurate to the contributions they have made. Most people, desiring to think of themselves as fair, therefore, would be loathe to think that any goal they might be pursuing has been reached by taking unfair advantage of someone else. Few could live comfortably with such a negative self-image— hence the need for finding justifications for one's behavior.

justifications or coping strategies frequently invoked by New Jersey males.[4] I shall label the first, and perhaps the most comforting one, the *"see-no-evil" strategy.* There the individual professes his desire to see women treated equally, but he happens to find no evidence of gender-based discrimination in his environment and hence experiences no distress in holding on to his privileged position. For example, several of the men we encountered compared their wives' lives with the position of their mothers and expressed the conviction that sufficient change had already taken place to wipe out former inequities. One blue-collar man recalled that his mother never knew how much money her husband earned or how he spent it and never thought to question him. She was given her weekly household allowance and "that was that," but his own wife "insists on keeping the checkbook"! So where is the inequality? he seems to say. A printer tells the group that he hears talk of employment discrimination and certainly would condemn it, but he has no personal experience with it. Apparently, he is oblivious of the fact that no woman works in his shop and that to this day printing and typesetting are among the most male-dominated trades. The engineer tells how he would like to hire women, but he operates from the assumption that there just are not any female engineers and gives no evidence of having made any efforts to verify his assumption. In making these assessments, the persons probably act in good faith. They have noted no discrimination because they have accepted appearance for reality and have asked no questions of themselves or others. When they are given evidence to the contrary, they are inclined to minimize it or to think it happens only to a certain type of woman—women who are difficult to work with or have a chip on their shoulders. Such blind spots have the advantage of permitting the individual to maintain a positive image of himself as a fair person without having to relinquish any advantages. I am reminded of a corporation president I once interviewed whose female employees felt denigrated because it was they and not the men who during company outings were always put in charge of refreshments. When I confronted him with the complaint, he was totally baffled and replied "but they enjoy doing this" and absolutely could not conceive of the practice as a form of sex-typing.

A second coping strategy can be called *inflation of one's deservingness.* Here a person exaggerates the value of his own contributions, perhaps by underestimating the other's accomplishments. It permits the person to retain the reward without having to admit to himself that he might have been overrewarded at the expense of someone else. Some

4. Several of the strategies which follow are adopted from the work of equity theorists, such as H. T. Reis (1987).

will explain the gender gap in income in this way. Whatever jobs are typically female, that is, performed by more females than males, are usually considered less difficult and less important. This then becomes the reason for allocating fewer monetary compensations to such jobs. The mechanic we cited in chapter 7 exemplifies this inflated deserving-ness strategy. Recall how he protested that even highly specialized sec-retaries should not get the same pay as he, because his work was dirty and greasy while they worked in clean offices! He thought it only fair that his wage should be higher. This strategy then permits him to con-tinue thinking of himself as a "fair guy" without having to yield his higher pay. Other men, as we saw, felt they deserved advantages simply because their work involved heavy labor. Another man gives such labor as justification why he should not be expected to help at home even though his wife also is employed full-time. Women, who work in air-conditioned banks, as one maintenance worker stated outright, don't deserve the same consideration at home as do men who work in hot, poorly ventilated plants. Definitions of equality like these serve the purpose of reducing

> some of the seeming tension between self-interest and justice. Unfairly large rewards might be desirable in and of themselves, but they would be unpalatable to the self, because they breach the prerequisites to long-term benefits that one must be a deserving person. However, both ten-dencies can be fulfilled to the extent that the latitude of acceptance for defining a fair reward can be stretched . . . thereby maintaining the self-perception of fairness while at the same time enhancing the rewards. (Reis 1987: 145)

The *blaming-the-victim strategy* as employed here constitutes a variation of the "inflation of deservingness" technique. I observed in-stances of this pattern now and then, as in the case of the young de-signer who attributes female architects' dissatisfaction with his work to their inferiority complex or the businessman who blames corporate women's employment difficulties on their touchiness. On the whole, however, this strategy was not much in evidence. For the individual who uses it, the technique serves the same purpose as do the other cop-ing techniques; it is a convenient rationalization for maintaining the current balance of rewards while protecting a good image of oneself.

Recourse to lofty principles, the fourth coping technique, permits a person to justify certain advantages he considers unfair because they serve a greater good, a loftier principle of which society approves. For example, the so-called protective legislation enacted earlier in this cen-tury had for a long time kept women out of certain lucrative occupa-tions because such work was said to endanger a woman's health. That type of "empathic" reasoning still has appeal. Latch-key kids and harried family lives were cited now and then by some of the men in our sample as justification for discouraging women with small children from accepting full-time employment. In the previous chapters we quoted from a conversation among several middle-class men who recognized women's legitimate interest in outside employment but asserted that meeting children's needs should have priority. Another lofty principle invoked by some is the chance that a woman's employment can endanger public safety or the safety of a fellow employee. That was the reason cited by the man who objects to women becoming roofers or policemen. "I don't think a woman should be a cop. I'm going to have a 120-pound woman save me from a 220-pound murderer? No way."[5] Recourse to lofty principles, whether for the sake of children or the public's safety, always implies that it is the woman who has to make a sacrifice not demanded of a man and that women should be willing to make it for the sake of the greater good.

More frequently invoked was a fifth technique, which I label the *"Why Punish Me?"* coping strategy. In this case, an individual absolves himself of personal responsibility for whatever inequities he readily observes in society. Why punish me, so the argument runs, for the sins of our fathers or the misdeeds of society? It is not my fault if the unions will not accept female apprentice bricklayers, I would give them a chance if it were up to me. But neither do I want to see my application passed over in preference for a female. As we have seen, blue-collar men frequently invoke this principle. The reader will recall the many objections they have to their companies' efforts to recruit and/or train women for previously all-male jobs. White-collar males express similar reservations. They object to the idea of paying a personal price in order to level the field for women, as when their companies promoted women over men or enacted affirmative action policies. Even though they may have been less reluctant than blue-collar men to acknowledge past injustices, they too are unwilling to pay a personal price for remedying past injustices. They raise the issue less frequently than blue-collar men, however, perhaps because they do not have to cope with the situation as often.

Of course, if men really feel uncomfortable about gender-based discrimination, one very direct strategy would be to cease discriminating and see that others do likewise. I found little evidence that many men in the sample even contemplated employing what I shall label a *distress*

5. While the reference to body strength may seem persuasive at first, one has to be permitted some skepticism about the man's concern for public safety since he concludes with a discussion of trades from which women should be excluded with: "You just can't keep going on and on. It has to be stopped somewhere. And they're trying to get hold of everything now. They're going to take the men out of employment."

and redress coping strategy. One or another man occasionally mentions how in his personal interactions with women he would never discriminate, or how he seeks to treat women fairly. But not a single man reports having made an attempt to stop someone else from discriminating against a woman or otherwise harassing her.[6] We need only to remember the business man who encouraged the young woman not to quit despite harassment by male colleagues. But did he offer to speak to these colleagues about it? No. The men, much like the women in the focus groups, refrain from considering new policies government might enact to promote gender equality, although, as we saw, they exhibit considerable ambivalence if not hostility with respect to affirmative action policies. Male telephone respondents support several policies designed to benefit women, albeit always with smaller margins than do women. Consequently, it comes as no surprise that not one single man, even when pressed by the moderator, ever even considered becoming politically active on behalf of equal rights. We need only to recall the civil servant who thinks he would be out there marching or protesting if he were a woman but, being a man, sees no reason for involving himself! We must, of course, remember that women too, for the most part, avoid taking public actions (chapters 5 and 6). What makes men's refusals different are the reasons they offer: Discrimination is someone else's business. So long as they personally do not deliberately discriminate, they do not have to reproach themselves.

Any one of the above six coping strategies may have helped men to avoid, or at least to minimize, distress over a situation they clearly perceived to be unfair and may help explain why so few were bothered by the discrimination they observed (see chapter 7). But personal relief from distress does little to ameliorate the social situation itself. Discrimination remained, as one of the previously cited women declared, "a fact of life." So how do women cope with this fact of life? What are their coping strategies?

WOMEN'S COPING STRATEGIES

Women, of course, have the opposite objective when they contemplate potential changes in gender relations. By and large, they have no need for coping strategies to justify continuing their subordinate status. On the contrary, their objective is to end their subordination and to bring

---

6. A recent case before the Office of Equal Employment Opportunities (reported in the *New York Times,* 10 January 1995) points to this pattern. After two women complained about their supervisor's sexual harassment of them, male fellow employees engaged in a campaign of verbal harassment and threats against the women which became so stressful that the women quit their jobs.

about true gender equality. Their task is to adopt coping strategies that will yield the desired benefits but attain them without inviting costly male resistance. Because they are convinced that men harbor much resistance to fundamental changes in gender relations, the women tend to rely on coping strategies that will minimize, if not actually avoid, male resistance. Avoiding open conflict with men becomes a paramount consideration in their choice of coping strategies. To gain a fuller understanding of the rationale for their choice of coping strategies, it is necessary to pause and describe how women view men or rather what motives they ascribe to them before we can begin with the analysis of female coping strategies.

Women's construction of men is that they are still governed by the macho ideal and hence have changed far less than women. Recent developments, they argue, threaten men, who will seek to resist change as best they can. In the women's construction of men, "maleness" and "macho" are all but synonymous. One young woman tells us, "men have terrible fear of being overpowered," and another asserts: "They are telling us that today we can have the best of both worlds. But it is really a special kind of partner to make it work and there aren't many around . . . no matter what they promised before marriage, it is still 'I'm going to lie down and watch the ball game while you make dinner.' It doesn't matter you've been on your feet all day." A woman in the military complains that men can only "see us in the kitchen and in front of the stove. I mean, you could come in with your briefcase, it would still be the same old story." These women are truly convinced that most men still subscribe to the notion that women should be kept barefoot and pregnant.[7] They often attribute this attitude to the ways mothers used to bring up boys. The reader may recall the discussion of the "prince" his mama brought up who now expects "the little wife" to become his new mama![8] And so they believe "we have to

7. Here is one such version: "I mean if you said to a man: 'do you want me to stay home and cook you a nice big meal and make you children?' Okay, three-quarters of them would probably say 'yes, I would like that. I need a woman at home to take care of my house and my kids and be there in the kitchen.'"

8. Only now and then does a woman in our groups or over the phone express much sympathy that the recent changes might involve some hardships for men as well. But calls for empathy don't find much ready acceptance as the following exchange illustrates. One woman asserts: "We, too, have to give up something." Another interjects: "And what do *men* give up?" To which the first woman replies: "Oh, they are giving up plenty. They are giving up a wife that is home constantly to greet them at the door when they walk in. They are giving up the security of knowing that their woman isn't going to go anywhere because where else could she go? What could she do? They have given up quite a bit, I think." But even this empathic comment recognizes that men have or have had a good life thanks to women's subservience.

see another generation of men in the marketplace, in the business world. Men who were raised by women like us." In the meantime, they will try to raise their own sons to respect women and not to become male chauvinists (a term used often). But they harbor considerable doubt that they will be successful, given the proclivities of a society dominated by males.[9] In making their choice of coping strategies, these pessimistic, even unflattering, views of men seem to have played a decisive role.

Two major and at times conflicting objectives guide women's choice of coping strategies: they must seek to equalize as much as possible their position vis-à-vis men but they must simultaneously seek not to jeopardize their relations with them, especially with those men who are important to their private lives. To the end of achieving these objectives, different women opt for different coping strategies, and a few combine several, but all seem to have these two goals in mind. A frequently invoked strategy is resort to the *not-me syndrome* (discussed in chapter 3). This strategy is adopted by women who are keenly aware of sex-based discrimination but consider themselves to have been exempt from it. They see other women being discriminated against at work or treated badly at home, but assure us that no one has ever done this to them, or if someone did it once upon a time, that person was quickly "put in his place," so that the behavior ceased. Exemption from personal discrimination, of course, does not prevent the woman in question from experiencing indignation over the treatment accorded her group. But the "not-me" strategy protects her from feeling personally victimized. Her pride and self-esteem are thus kept intact. The telephone respondents, as we saw, had frequent recourse to the "not-me" technique; focus group members resorted to it less, perhaps because the group setting was more conducive to the voicing of complaints.

Another way of coping with discrimination is the *refusal-to-be-bothered strategy*. Here the woman recognizes that she is the target of discrimination but refuses to "let it get me." This is another tactic for avoiding feeling victimized or having one's self-image diminished. Moreover, it protects the individual from the corrosive force of anger and resentment. The debilitating effect is a cost women quite consciously seek to avoid. In addition, women, as we saw in chapter 4, have been brought up not to show anger or to complain because men are alleged to dislike it. As focus groups pointed out, showing pain only

---

9. One woman tells of her efforts to encourage cooperation rather than aggression in her four-year-old but expresses her fear that it will come to naught when he enters public school because the other children will call him a sissy.

encourages further male harassment and the impression that women "just can't take it." Much like the stewardesses in Hochschild's study, they are keenly aware that complaints often are counterproductive. Recall the woman who works with "some pretty tough men" who constantly seek to trip her up. She chooses not to let it bother her, so that now, in her view, it has made her "very strong."

Three coping strategies do *not* find favor (or find very little favor) with the women in our sample. They are: compliance, confrontation, and collective action. Not one woman advocates giving up and resigning herself to or willingly accepting being treated as less worthy than a man. Although a few women complain that "we all appear so resigned," I found no evidence that they had resigned themselves to the point of accepting genuine subservience to male domination, either for themselves or their daughters. But they also avoid the very opposite strategy of challenging men's alleged superiority: only an occasional woman reports choosing a confrontational strategy, challenging men whenever she felt discriminated or demeaned by them. The woman in one of our groups who reports how she matched insult with insult and refuses "to let men get away with it" is a distinct exception, and her strategy was rejected by the group. And, as exemplified in chapter 6, virtually no one suggests that the way to cope with the injustice done to her individually or to the group is to take collective action in order to bring about systemic change.

In lieu of collective action, they offer a uniquely American, individualistic solution; namely, if women want to succeed, they have to do it on their own, even if it might require sacrifices or accommodations. I have labeled this the coping strategy of *accommodation for a purpose*. In the focus groups, this is the preferred coping strategy. It is prompted by women's perception that men are not inclined to lend them a helping hand in their search for equal opportunity. Nor do women have much faith that laws or government regulations will be effective in promoting it. Hence, if they want to obtain the same opportunities and rewards routinely granted men, they have to do it on their own. They will have to prove themselves by working twice as hard as any man and by equalling or exceeding his competencies. They leave no doubt that this is grossly unfair and that it distresses them, but for the time being they see no other option. They think it is "a waste of energy to ask oneself how certain men got to the top, instead . . . if you're serious about your career, don't waste time looking back. Yeah, just keep going." What "just keeping going" entails is making accommodations no man is expected to make. Lois's advice to a friend exemplifies one such accommodation. Her friend, a recent law school graduate, refused to take a typing test before being hired by a law firm because she believed no such demand was made of men. Lois reports counselling her to take the test nonetheless. "I said: Well, then you are going to baby-sit for the rest of your life. Because, you know, those are the facts, man. Discrimination is standard procedure—just forget it." Lois does not advise her friend to comply simply to be cooperative or "to be a good girl," but rather so that she can become a practicing lawyer in a good law firm. Essentially, she is saying to her friend: If you want to gain equal status with men, you have to play the game according to the rules men have stipulated for women even though the rules may be unfair or even rigged against women. Just try to beat them at their own game.

Accommodation is not restricted to the workplace. Another front where women do most of the accommodating is the home. As we saw earlier, even when a woman is employed full-time, she probably still performs most of the major domestic chores and does so with but mini-mal assistance from other family members.[10] It is an unfair arrange-ment, and she feels she deserves more help, but often she does not insist on securing it in order to avoid as much as possible the confronta-tion and conflict she knows are likely to follow. It has the added advan-tage, as she knows only too well, of not diminishing the man's ego, his sense of self.[11] So, unlike her partner who works one shift, she works two. Apparently even today "men expect to *receive* at home but to *give* at work" (Hertz 1986: 125). Although the woman also gives at work, she has to give at home as well. As a result, she gets very tired and often feels unappreciated.[12] We see here a pattern not very different from what we observed in the workplace. Women meet male resistance not by giving up nor by engaging in open combat but by persisting and perhaps outperforming men, (the supermom syndrome). They are "proving themselves," as they are wont to say. Thus they seek an indi-vidualistic solution to a problem that in reality is a social one.

This individualistic approach, besides being congenial to the Ameri-

10. During the telephone survey, a robust majority declares that in their own home the division of labor was fairly equitable but that such a fair balance clearly did not prevail in other households. So once more we see the "not-me syndrome" at work. Stanley and Wise (1983) noted a similar phenomenon and argued that many women distinguish be-tween the family as an institution and *their* family; *the* family is oppressive but *their* family is not.

11. Several authors (Crosby 1991; Epstein 1988) liken these accommodations to a type of conspiracy in which women seek to "protect men and help to maintain the myth [of male superiority]" (Epstein 1988: 237).

12. A young bank employee graphically illustrates the dilemma. "I would like to have things maybe shared a little more . . . I would like him [her husband] to appreciate that I work a hard day too. I would like other people [to appreciate it]. There is this bar we frequent, it's a local bar, you know everybody . . . and I still get that stuff like 'what did you make for dinner tonight'? . . . and 'is that all you made'? I get tired too, you know."

can way of thinking, has the added advantage of avoiding conflict with members of the opposite sex. Insistence on total equality with "the men still brought up by their mommies" would, at least at this time, only lead to the proverbial "tug-of-war," they tell each other, and they are by no means sure they could win that war. As for the family, they have much too much invested in its survival to insist on the genuine equality to which they feel entitled.[13] After all, inequality based on sex "is the only instance in which representatives of unequal groups live in more intimate association with each other than with members of their own group" (Rossi 1965: 101). This intimate association is of the utmost importance to many women in our study—so much so that they are willing, gladly or reluctantly, to make the required accommodations. Notwithstanding the many complaints they voice about men, these women are not antimale (as antifeminists so often charge). Far from it, they value the intimate as well as the formal associations with men, but they wish they could take place on a more level field. Accommodation for a purpose as well as the other coping techniques thus meet (some more than others) women's main objective, namely, to enhance their chances for equal opportunity without jeopardizing their relations with the opposite sex. The avoidance of open conflict with males probably reduces the strain or cost (psychological and otherwise) for women, but the cost is considerable, for inequality continues to persist. The glass is still half empty.

To conclude, men and women alike have found ways to reduce for themselves the cost of coping with a process from which one group stands to gain while another believes it stands to lose. Those who perceive of themselves or their group as potential losers—women as well as men—found ways for resisting or at least stalling change by justifying the status quo. The beneficiaries of future change, by contrast, employed strategies to alter the status quo but made concessions and accommodations in order not to increase the resistance of the defenders of the status quo. The question which remains unanswered is: Do the participants in this dance of strategies—male as well as female—perhaps pay too high a price for coping?

13. Only a few women expressed their lack of interest in marriage and family life. Far more frequent were expressions of fear of divorce. Although the focus group participants featured divorced and single as well as married women, only two single women took the opportunity to state that marriage does not interest them, "at least not yet," as one said.

Epilogue

It is important that we do not regard perceptions and cognitions about sex and gender as individualistic phenomena. . . . People can not alter their inadequate or inappropriate views of the world at will. It is also important that we not neglect the role of the social framework in creating these perceptions. Each of these caveats is important.

—Rhoda K. Unger (1990)

The over 650 men and women who shared with us their thoughts on gender relations came from small towns, teeming urban centers, and affluent suburbs. They are high school dropouts and people with advanced degrees, prosperous professionals and individuals working for a minimum wage. As different as their backgrounds might be, they all have one thing in common: they know they are living in a transitional period, a period of rapid change where many of the old norms governing gender relations no longer apply. Both the men and women strive bravely to adapt to the new realities, although the women find it considerably easier.

For women, the change often proves liberating and empowering. For the most part, they still do more of the giving and less of the receiving than their male partners and co-workers. They do feel, however, that over the last decades their position has improved and that their rights, needs, and wants are beginning to count for more than did their mothers' and grandmothers'. They now have choices their mothers and grandmothers never had, and they consider this an important achievement. But they also know they have a long way to go before they can catch up with men. They attribute the progress achieved so far entirely to their own efforts and believe further progress is possible so long as they continue to depend on their own individual efforts, so long as they do not entertain the futile hope that men or governments might help them. A mixture of pride, pessimism, and optimism characterizes these women, young and old alike—pride in what women have accomplished so far and pessimism that matters will improve greatly in the near future but optimism that the march toward equality cannot be halted, though it will progress slowly "one inch at a time" (from a focus group member).

And what is it that these women want? Put at its simplest, they want what most men consider their natural birthright by virtue of being a male (though realized by but a few), namely to enjoy simultaneously the opportunity for meaningful, rewarding work beyond the confines of the home *and* to have a satisfactory family life without having to ask whether the two roles are compatible and without having to feel guilty for wishing to have a life outside the confines of the home. Women fervently wish that men and society accorded them more respect and ceased treating them as though they were inferior to men, and they can find no reason why women should not receive equal treatment with men. In that respect, their agenda bears strong resemblances to the feminist agenda.

But does their agenda make the New Jersey women feminists? I think not. To be sure, these women desire equality as much as do the feminists, and both are convinced that women do not as yet enjoy it. They also share the feminists' sense of minority consciousness, in that they believe that society treats women, notwithstanding their numerical majority, much as it treats disadvantaged minorities. They also share the feminists' opinion that many of the institutional structures of our society are arranged to meet the needs of men and to benefit them rather than women. Like feminists, the women who participated in this study want to see an end to violence against women and to gender-based discrimination; like them they favor equal pay for equal work, equal access to the labor market, and related social and economic policies designed to improve women's lives.

But they are far less concerned than are feminists with gaining access to power, nor do they share the feminists' commitment to fundamental social change in the system's major institutions, least of all in the family. With a few exceptions, the women we talked with want to see the traditional nuclear family left almost unaltered (except for a bit more help from family members as well as appreciation for the work women perform at home).[1] Neither the focus group conversations nor their telephone responses articulate a politicized critique of the gendered system. They also strongly reject some feminists' insistence on female solidarity and the willingness to resort to collective action in order to improve women's position.

Their desire for marriage, or at least male partnership and family, takes precedence over solidarity with women as a group. They lack the

1. Even though the traditional family is fast becoming an anachronism, the above statement is not meant to imply that feminists are anti-family. That is patently not the case, but the desire to restructure the family constellation and to bring an end to patriarchy and other gender-based hierarchies features far more prominently in their concerns than in those of the New Jersey women we interviewed.

group consciousness so characteristic of committed feminists because they think that individually they have more in common with some men than they have with women as a group. They may share with the group a common sense of indignation over the treatment accorded women, but they also know that they are separated from each other by virtue of the differences in the circumstances of their daily lives, lives that they share with men.

Paramount for them is the need to avoid open conflict with the men with whom they live or work. Not that they would not welcome the chance for the relationship to proceed on a more egalitarian basis, but if that cannot be achieved, they are willing to be the accommodator by taking on the second shift at home or working harder than a man on the shop floor. Their whole approach to dealing with gender-based inequality is neither rebellious nor passive but essentially pragmatic. New Jersey women are both traditional and egalitarian, causing them to experience considerable ambivalence as they strive for more equitable treatment.

The New Jersey men are ambivalent as well. They acknowledge that gender relations have changed quite dramatically during the past few decades and, in all likelihood, will change even more in the future. They recognize the fairness of many of the demands made by women, but they are also apprehensive if not outright afraid as to what gender equality will entail for them. So they are having a harder time than women adjusting to the new social realities, especially if they believe that these will erode their power and related male prerogatives.[2] Being in control and the fear of losing it disquiets them as they contemplate the changing gender scene. But they too are trying to cope. R. W. Connell's description (1991: 13) of the men he interviewed fits our sample perfectly: "Every man we interviewed has been conscious of [the cultural force of modern feminism]. Some are receptive and some hostile, all feel the mobilization of women as a presence. In the lives of some men it is a decisive presence." That "mobilized presence" is here to stay—on that the men and women in this study can agree—but neither can predict what direction or shape it will take next.

---

2. Mathews and DeHart (1990) attributed defeat of the ERA in part to men's dislike of being challenged by women and having to share power with them.

THE INTERVIEW SCHEDULE

1. To begin with, for how many years have you lived in New Jersey, or have you lived here all of your life?
   1. Less than one
   2. One or two
   3. 3–5
   4. 6–10
   5. 11–20
   6. 21–30
   7. More than 30
   8. All my life
   9. Don't know

2. Overall, how would you rate the job Ronald Reagan is doing as president—excellent, good, only fair, or poor?
   1. Excellent
   2. Good
   3. Only fair
   4. Poor
   9. Don't know

3. In dealing with the Soviet Union, which do you think is a more effective way to keep the peace—by demonstrating our friendly intentions, or by demonstrating our willingness to use force?
   1. Friendly intentions
   2. Willingness to use force
   (Vol) 3. Both
   9. No opinion

4. Do you favor or oppose the United States agreeing to a "nuclear freeze" with the Soviet Union—that is, putting a stop to the testing, production, and installation of additional nuclear weapons by both sides?
   1. Favor
   2. Oppose
   (Vol) 8. Depends
   9. No opinion

5. If you had to choose between more government services and higher taxes, or less government services and lower taxes, which would you choose? (If choice made, probe: Do you feel strongly about this?)
> 1. More services/taxes—strongly
> 2. More services/taxes—not strongly
> 3. Less services/taxes—not strongly
> 4. Less services/taxes—strongly
> 9. No opinion

6. As you know, most of the money government spends comes from taxes you and others pay. For each of the following, please tell me whether you think government should be spending more, less, or the same as now. First, how about [designated point]—should we spend more, less, or the same? (Repeat response options every three items, "should we spend more, less, or the same?")

	More	Less	Same	No Opinion
( ) a. College loans for minority students	1	3	2	9
( ) b. Aid to the elderly	1	3	2	9
( ) c. The space weapons defense program known as "Star Wars"	1	3	2	9
( ) d. Housing for low-income families	1	3	2	9
( ) e. Shelters for battered women	1	3	2	9
( ) f. Protecting the environment	1	3	2	9
( ) g. Colleges and universities	1	3	2	9
( ) h. Day care centers for children of working mothers	1	3	2	9

7. How important do you think it is for government to help disadvantaged groups—very important, somewhat important, or not very important?
> 1. Very important
> 2. Somewhat important
> 3. Not very important
> 9. Don't know

8. Many people share common experiences with or feel close to certain groups. Please tell me whether you feel particularly close to any of the groups I read: First [designated point] do you feel close to this group or not? Next, do you feel close to . . .

	Close	Not Close	Depends/ Maybe (Vol)	Inap. No Opinion
( ) a. People of your own religion	1	3	8	9
( ) b. People with similar occupations	1	3	8	9
( ) c. Ask WOMEN: Other women Ask MEN: Other men	1	3	8	9
( ) d. People of your own race or ethnic group	1	3	8	9
( ) e. People in the same social class or with similar household incomes	1	3	8	9

9. If a woman leaves her job to have a baby do you think she has a *right* to get her job back, or should this be left up to the employer to decide? (If choice made, probe: Do you feel strongly about this?)
    1. Right—strongly
    2. Right—not strongly
    4. Employer decision—not strongly
    5. Employer decision—strongly
(Vol) 8. Depends on circumstances/situation
    9. Don't know

10. As you know, the Equal Rights Amendment was not approved by enough states to make it part of the Constitution. Do you think it is important that another effort be made to ratify the E.R.A., or not?
    1. Yes, important
    2. No, not important
(Vol) 3. Against E.R.A.   Go to Q.12
(Vol) 8. Depends
    9. Don't know

11. Do you personally favor or oppose the Equal Rights Amendment? (If favor or oppose, probe: Are you strongly [opposed to it/in favor of it], or not so strongly.
    1. Favor—strongly
    2. Favor—not strongly
    4. Oppose—not strongly
    5. Oppose—strongly
(Vol) 8. Depends/both pro and con
    9. Don't know/undecided

12. How much interest do you have in how women as a whole are getting along in this country? Do you have a great deal of interest, some interest, just a little, or not much?
    1. Great deal
    2. Some
    3. A little
    4. Not much
    9. Don't know

13. In general, who would you say gets treated better by society—men, women, or are they treated the same?
    1. Men
    2. Women
    3. The same
(Vol) 8. Depends   Go to Q.16
    9. Don't know

(If "Men" or "Women" is the answer to Q.13, ask:)

14. Do you think this is fair, unfair, or isn't this the way you think about it?
    1. Unfair
    2. Fair
    3. Not how I think about it   Go to Q.16
    9. Don't know

(If "Unfair" to Q.14, ask:)

15. Is this something that really bothers you, or is this just the
    way society is?
    1. Bothers
    2. Accepts
(Vol) 8. Both
    9. Don't know

16. How much sex discrimination would you say there is in American soci-
    ety—where women are not treated as equals because of their sex—a lot,
    a fair amount, some, just a little, or none at all?
    1. Lot
    2. Fair amount
    3. Some
    4. Just a little
    5. None   Go to Q.20
    6. Depends (Vol)
    9. Don't know

(If #1, 2, 3, or 4 to Q.16, ask:)

17. How do you feel about this *yourself*—does this bother you a lot, some, a
    little, or not at all?
    1. Lot
    2. Some
    3. Little
    4. Not at all
    9. Don't know

18. And how do you think most *women* feel about this—is sex discrimina-
    tion something that bothers them a lot, some, a little, or not at all?
    1. Lot
    2. Some
    3. Little
    4. Not at all
    9. Don't know

19. What about most *men*—are they bothered a lot, some, a
    little, or not at all?
    1. Lot
    2. Some
    3. Little
    4. Not at all
    9. Don't know

20. Some people do not feel the issue of sex discrimination is very impor-
    tant, saying it doesn't affect them directly. Others feel it is very impor-
    tant, saying they experience sex discrimination in everyday life.
    How about you—is sex discrimination a problem you encounter every
    day, pretty often, just once in a while, or rarely?
    1. Every day
    2. Pretty often

3. Once in a while
4. Rarely/never
9. Don't know

21. In society today would you say that women's opinions are given equal respect to men's, less respect, or more?

    1. Equal
    2. Less   For male respondents, skip to Q.23
    3. More
    9. Don't know

22. *ASK WOMEN ONLY:* How about yourself—do you feel your opinions are treated with equal respect, less respect, or more?

    1. Equal
    2. Less
    3. More
    9. Don't know

ASK EVERYONE:

23. For each of the following, please tell me if you think <u>men</u> are treated better, <u>women</u> are treated better, or if they are treated the same. First, [designated point] who's treated better—men, women, or the same? (Repeat options every 3 questions and as otherwise needed)

	Men	Women	Same	Depends (vol)	No Opinion
( ) a. When applying for a loan or mortgage by themselves	1	3	2	8	9
( ) b. In getting management jobs in business	1	3	2	8	9
( ) c. In divorce settlements	1	3	2	8	9
( ) d. When it comes to income or pay	1	3	2	8	9
( ) e. In getting top jobs in government	1	3	2	8	9

   f. When a woman believes she has been discriminated against in one of these areas, what would you advise her do about it? (Probe: What actions could she take?)

   _____
   _____
   _____

24. I'm going to read you some statements. For each, please just tell me if you agree a lot, agree a little, or disagree. (Repeat options as necessary—"Do you agree a lot, a little, or disagree?") [Designated point A—E]

	Agree Lot	Little	Disagree	No Opinion
( )a. Despite the recent gains of women, when all is said and done, it's still a man's world.	1	2	3	9

	Agree			
	Lot	Little	Disagree	No Opinion
( ) b. Even if a woman is as accomplished as a man in what she does, she does not seem to get the same amount of recognition.	1	2	3	9
( ) c. To get ahead in the world, a woman has to be much better at what she does than a man.	1	2	3	9
( ) d. ASK WOMEN ONLY: Being a woman has prevented me from doing some of the things I wanted to do in life.	1	2	3	9
( ) e. When a woman seeks public office or a job formerly held by a man, most people are more concerned with the fact that she is a woman than with her individual qualifications.	1	2	3	9
f. Even though women are a majority of the population, they are often treated as second-class citizens or as a minority.	1	2	3	9

g. How about most of the women you know? Do you think they feel they are often treated as second-class citizens? (If yes, probe: Does this happen a lot or just a little?)

    1. Yes—lot
    2. Yes—little
    3. No   All men skip to Q.26
    9. Don't know

h. ASK WOMEN ONLY: And how about yourself—do you ever feel as if you are treated as a second-class citizen? (If yes, probe: Do you feel this way often, sometimes, or just once in a while?)

    1. Often
    2. Sometimes
    3. Once in a while
    4. No
    9. Don't know

25. *ASK WOMEN ONLY:* When a woman achieves something important and gets recognition, do you feel <u>proud</u> because another woman accomplished something, or isn't this something you think about?

    1. Proud   3. Don't think about it/no, not proud
(Vol) 8. Depends   9. No opinion

ASK EVERYONE:

26. Thinking back over the past ten to twenty years, how much change do you think there has been in the position of women in this country—a lot, some, just a little, or none at all?

    1. Lot
    2. Some
    3. Just a little
    4. None   Skip to Q.32
    9. Don't know

27. Speaking for yourself, would you say that these changes have been coming too fast, too slow, or at about the right pace?

    1. Too fast
    2. Too slow
    3. About right
    9. No opinion

28. What do you think is the *most important* reason these changes have happened? (Probe: What do you mean by this; why do you think this happened?)

    _____
    _____
    _____
    _____
    _____

29. How do you *personally* feel about what's been happening—have these changes been for the better or the worse?

    1. Better
    2. Worse
    3. Some of both/depends
    9. Don't know

30. Do you feel *your* life has been affected by any of these changes? (If yes, probe: For the better or for the worse?)

    1. Not affected
    2. Better
    3. Worse
    4. Affected (both)/don't know how
    9. Don't know

31. How much of the recent change in the position of women is due to government actions or policies—a great deal, some, a little, or would these changes have happened no matter what the government did?

    1. Great deal
    2. Some
    3. A little
    4. No matter what
    9. Don't know

32. Some people think the government should make every effort to improve the social and economic position of women. Others feel women should help themselves and that government should make no special effort. Should government be more active in trying to improve the status of women, less active, or continue as it has?

    1. More active
    2. Less active
    3. Continue
    9. Don't know

33. Do you think the gains made by women in the direction of greater freedom and full equality are secure, or could things go back to the way they were some years ago?

    1. Secure
    2. Change back
    9. Don't know

34. And what would you *like* to see in the future—change in the direction of fully equal treatment of men and women in all areas, change back in the direction of how things were some years ago, or should things stay pretty much the way they are today?

    1. Change to more equal treatment
    2. Change back to how things were
    3. Stay as is today
(Vol) 8. Depends   Go to Q.36
    9. Don't know

               (If "Change #1 or #2" to Q.34, ask:)

35. Would you like to see a *major* change or *minor* one from how things are now?

    1. Major
    2. Minor
(Vol) 8. Both/depends
    9. No opinion

36. Some people feel there are traditional roles for men and women—with men's place in the workforce and women's in the home. Others feel there should not be roles based on sex—that men and women should do whatever they want as individuals. Which of these views is closest to your own, or are you somewhere in the middle?

    (If choice made, probe: Do you feel strongly about this, or not too strongly?) (If middle, probe: Which side do you lean more toward—traditional roles or individual choice?)

    1. Traditional roles—strongly
    2. Traditional roles—not strongly
    3. Middle, then lean toward traditional roles
    4. Middle, doesn't lean
    5. Middle, then lean toward individual choice
    6. Individual choice—not strongly
    7. Individual choice—strongly
    9. Don't know

37. Thinking about how <u>you</u> were taught to behave and things you did when you were growing up, were you treated very differently, somewhat differently, or pretty much the same as:

    FOR FEMALE R's: Your brothers or other boys your age?
    FOR MALE R's: Your sisters or other girls your age?
    1. Very differently
    2. Somewhat differently
    3. Same
    9. Don't know

38. If money were no object, do you think most women would *prefer* to have a job outside the home, or would they prefer to stay home and take care of a house and family?
    1. Job
    2. House/family
    (Vol) 3. Both   All men go to Q.40
    (Vol) 4. Work part-time
    9. Don't know

ASK WOMEN ONLY:

39. And if <u>you</u> were free to do either, would you prefer to have a job outside the home or to take care of a house and family?
    1. Job
    2. House/family
    (Vol) 3. Both
    (Vol) 4. Work part-time
    9. Don't know

ASK EVERYONE:

40. In politics and government, do you think that as a group, women have less influence than men, more influence, or *exactly* the same amount?
    1. Less
    2. More
    3. Same
    8. Depends (Vol)   Go to Q.42
    9. Don't know
    (If "Less" to Q.40, ask:)

41. Some blame women themselves for their lack of influence, while others blame men, government, or society in general.
    a. Do women deserve most, some, a little, or none of the blame for their lack of influence in government and politics?
    b. Should most, some, a little, or none of the blame for women's lack of influence be placed on men?
    c. How much blame for women's lack of influence is because of the government itself—most, some, a little, or none?
    d. How responsible is society in general for women's lack of influence—should society get most, some, a little, or no blame?

	Most	Some	Little	None	No Opinion
a. Women	1	2	3	4	9
b. Men	1	2	3	4	9
c. Government	1	2	3	4	9
d. Society	1	2	3	4	9

42. Now I'm going to read you a short list of reasons some people have given for why women have less influence in business and earn less than men. Please just tell me if you think each is or is not a reason why women are less successful.

First . . . [designated point], is this a reason or not?
Second . . . is this a reason why women have less influence and earn less, or not? (Repeat options as necessary.)

	Is	Is Not	Don't Know
( ) a. Women tend to be less qualified	1	2	9
( ) b. Men have held women back	1	2	9
( ) c. Women have too many household obligations	1	2	9
( ) d. Women are not as ambitious or aggressive	1	2	9
( ) e. Government policy has held women back	1	2	9

If two or more circled, ask Q.43   If one or none circled, go to Q.44

43. I'm going to read back the statements you agreed with. Please tell me which one you think is the most important reason why women have less influence and earn less than men. (Read all circled in boxed "Is" column above . . . which is most important?)
   1. Less qualified
   2. Men have held women back
   3. Household obligations
   4. Less ambitious/aggressive
   5. Government policy
   8. Other
   9. Don't know/can't choose

44. Some people tell us that too much is expected of today's women because most work outside the home and still are expected to be good homemakers and parents. Do you think young women today have a tougher life than women use to have, or not?
   1. Yes
   2. No
   (Vol) 8. Depends
   9. Don't know

45. Which do you think is the best way for women to get equal treatment with men—by working *together as other groups do,* or by each individual working to get ahead on her own?
   1. Women working together
   2. Women working as individuals
   (Vol) 3. No change necessary
   (Vol) 4. Both 1 and 2   9. Don't know

46. I'm going to read three statements to you about groups trying to change women's status in society. Please tell me which view is closest to your own. (Read options 1–3.)
    1. First, the women's movement has done more harm than good to advance the position of women.
    2. Second, while the women's movement was necessary years ago to advance women, it is no longer necessary today, or
    3. Third, the women's movement is still necessary if women are to continue to advance.
    9. No opinion

47. Do you know of any women who have applied for jobs they were qualified for but did not get just because they were women?
    1. Yes
    2. No
    9. Don't know

48. Have you been regularly employed full- or part-time in the last few years?
    1. Yes
    2. No
    9. Don't know If 2 or 9 are circled, go to Q.56
    (If "Yes" to Q.48, ask:)

49. In the place where you work, do women generally stand an equal chance with men in terms of pay, job assignments, and promotions, or not?
    1. Yes, equal
    2. No
    7. Not appropriate
    8. Depends
    9. Don't know
    (If "No" to Q.49, ask Q.50. All other answers: *men* skip to Q.56; working *women* go to Q.51.)

50. How do you feel about this? Is this something that bothers you a lot, a little, or do you just accept it as the way things work?
    1. Lot
    2. Little
    3. Way things work. All men skip to Q.56
    9. Don't know

ASK WOMEN ONLY:
51. In the place where you work now, do you think you've ever been discriminated against because you're a woman in terms of pay, job assignments, or promotion?
    1. Yes
    2. No
    9. Don't know

52. At work, do you think your opinions and suggestions are given as much attention as men who hold the same type of position as you, more attention, or less?

    1. Same   Go to Q.54
    2. More
    3. Less
    9. Don't know   Go to Q.54
    (If "Less" to Q.52, ask:)

53. Is this something you feel angry about, something you have learned to accept, or both?

    1. Angry
    2. Learned to accept
    3. Both
    9. Don't know

54. Some women we talk to say they are made to feel like "outsiders" by the men they work with just because they are women. Do you feel this way, or not?

    1. Do
    2. Do not
    8. Sometimes
    9. Don't know

55. Have you ever been the object of an unwanted sexual advance or been made to feel uncomfortable at work by such things as men putting their arm around you or sex-related teasing?

    1. Yes
    2. No
    9. Don't know If 2 or 9 are circled, go to Q.56
    (If "Yes" to Q.55, ask:)

55A. How do you feel about this? Is this something that bothers you a lot, a little, or do you just accept it as the way things work?

    1. Lot
    2. Little
    3. Way things work
    9. Don't know

ASK EVERYONE:

56. If both a man and woman work full-time, do you think that the man should do most, half, or only some of the household chores? (If necessary, explain: "By household chores I mean things like cooking, cleaning, and making minor repairs.")

    1. Most
    2. Half
    3. Some
(Vol)   4. None
    9. Don't know

57. And what do you think actually happens when both people work full-time? In most households, does the man do most, half, only some, or none of the housework?

    1. Most   If 2 or 9 are circled, go to Q.59
    2. Half
    3. Some
    4. None
    9. Don't know
    (If #3, 4, or 9 to Q.57, ask:)

58. Do you think of this as something that is very unfair to working women, a little unfair, or don't you think of it in terms of fairness?

    1. Very unfair
    2. A little
    3. Not in terms of fairness
    9. Don't know

59. Are you married, widowed, divorced, separated, or have you never been married?

    1. Married
    2. Widowed
    3. Divorced
    4. Separated
    5. Never married
    9. Don't know
    (If 2, 3, or 4 are circled, go to Q.61; if 5 or 9, go to Q.62.)
    (If "Married" to Q.59, ask:)

60. Does your (husband/wife) do (his/her) fair share of the household chores such as cooking, cleaning, and fixing things?

    1. Yes
    2. No
    9. Don't know

61. Do you have children?

    1. Yes
    2. No   If 2 or 9 are circled, go to Q.62
    9. Don't know/refused
    (If "Yes" to Q.61, ask:)

61A. And how old is your youngest child?   _____

Now just a few more questions so we can classify your answers.

62. In politics as of today, do you consider yourself a Democrat, Republican, Independent, or something else?

    1. Democrat   If 2 is circled, skip to Q.64
    2. Republican
    3. Independent
    4. Something else/other
    9. Don't know/no opinion
    (If #3, 4, or 9 to Q.62, ask:)

63. Do you lean more toward the Democratic Party or more toward the Republican Party?

    1. Democratic Party
    2. Republican Party
    3. Other
    4. Neither
    9. Don't know/no opinion

64. Regardless of the political party you might favor, do you consider yourself to be a liberal, conservative, or somewhere in between?

    1. Liberal   If 1 or 2 is circled, skip to Q.66
    2. Conservative
    3. Somewhere in between
    9. Don't know/no opinion
    (If 3 or 9 is the answer to Q.64, ask:)

65. Do you lean more toward the liberal side or more toward the conservative side?

    1. Liberal
    2. Conservative
    3. Other/neither
    9. Don't know/no opinion

66. Do you own or rent your apartment or house?

    1. Own
    2. Rent
    3. Live rent-free with parents/relatives
    4. Both own and rent
    9. Not determined

67. Are you currently employed, laid off, retired, or not employed?

    1. Employed
    2. Temporarily laid off   Say, "When working," then go to Q.69
    3. Retired
    4. Not employed   Go to Q.72
    5. Other/refused
    (If "Employed" to Q.67, ask:)

68. Do you work full-time or part-time?

    1. Full-time
    2. Part-time
    9. Other/don't know

69. What do you do for a living? _____

70. Do you think of your work as a career or as a job?

    1. Career
    2. Job
    3. Both/other, specify: _____
    9. Don't know

71. Do you get paid at an hourly rate, a salary, or are you self-employed?

    1. Hourly (and piecework)
    2. Salaried (and commissions)

3. Self-employed
9. Don't know

72. Are you the chief wage-earner in your household?

    1. Yes   Go to Q.75
    2. No
    (If "No" to Q.72, ask:)

73. Is the chief wage-earner in your household currently employed, temporarily laid off, retired, or not employed?

    1. Employed
    2. Temporarily laid off
    3. Retired
    4. Not employed   If 3, 4, or 5 is circled, go to Q.75
    5. Other/refused
    (If 1 or 2 is the answer to Q.73, ask:)

74. Does/did the chief wage-earner get paid at an hourly rate, paid a salary, or is the chief wage-earner self-employed?

    1. Hourly (and piecework)
    2. Salaried (and commissions)
    3. Self-employed
    9. Don't know

75. Are you or anyone in your household a member of a union? (If yes, probe: Is that you, someone elsse, or both?)

    1. No
    2. Respondent only
    3. Other only
    4. Respondent and other
    5. Used to be in the past
    9. Don't know

76. What was your age on your last birthday?

    1. 18–20
    2. 21–24
    3. 25–29
    4. 30–39
    5. 40–49
    6. 50–59
    7. 60–64
    8. 65 and over
    9. No answer/refused

77. Are you white, black, or of Hispanic origin?

    1. White
    2. Black
    3. Hispanic
    4. Other (Specify:_____)
    9. Not determined

78. Do you consider yourself to be Catholic, Protestant, Jewish, or something else?

    1. Protestant

2. Catholic
3. Jewish
4. None/Atheist/Agnostic
5. Other
9. Don't know/refused

79. Where do you live—in what township or municipality? In what county is that?

_____   _____

County   Town

80. So that we can group all answers, what is your total annual <u>family income</u> before taxes: Under $10,000; $10,000 to $15,000; $15,000 to $20,000; $20,000 to $30,000; $30,000 to $50,000; over $50,000?

    1. Under $10,000
    2. $10,001–$15,000
    3. $15,001–$20,000
    4. $20,001–$30,000
    5. $30,001–$50,000
    6. Over $50,000
    8. Don't know
    9. Refused   Go to Q.82

81. And what is your personal income before taxes: Under $5,000; $5,000 to $10,000; $10,000 to $15,000; $15,000 to $20,000; $20,000 to $30,000; $30,000 to $50,000; over $50,000?

    1. Under $5,000
    2. $5,001–$10,000
    3. $10,001–$15,000
    4. $15,001–$20,000
    5. $20,001–$30,000
    6. $30,001–$50,000
    7. Over $50,000
    9. Refused/don't know

81A. Did you receive a high school diploma?
    1. No   Go to Q.82
    2. Yes   Ask Q.81B

81B. Did you ever attend college? (If yes, did you graduate from college?)
    2. Yes, did not graduate
    3. Yes, graduated
    4. No/don't know

82. You've been very helpful. Sometimes we need to recontact people to ask one or two followup questions. Could I please have just your first name?

_____

83. Just so I am sure I dialed correctly, is your home phone number: (Record phone number legibly below.) (If not, record actual number dialed.)

_____ – _____ – _____

Thank respondent; terminate interview; and rate the respondent's level of interest in the survey and level of caring about or involvement with the general topic of "Gender and Politics."

    1. Very high
    2. Above average
    3. Average
    4. Below average
    5. Very low

Sex of interviewer:

    1. Male
    2. Female
    ____ # of call attempts

RESEARCH PROCEDURE

INDICES

The Discrimination Awareness Index (DA)

The DA Index was created from the twelve items listed below:

AMT — How much sex discrimination would you say there is in American society—where women are not treated as equals because of their sex—a lot, a fair amount, some, just a little, or none at all?

RESP — In society today, would you say that women's opinions are given equal respect to men's, less respect, or more?

SOC — In general, who would you say gets treated better by society—men, women, or are they treated the same?

For each of the following, please tell me if you think men are treated better, women are treated better, or if they are treated the same:

LOANS — when applying for a loan or mortgage by themselves;

BUS — in getting management jobs in business;

GVT — in getting top jobs in government;

INC — when it comes to income or pay.

I'm going to read you some statements. For each, please just tell me if you agree a lot, agree a little, or disagree.

NW — Despite the recent gains of women, when all is said and done, it's still a man's world.

REC — Even if a woman is as accomplished as a man in what she does, she does not seem to get the same amount of recognition.

ACH — To get ahead in the world, a woman has to be much better at what she does than a man.

QUAL — When a woman seeks public office, or a job formally held by a man, most people are more concerned with the fact that she is a woman than with her individual qualifications.

2ND CL   Even though women are a majority of the population, they are often treated as second-class citizens or as a minority.

The Affect Index (AI)

The AI Index was created from six items; three of them were asked as follow-up questions to a DA item. The DA variable name to which the affect question refers is listed prior to the affect variable name.

AI UNEQ TREAT   Do you think this is fair, unfair, or isn't this the way you think about it?

                    combined with

                    Is this something that really bothers you, or is this just the way society is?

(Note: UNEQ TREAT was created from a combination of responses to the prior two items. Possible responses are "unfair-bothered," "unfair-not bothered," or "not unfair, "not bothered.")

AI AMT SD   How do you feel about this yourself—does this bother you a lot, some, a little or not at all?

AI HH DL was asked as a follow-up question in the following series of questions:

If both a man and woman work full-time, do you think that the man should do most, half, or only some of the household chores?

And what do you think actually happens when both people work full-time? In most households does the man do most, half, only some, or none of the housework?

AI HH DL   Do you think of this as something that is very unfair to working women, a little unfair, or don't you think of it in terms of fairness?

AI CLOSE   Many people share common experiences with, or feel close to, certain groups. Please tell me whether you feel particularly close to other women. (Respondents were asked the same about five other groups.)

AI ESP   Some people do not feel the issue of sex discrimination is very important, saying it doesn't affect them directly. Others feel it is very important, saying they experience sex discrimination in everyday life. How about you—is sex discrimination a problem you encounter everyday, pretty often, just once in a while, or rarely?

AI INTEREST   How much interest do you have in how women as a whole are getting along in this country? Do you have a great deal of interest, some interest, just a little, or not much?

Table B1: Measures of Association (Kendall's Tau$_b$) Between Discrimination Awareness Index Items

	A. WOMEN											
	AMT	RESP	SOC	LOANS	BUS	GVT	INC	MW	REC	ACH	QUAL	2ND CLASS
Amount of sex discrimination (AMT)		.30	.38	.28	.27	.12	.26	.29	.38	.40	.26	.37
Respect for women's opinions (RESP)			.32	.21	.34	.19	.23	.31	.28	.31	.23	.33
Who's treated better in "Who's treated better in society?" (SOC)				.24	.34	.21	.35	.36	.29	.37	.27	.35
Who's treated better in getting loans (LOANS)					.27	.09*	.26	.25	.20	.26	.19	.26
Who's treated better in management jobs in business (BUS)						.29	.31	.30	.31	.28	.26	.32
Who's treated better in top government jobs (GVT)							.30	.17	.21	.28	.29	.17
Who's treated better income-wise (INC)								.28	.22	.28	.22	.28
Still a man's world (MW)									.48	.44	.40	.44
Recognition for women's accomplishments (REC)										.45	.44	.46
Achievement has to exceed men's (ACH)											.35	.46
Society concerned with sex, not qualifications (QUAL)												.33
Treated as second-class citizen (2ND CLASS)												

n = sizes vary between 359 and 399
All correlations significant at .01 level unless noted
* significant .05
See the questionnaire (Appendix A) for complete questions and response categories.

	AMT	RESP	SOC	LOANS	BUS	GVT	INC	MW	REC	ACH	QUAL	2ND CLASS
B. MEN												
Amount of sex discrimination (AMT)		.34	.27	.09†	.21	.20	.16	.21	.14*	.12*	.14	.22
Respect for women's opinions (RESP)			.30	.05†	.18	.17	.05†	.26	.19	.13*	.22	.32
Who's treated better in "Who's treated better in society?" (SOC)				.14*	.21	.15*	.12*	.29	.09†	.08†	.19	.24
Who's treated better in getting loans (LOANS)					.21	.11†	.05*	.12†	.19	.26	.15*	.12*
Who's treated better in management jobs in business (BUS)						.27	.13*	.11*	.17	.15*	.15	.19
Who's treated better in top government jobs (GVT)							.21	.16	.03†	.08†	.07†	.26
Who's treated better income-wise (INC)								.13*	.09†	.10†	.16	.08†
Still a man's world (MW)									.25	.26	.31	.40
Recognition for women's accomplishments (REC)										.40	.26	.31
Achievement has to exceed men's (ACH)											.32	.39
Society concerned with sex, not qualifications (QUAL)												.35
Treated as second-class citizen (2ND CLASS)												

n = sizes vary between 179 and 200
All correlations significant at .01 level unless noted
* significant .05
† not significant
See the questionnaire (Appendix A) for complete questions and response categories.

Table B2: Measures of Association (Kendall Tau$_b$) Between Affect Index Items

A. WOMEN						
Affect	UNEQ Treat	AMT SD	HH DL	Close	Interest	Exp.
Unequal treatment		.41	.30	.18	.25	.39
Amount of sex discrimination			.20	.17	.26	.37
Household division of labor				.07*	.12	.25
Closeness to other women					.05†	.12
Interest in other women						.25
Sex discrimination is common experience						

n = sizes vary between 380 and 399
All correlations significant at .01 level unless noted
* significant .05
† not significant
See the questionnaire (Appendix A) for complete questions and response categories.

B. MEN						
Affect	UNEQ Treat	AMT SD	HH DL	Close	Interest	Exp.
Unequal treatment		.25	.16	.05†	.14*	.12†
Amount of sex discrimination			.16	.19	.34	.11
Household division of labor				−.01†	.14	.09†
Closeness to other women					.02†	.02†
Interest in other women						.11†
Sex discrimination is common experience						

n = sizes vary between 182 and 200
All correlations significant at .01 level unless noted
* significant .05
† not significant
See the questionnaire (Appendix A) for complete questions and response categories.

CODING

Each of the items was rank-ordered with "1" as the response demonstrating the most awareness of sex discrimination or the most "anger" over sex discrimination, and the highest number representing little or no awareness or no anger over sex discrimination. The affect items were recoded to include those respondents who were originally skipped out because of a prior response. For example, those who said there was no sex discrimination in American society and were therefore not asked if sex discrimination bothered them, were coded as being bothered "not at all." Those respondents with missing values for any of the items were assigned a "0" (or, because of standardization, the mean score) for the item(s) on which they had a missing value. This would not appear to significantly affect the indices, as only eight persons had three or more missing on the twelve-item DA index, and six had two or more missing on the six-item affect index.

A correlation (Kendall's taub) between each item and the remaining items was performed in order to test for convergent validity. An average of the correlation of each item with the other seventeen items was then created. If the average inter-item (taub) for any of the indicators was below .20, the item was dropped from the index as there was not sufficient evidence of convergent validity (Campbell and Fiske 1959). On this basis, twelve items were included in the DA index.

MINORITY CONSCIOUSNESS

In order to create the MC index, new variables were first created for the DA and AI indices. The additive DA and AI indices were broken into equal thirds, representing high, medium, and low levels of discrimination awareness and affect. The MC index was created from a combination of responses of the tricotomized DA and AI rank-ordered variables. Levels of MC were based on the conditional distribution of scores of DA and AI as shown below. In table B3, the column variable, DA, shows the original position of respondents on the DA scale, as the row variable, AI, does for the AI index. The numbers in the nine internal cells represent the level of MC of those respondents having that particular combination of DA and AI levels.

Table B3: Minority Consciousness (MC)

			DA	
		HI	Med	Lo
	Hi	1	1	2
AI	Med	1	2	3
	Lo	3	3	3

	MC Frequency Distribution	
Hi (1)	38%	
Med (2)	17%	
Lo (3)	45%	
TOTAL	100%	$n = 600$

STANDARDIZATION[1]

Each of the variables was standardized prior to being included in the additive index. While this operation makes interval level assumptions about the component variables, which were collected in ordinal fashion, we feel tradeoffs in a number of areas combine to justify this decision. First, the ordinal properties are preserved within each of the variables used.

The primary reason for this operation lies in the nature of the measurement process and concern with minimizing nonrandom error. Ideally, one would want a sufficiently large number of indicators to assure that error would be normally distributed, much like a distribution of sample means in a

1. The above section on standardization was written by Cliff Zukin.

sampling distribution. Given the limited number of indicators we are forced to rely on, however, there is no such guarantee.

Moreover, much as we would expect different indicators to tap different dimensions of a concept, we might also expect different indicators to tap different segments of a single dimension. Thus, for example, we may have two indicators of the concept "discrimination awareness," one of which records 45 percent of the sample at the "most aware" point on the scale, while the other records only 20 percent at a similar point. The second indicator is thus a "harder" test, and we would not want to give it the same numerical score or "weight" as an indicator of this concept as we did the first.

By standardizing each variable prior to combining them, we are attempting to remove some of the "noise" that may be expected to result from the fact that they differ in their sensitivity as measuring instruments coupled with the fact that we do not have an infinite number of indicators. Thus, we are effectively combining an individual's score on a variable after it has been adjusted to the mean of the distribution on that variable. While this is not an entirely standard technique to be performed on ordinal data, we believe it to be a reasonable decision and the "lesser of evils" in terms of the particular measurement problem facing us.

References

Andersen, K. 1975. "Working Women and Political Participation, 1952–1972." *American Journal of Political Science* 19: 439–53.

Andersen, K., and E. A. Cook. 1985. "Women, Work and Political Attitudes." *American Journal of Political Science* 29: 606–25.

Ashmore, R. D. 1990. "Sex, Gender, and the Individual." In *Handbook of Personality: Theory and Research,* edited by L. A. Pervin, pp. 486–526. New York: Guilford Press.

Ashmore, R. D., and F. K. Del Boca, eds. 1986. *The Social Psychology of Female-Male Relations: A Critical Analysis of Central Concepts.* New York: Academic Press.

———. 1979. "Sex Stereotypes and Implicit Personality Theory: Toward a Cognitive-Social Psychological Conception." *Sex Roles* 5: 219–48.

Axelrod, M. D. 1975. "Marketers Get an Eyeful when Focus Groups Expose Products, Ideas, Images, Ad Copy, etc to Consumers." *Marketing News,* 28 February 1975.

Ballou, J. 1990. "Respondent/Interviewer Gender Interaction Effects in Telephone Surveys." Paper presented at the 1990 International Conference on Measurement Errors in Surveys, Tucson, Arizona, 11–14 November 1990.

Ballou, J., and F. Del Boca. 1980. "Gender Interaction Effects on Survey Measures in Telephone Interviews." Paper presented at the 35th Annual Conference of the American Association of Public Opinion Research, Mason, Ohio, 29 May–1 June 1980.

Baltes, P. B., and K. W. Schaie, eds. 1973. *Lifespan Psychology: Personality and Socialization.* New York: Academic Press.

Baxter, S., and M. Lansing. 1983. *Women and Politics: The Invisible Majority.* Ann Arbor: University of Michigan Press.

Belenky, M. F., et al. 1986. *Women's Way of Knowing: The Development of Self, Voice and Mind.* New York: Basic Books.

Bem, S. L. 1975. "The Measurement of Psychological Androgyny." *Journal of Consulting and Clinical Psychology* 42: 155–62.

Bernard, J. 1981. *The Female World.* Glencoe, IL: Free Press.

————. 1974. *Academic Women.* New York: Mendosa Book.

————. 1972. *The Future of Marriage.* New York: World.

————. 1971. *Women and the Public Interest.* Chicago: Aldine Atherton.

Biemer, P., et al. 1991. *Measurement Error in Surveys.* New York: John Wiley.

Blechman, E. A. 1984. "Women's Behavior in a Man's World: Sex Differences in Competence." In *Behavior Modification with Women,* edited by E. A. Blechman, pp. 1–33. New York: The Guilford Press.

Blydenburgh, J. C., and R. S. Sigel. 1983. "Key Factors in the 1982 Elections as Seen by Men and Women Voters. An Exploration into the Vulnerability Thesis." Paper delivered at the Annual Meeting of the American Political Science Association.

Bourque, S., and J. Grossholtz. 1974. "Politics and Unnatural Practice: Political Science Looks at Female Participation." *Politics and Society* 4 (Winter 1974): 225–66.

Broverman, I. K., et al. 1972. "Sex-Role Stereotypes: A Current Appraisal." *Journal of Social Issues* 28 (2): 59–78.

Calder, B. J. 1977. "Focus Groups and the Nature of Qualitative Marketing Research." *Journal of Marketing Research* 14: 353–64.

Carter, D. B., ed. 1987. *Current Conceptions of Sex Roles and Sex Typing: Theory and Research.* New York: Praeger.

Center for Public Interest Polling: Eagleton Institute of Politics, Rutgers University. 1990. "Overview of Focus Group Techniques: Collection of Relevant Materials." Mimeo prepared for Livingstone Public Library.

Chafe, W. H. 1977. *Women and Equality: Changing Patterns in American Culture.* Oxford: Oxford University Press.

————. 1972. *The American Woman: Her Changing Social, Economic and Political Roles, 1920–70.* London: Oxford University Press.

Clelland, J. 1988. "Gender and the U.S. Welfare State: Women's Experiences During the Depression in Minneapolis." Paper presented at the Annual Meeting of the American Political Science Association.

Connell, R. W., and associates. 1991. Untitled Research Draft.

Connell, R. W. 1989. "Cool Guys, Swots and Wimps: The Interplay of Masculinity and Education." *Oxford Review of Education* 15: 291–303.

————. 1987. *Gender and Power.* Stanford, CA: Stanford University Press.

————. 1985. "Theorizing Gender," *Sociology* 19(2): 260–72.

Conover, P. J. 1987. "Gender Identities and Basic Political Orientations." Paper presented at the Annual Meeting of the Midwest Political Science Association.

————. 1986. "Group Identification and Group Sympathy: Their Political Implications." Paper presented at the Annual Meeting of the Midwest Political Science Association.

Conover, P. J., I. Crewe, and D. Searing. 1991. "The Nature of Citizenship in the United States and Great Britain: Empirical Comments on Theoretical Themes." *Journal of Politics* 53: 800–832.

Conover, P. J. and Feldman, S. 1983. "Group Identification Values and the Organization of Political Beliefs." Paper presented at the Annual Meeting of the Midwest Political Science Association.

Conover, P. J., and V. Sapiro. 1993. "Gender Consciousness and Gender Politics in the 1991 Pilot Study: A Report to the ANES Board of Over-Seers." Ann Arbor: University of Michigan.
———. 1992. "Gender, Feminist Consciousness, and War." Paper presented at the Annual Meeting of the Midwest Political Science Association, Chicago.
Conway, J. F., S. C. Bourque, and J. W. Scott, eds. 1992. *Learning about Women, Gender, Politics, and Power.* Ann Arbor: University of Michigan Press.
Conway, J. K. 1989. *The Road from Coorain.* New York: Vintage Books.
Crosby, F. J. 1991. *Juggling: The Unexpected Advantages of Balancing Career and Home for Women and Their Families.* New York: The Free Press.
———. 1982. *Relative Deprivation and Working Women.* New York: Oxford University Press.
———, ed. 1987. *Spouse, Parent, Worker: On Gender and Multiple Roles.* New Haven: Yale University Press.
Crosby, F., S. Clayton, C. Alknis, and K. Hemker. 1988. "Cognitive Biases in the Perception of Discrimination: The Importance of Format." *Sex Roles* 14: 637–46.
Crosby, F., J. Golding, and A. Reswick. 1983. "Discontent among Male Lawyers, Female Lawyers, and Female Legal Secretaries." *Journal of Applied Social Psychology* 13: 183–90.
Crosby, F. J., and A. M. Gonzales-Intal. 1984. "Relative Deprivation and Equity Theories: Felt Injustice and the Undeserved Benefits of Others." In *The Sense of Injustice,* edited by R. Folger, pp. 141–66. New York: Plenum Press.
Crosby, F., and G. M. Herek. 1986. "Male Sympathy with the Situation of Women: Does Personal Experience Make a Difference?" *Journal of Social Issues* 42, no. 2: 55–66.
Crosby, F., J. P. Muehrer, and G. Loewenstein. 1986. "Relative Deprivation and Explanation: Models and Concepts." In *Relative Deprivation and Social Comparison,* edited by J. M. Olson, C. P. Herman, and M. P. Zanna, pp. 17–32. Hillsdale, NJ: Lawrence Erlbaum Associates.
Cutler, N. E. 1982. "Subjective Age Identification." In *Research Instruments in Social Gerontology,* edited by J. D. Mangen and W. A. Peterson, pp. 731–87. Minneapolis: University of Minnesota Press.
Davis, J. A. 1959. "A Formal Interpretation of the Theory of Relative Deprivation." *Sociometry* 22: 280–96.
Deaux, K. 1987. "Psychological Constructs of Masculinity and Femininity." In *Masculinity/Femininity,* edited by J. M. Reichisch, L. A. Rosenblum, and S. A. Shields. New York: Oxford University Press.
———. 1985. "Sex and Gender." In *Annual Review of Psychology 36,* edited by M. Rosenzweig and L. Porter. Palo Alto, CA: Annual Reviews Inc.
———. 1984. "From Individual Differences to Social Categories: Analysis of a Decade's Research on Gender." *American Psychologist* 39: 105–16.
Deaux, K., and M. E. Kite. 1987. "Thinking about Gender." In *Analyzing Gender: A Handbook of Social Science Research,* edited by B. B. Hess and M. M. Ferree, pp. 322–47. Newburg Park, CA: Sage Publications.

Deaux, K., and B. Major. 1987. "Putting Gender into Context: An Interactive Model of Gender-Related Behavior." *Psychological Review* 94: 369–89.

Delli Carpini, M. X., and B. A. Williams. 1991. "Methods, Metaphors, and Media Messages: The Uses of Television in Conversations about the Environment." Paper presented at the Annual Meeting of the Political Science Association in Washington, DC.

De Tocqueville, A. 1955. *The Old Regime and the French Revolution.* Garden City: Doubleday.

Deutsch, M. 1975. "Equity, Equality, and Need: What Determines Which Value Will Be Used as the Basis of Distributive Justice?" *Journal of Social Issues* 31: 137–49.

Eagly, A. H. 1987. *Sex Differences in Social Behavior: A Social Role Interpretation.* Hillsdale, NJ: Lawrence Erlbaum Associates.

Easton, D. 1965. *A Framework for Political Analysis.* Englewood Cliffs, NJ: Prentice-Hall.

Easton, D., and J. Dennis. 1969. *Children in the Political System.* New York: McGraw Hill.

Epstein, C. F. 1988. *Deceptive Distinctions: Sex, Gender, and the Social Order.* New Haven: Yale University Press.

Epstein, L. K., and S. J. Carroll. 1983. "Sex and the Vote: The 1982 Election Day Voter Polls." Paper presented at the Annual Meeting of the American Political Science Association.

Faludi, Susan. 1991. *Backlash: The Undeclared War Against Women.* New York: Crown Publishers.

Feldman, S., and J. Zaller. 1988. "The Political Culture of Ambivalence: Ideological Responses to the Welfare State." Paper presented at the Annual Meeting of the Midwest Political Science Association in Chicago.

Ferree, M. M. 1987. "She Works Hard for a Living: Gender and Class on the Job." In *Analyzing Gender: A Handbook of Social Science Research,* edited by B. B. Hess and M. M. Ferree, pp. 322–47. Newbury Park, CA: Sage Publications.

———. 1976. "Working Class Jobs: Housework and Paid Work as Sources of Satisfaction." *Social Problems* 23: 431–41.

Ferree, M. M., and B. B. Hess. 1987. "Introduction." In *Analyzing Gender: A Handbook of Social Science Research,* edited by B. B. Hess and M. M. Ferree, pp. 9–30. Newbury Park, CA: Sage Publications.

Folger, R. G. 1987. "Reformulating the Preconditions of Resentment: A Referent Cognition Model." In *Social Comparison, Social Justice, and Relative Deprivation,* edited by J. C. Masters and A. P. Smith, pp. 183–216. Hillsdale, NJ: Lawrence Erlbaum Associates.

———. 1984. *The Sense of Injustice: Social Psychological Perspectives.* New York: Plenum.

Frankovic, K. A. 1982. "Sex and Politics: New Alignments, Old Issues." *PS* 15: 439–48.

Freeman, J. 1975. *The Politics of Women's Liberation.* New York: David McKay.

Friedan, Betty. 1963. *The Feminine Mystique.* New York: W. W. Norton & Company.

Fulenwider, C. K. 1980. *Feminism for American Politics: A Study of Ideological Influence.* New York: Praeger Publishers.

Gailey, C. W. 1987. "Evolutionary Perspectives on Gender Hierarchy." In *Analyzing Gender: A Handbook of Social Science Research,* pp. 3–67. Ann Arbor: University of Michigan Press.

Gerson, Kathleen. 1985. *Hard Choices: How Women Decide about Work, Career, and Motherhood.* Berkeley: University of California Press.

Gilbert, L. A. 1985. *Men in Dual-Career Families: Current Realities and Future Prospects.* Hillsdale, NJ: Lawrence Erlbaum Associations.

Gilligan, C. 1982. *In a Different Voice: Psychological Theory and Women's Development.* Cambridge, MA: Harvard University Press.

Glazer, P. M., and M. Slater. 1986. *Unequal Colleagues: The Entrance of Women into the Professions, 1890–1940.* New Brunswick, NJ: Rutgers University Press.

Glenn, E. N. 1987. "Gender and the Family." In *Analyzing Gender: A Handbook of Social Science Research,* edited by B. B. Hess and M. M. Ferree, pp. 348–80. Newbury Park, CA: Sage.

Glenn, N. D. 1974. "Aging and Conservatism." *Annals of the American Academy of Social and Political Science* 1515: 176–86.

Graubard, S. R. 1987. "Preface." In *Learning about Women: Gender, Politics, and Power,* edited by J. K. Conway, S. C. Bourque, and J. W. Scott, pp. v–xxix. Ann Arbor: University of Michigan Press.

Greenberg, E. S. 1970. *Political Socialization.* New York: Atherton.

Greenstein, Fred I. 1965. *Children and Politics.* New Haven: Yale University Press.

Grossman, H., and N. L. Chester, eds. 1990. *The Experience and Meaning of Work in Women's Lives.* Hillsdale, NJ: Lawrence Erlbaum Associates.

Gruberg, M. 1968. *Women in American Politics.* Oshkosh: Academia Press.

Gurin, P. 1987. "The Political Implication of Women's Multiple Statuses." In *Spouse, Parent, Worker: On Gender and Multiple Roles,* edited by F. J. Crosby, pp. 167–96. New Haven: Yale University Press.

Gurin, P. 1985. "Women's Gender Consciousness." *Public Opinion Quarterly* 49: 143–63.

Gurin, P., A. H. Miller, and G. Gurin. 1980. "Stratum Identification and Consciousness." *Social Psychological Quarterly* 43: 30–47.

Gurr, T. R. 1970. *Why Men Rebel.* Princeton, NJ: Princeton University Press.

Guttentag, M., and P. F. Secord. 1983. *Too Many Women? The Sex-ratio Question.* Beverly Hills, CA: Sage Publishers.

Hacker, H. M. 1951. "Women as a Minority Group." *Social Forces* 30: 60–69.

Hare-Mustin, R. T., and J. Maracek. 1988. "The Meaning of Difference: Gender Theory, Postmodernism, and Psychology." *American Psychologist* 43, no. 6: 455–64.

Harrison, Cynthia. 1988. *On Account of Sex: The Politics of Women's Issues, 1945–1968.* Berkeley: University of California Press.

Hertz, Rosanna. 1986. *More Equal Than Others: Women and Men in Dual-Career Marriages.* Berkeley: University of California Press.

Hess, B. B., and M. M. Ferree, eds. 1987. *Analyzing Gender: A Handbook of Social Science Research.* Beverly Hills, CA: Sage Publications.

Hess, R. D., and J. V. Torney. 1968. *The Development of Political Attitudes in Children.* Chicago: Aldine.

Higgenbotham, J. B., and K. K. Cox, eds. 1979. *Focus Group Interviews: A Reader.* Chicago: American Marketing Association.

Hochschild, Arlene R. 1989. *Second Shift: Working Parents and the Revolution at Home.* New York: Viking Press.

———. 1981. *The Managed Heart: Commercialization of Human Feeling.* Berkeley: University of California Press.

———. 1973. "Review of Sex Role Research." *American Journal of Sociology* 78: 1011–28.

Hochschild, Jennifer L. 1981. *What's Fair? American Beliefs about Distributive Justice.* Cambridge, MA: Harvard University Press.

Hoffman, L. W. 1977. "A Follow-up Study." *Journal of Consulting Clinical Psychology* 45: 310–21.

———. 1974. "Fear of Success in Males and Females: 1965 and 1971." *Journal of Consulting Clinical Psychology* 42: 353–58.

Horney, K. 1967. *Feminine Psychology.* New York: W. W. Norton.

Huddy, L., and J. Bracciodieta. 1992. "Feminists Under Siege: The Origins and Consequences of Public Opposition Toward Feminists." Paper presented at the Annual Meeting of the Midwest Political Science Association, Chicago, 9–11 April.

Hyman, H. 1959. *Political Socialization.* Glencoe, IL: Free Press.

Inwold, R. H., and N. D. Bryant. 1981. "The Effect of Sex of Participants on Decision-making in Small Teacher Groups." *Psychology of Women Quarterly* 5: 532–42.

Jaros, D., H. Hirsch, and F. Fleron. 1968. "The Malevolent Leader: Political Socialization in an American Subculture." *American Political Science Review* 62: 564–75.

Jennings, M. K., and R. Niemi. 1974. *The Political Character of Adolescence.* Princeton, NJ: Princeton University Press.

Kagan, J., and O. Brim, eds. 1980. *Constancy and Change in Human Development.* Cambridge: Harvard University Press.

Kahn, A. 1984. "The Power War: Male Responses to Power Loss Under Equality." *Psychology of Women Quarterly* 8: 234–47.

Kane, E. W., and L. J. Macauley. 1993. "Interviewer Gender and Gende tudes." *Public Opinion Quarterly* 57: 1–28.

Kanter, R. M. 1977a. *Men and Women of the Corporation.* New York: Basic Books.

———. 1977b. *Work and Family in the U.S.* New York: Russell Sage.

Katzenstein, M. F. 1984. "Feminism and the Meaning of the Vote." *SIGNS* 10: 4–26.

Kessler-Harris, A. 1982. *Out to Work: A History of Wage-Earning Women in the United States.* New York: Oxford University Press.

Klein, Ethel. 1984. *Gender Politics.* Cambridge, MA: Harvard University Press.

Komarovsky, M. 1991. "Some Reflections on the Feminist Scholarship in Sociology." *Annual Review of Sociology* 17: 1–25.

———. 1988. "The New Feminist Scholarship: Some Precursors and Polemics." *Journal of Marriage and the Family* 50: 585–93.

———. 1985. *Women in College Shaping New Feminine Identities.* New York: Basic Books.

———. 1976. *Dilemmas of Masculinity: A Study of College Men.* New York: W. W. Norton.

———. 1959. "Functional Analysis of Sex Roles." *American Sociological Review* 15: 508–16.

Krueger, R. A. 1988. *Focus Groups: A Practical Guide for Applied Research.* Beverly Hills, CA: Sage Publications.

Kuppersmith, J. 1987. "The Double Bind of Personal Striving: Ethnic Working Class Women in Psychotherapy." *Journal of Contemporary Psychotherapy* 17: 204–16.

Lane, R. 1962. *Political Ideology: Why the American Common Man Believes What He Does.* New York: Free Press.

Langland, E., and W. Gove, eds. 1981. *A Feminist Perspective in the Academy: The Difference It Makes.* Chicago: University of Chicago Press.

Laws, J. L. 1975. "The Psychology of Tokenism: An Analysis." *Sex Roles* 1: 51–67.

Levinson, D. J. 1971. "Role, Personality and Social Structure in the Organizational Setting." In *A Source Book for the Study of Personality and Politics,* edited by F. I. Greenstein and D. Lerner, pp. 61–74. Chicago: Markham Publications.

Lipset, M. 1960. *Political Man: The Social Bases of Politics.* Garden City, NY: Doubleday.

Lopata, H. Z. 1987. "Women's Family Roles in Life Course Perspective." In *Analyzing Gender: A Handbook of Social Science Research,* edited by B. B. Hess and M. M. Ferree, pp. 381–407. Beverly Hills: Sage Publications.

Lydecker, T. H. 1986. "Focus Group Dynamics." *Association Management* 38 (3): 73–78.

Maccoby, E. E., and C. N. Jacklin. 1974. *The Psychology of Sex Differences.* Stanford, CA: Stanford University Press.

Mainero, L. A. 1986. "Coping with Powerlessness: The Relationship of Gender and Job Dependency to Empowerment Strategy Usage." *Administrative Science Quarterly* 31: 633–53.

Major, B., and K. Deaux. 1982. "Individual Differences in Justice Behavior." In *Equity and Justice in Social Behavior,* edited by J. Greenberg and P. L. Cohen, pp. 43–76. New York: Academic Press.

Mansbridge, Jane. 1986. *Why We Lost the ERA.* Chicago: University of Chicago Press.

Marini, M. M. 1978. "Sex Differences the Determination of Adolescent Aspirations: A Review of Research." *Signs* 4: 723–53.

Marini, M. M., and M. Brinton. 1984. "Sex Typing in Occupational Socialization." In *Sex Segregation in the Workplace: Explanations and Remedies,* edited by B. F. Reskin, pp. 723–53. Washington, DC: National Academy Press.

Martin, C. L. 1987. "A Ratio Measure of Sex Stereotyping." *Journal of Personality and Social Psychology* 52: 489–99.

Martin, J. 1987. "The Tolerance of Injustice." In *Relative Deprivation and Social Comparison,* edited by J. Olson, C. P. Herman, and M. P. Zanna, pp. 217–42. Hillsdale, NJ: Lawrence Erlbaum Associates.

———. 1981. "Relative Deprivation: A Theory of Distributive Injustice for an Era of Shrinking Resources." *Research in Organizational Behavior* 3: 53–107.

Mason, K. O., J. L. Czajak, and S. Albert. 1976. "Change in U.S. Women's Sex-Role Attitudes." *American Sociological Review* 41: 573–96.

Mathews, D. G., and J. S. De Hart. 1990. *Sex, Gender, and the Politics of the ERA.* New York: Oxford University Press.

McDonagh, E. L. 1982. "To Work or Not to Work: The Differential Impact of Achieved and Derived Status upon the Political Participation of Women, 1956–1976." *American Journal of Political Science* 26: 280–97.

McGlen, N. E., and K. O'Connor. 1983. *Women's Rights: The Struggle for Equality in the 19th and 20th Centuries.* New York: Praeger.

Mead, M. 1935. *Sex and Temperament for Three Primitive Societies.* New York: William Morrow.

Merelman, R. M. 1986. "Revitalizing Political Socialization." In *Political Psychology,* edited by M. A. Hermann, pp. 279–319. San Francisco: Jossey-Bass Publications.

Miller, A., P. Gurin, G. Gurin, and O. Malanchuk. 1981. "Group Consciousness and Political Participation." *American Journal of Political Science* 25: 494–511.

Miller, A., P. Gurin, and G. Gurin. 1978. "Electoral Implications of Group Identification and Consciousness: The Reintroduction of a Concept." Paper presented at the Annual Meeting of the Political Science Association.

Miller, J. B. 1976. *Toward a New Psychology of Women.* Boston: Beacon Press.

Molyneux, M. C. 1985. "Mobilization Without Emancipation? Women's Interests, the State and Revolution in Nicaragua." *Feminist Studies* 11, no. 2 (Summer 1985): 227–54.

Morgan, D. L. 1988. *Focus Groups as Qualitative Research.* Newbury Park, CA: Sage Publications.

Morgan, D. L., and M. T. Spanish. 1984. "Focus Groups: A New Tool for Qualitative Research." *Qualitative Sociology* 7 (3): 253–70.

Morris, A. D., J. J. Hatchett, and R. E. Brown. 1989. "The Civil Rights Movement and Black Political Socialization." In *Political Learning in Adulthood: A Sourcebook of Theory and Research,* edited by R. S. Sigel, pp. 272–305. Chicago: University of Chicago Press.

Myrdal, G. 1944. *An American Dilemma: The Negro Problem and Modern Democracy*, 2 vols. New York: Harper and Brothers Publishers.

Neugarten, B. 1968. *Middle Age and Aging*. Chicago: University of Chicago Press.

Nie, N. H., S. Verba, and J. R. Petrocik. 1976. *The Changing American Voter*. Cambridge, MA: Harvard University Press.

Norris, P. 1994. "Gender-Related Influences on Voting Behavior and Public Opinion." Paper presented at the Conference on Research on Women and American Politics: Agenda Setting for the 21st Century. New Brunswick, NJ: The Center for the American Woman in Politics, Rutgers University.

Olson, J. M., C. P. Herman, and M. P. Zanna, eds. 1986. *Relative Deprivation and Social Comparison*. Hillsdale, NJ: Lawrence Erlbaum Associates.

Parsons, T. 1951. *The Social System*. Glencoe, IL: The Free Press.

Parsons, T., and R. Bales. 1955. *Family Socialization and Interaction Process*. Glencoe, IL: The Free Press.

Pettigrew, T. 1967. "Social Evaluation Theory." In *Nebraska Symposium on Motivation*, vol. 15, edited by D. Levine, pp. 241–311. Lincoln: University of Nebraska Press.

Pettigrew, T. 1964. *A Profile of the Negro American*. Princeton, NJ: D Van Norstrand.

Pleck, J. H. 1985. *Working Wives, Working Husbands*. Newbury Park, CA: Sage Publications.

———. 1983. "Husband's Paid Work and Family Roles: Current Research Issues." In *Research in the Interweave of Social Roles: Families and Jobs*, vol. 3, edited by H. Lopata and J. H. Pleck, pp. 251–333. Greenwich, CT: JAI Press.

Poole, K. T., and L. H. Zeigler. 1987. *Women and Political Life*. New York: Longmans.

———. 1981. "The Diffusion of Feminist Ideology." *Political Behavior* 3: 229–56.

Ragins, B. R., and E. Sundstrom. 1989. "Gender and Power in Organizations: A Longitudinal Perspective." *Psychological Bulletin* 105: 51–88.

Reis, H. T. 1987. "The Nature of the Justice Motive: Some Thoughts on Operation, Internalization, and Justification." In *Social Comparison, Social Justice, and Relative Deprivation*, edited by J. C. Masters and W. P. Smith, pp. 131–50. Hillsdale, NJ: Lawrence Erlbaum Associates.

Rhodebeck, L. 1981. "Group-Deprivation: An Alternate Model for Explaining Collective Political Action." *Micropolitics* I: 239–67.

Robinson, H. 1993. "Faces of Feminism: Four Clark Professors Ponder the Future of the Women's Movement." *Clark University News* 16: 13–16.

Rokeach, M. 1973. *The Nature of Human Values*. New York: The Free Press.

Rosaldo, M. Z., and L. Lamphere. 1974. *Woman, Culture and Society*. Stanford, CA: Stanford University Press.

Rossi, A. 1965. "Equality between the Sexes: An Immodest Proposal." In *The American Woman*, edited by R. J. Lifton, pp. 93–143. Boston: Beacon Press.

Rubin, G. R. 1975. "The Traffic in Women: Notes on the Political Economy of

Sex." In *Toward an Anthropology of Women,* edited by R. Reiter, pp. 157–210. New York: Monthly Review Press.

Rubin, L. R. 1976. *Worlds of Pain: Life in the Working Class Family.* New York: Basic Books.

Ruble, D. N., and T. L. Ruble. 1982. "Sex Stereotypes." In *In the Eye of the Beholder: Contemporary Issues in Stereotyping,* edited by A. G. Miller, pp. 188–252. New York: Praeger.

Runciman, W. G. 1966. *Relative Deprivation and Social Justice.* Berkeley: University of California Press.

Sapiro, V. 1991. "Feminism: A Generation Later." Philadelphia: *The Annals of the American Academy of Social and Political Science,* 515: 10–22.

———. 1988. "Life Course, Gender, and Individual Political Development." Paper presented at the Annual Meeting of the International Political Science Association.

———. 1983. *The Political Integration of Women: Roles, Socialization and Politics.* Urbana: University of Illinois Press.

———. 1982. "Private Costs of Public Commitment or Public Costs of Private Commitments? Family Roles Versus Political Ambition." *American Journal of Political Science* 26: 265–79.

———. 1981. "Ideology and Utopia in Mass Politics: A Comparative Study of Left, Right, and Center on the 'Woman Question.'" Paper presented at the Annual Meeting of the American Political Science Association.

———. 1980. "News from the Front: Intersex and Inter-Generational Conflict Over the Status of Women," *Western Political Quarterly* 33: 260–77.

Sapiro, V., and B. G. Farah. 1980. "New Pride and Old Prejudice: Political Ambition and Role Orientations among Female Partisan Elites." *Women and Politics* 1: 13–36.

Schroedel, J. R. 1990. "Blue-Collar Women: Paying the Price at Home and on the Job." In *The Experience and Meaning of Work in Women's Lives,* edited by H. Y. Grossman and L. N. Chester, pp. 241–60. Hillside, NJ: Lawrence Erlbaum Associates.

Searing, D. D., J. J. Schwartz, and A. E. Lind. 1973. "The Structuring Principle: Political Socialization and Belief Systems." *American Political Science Review* 67: 415–42.

Sherif, C. W. 1982. "Needed Concepts in the Study of Gender Identity." *Psychology of Women Quarterly* 6: 375–98.

Sheriffs, A. C., and J. P. McKee. 1957. "Qualitative Aspects of Beliefs about Men and Women." *Journal of Personality* 25: 451–64.

Sigel, R. S. 1992. "How Men and Women Cope When Gender Role Orientations Change." *Political Psychology* 13 (3): 337–51.

———. 1989. "Feelings of Deprivation and Feeling Resentful: An Inevitable Sequence?" Paper presented at the Annual Meeting of the International Society for Political Psychology.

———. 1988. "Female Perspectives on Gender Relations." Paper presented at the Annual Meeting of the American Political Science Association.

———. 1984. "Minority Consciousness and the Gender Gap: A Preliminary

Test." Paper presented at the Annual Meeting of the American Political Science Association.

―――. 1975. "The Adolescent in Politics: The Case of American Girls." Paper presented at the Annual Meeting of the American Political Science Association.

―――, ed. 1965. *Political Socialization: Its Role in the Political Process*. Philadelphia: *The Annals of the American Academy of Social and Political Science,* vol. 361.

Sigel, R. S., and L. D. Burnbauer. 1989. "The 'Not-Me' Syndrome: A Paradox in Search of an Explanation." Paper presented at the Annual Meeting of the American Political Science Association.

Sigel, R. S., and K. J. Casey. 1991. "Group Consciousness and Identification: Gender Consciousness vs. Feminist Consciousness." Paper presented at the Annual Meeting of the American Political Science Association.

Sigel, R. S., and M. B. Hoskin. 1981. *The Political Involvement of Adolescents.* New Brunswick, NJ: Rutgers University Press.

―――. 1977. "Perspectives on Adult Political Socialization." In *Handbook of Political Socialization: Theory and Research,* edited by Stanley A. Renshon, pp. 259–93. New York: The Free Press.

Sigel, R. S., and J. Reynolds. 1979/1980. "Generational Differences and the Women's Movement: A Test of Two Competing Hypotheses." *Political Science Quarterly* 94: 635–48.

Sigel, R. S., and L. A. Sernekos. 1992. "Choosing Domesticity: An Analysis of Women Whose Preference Is for the Exclusively Domestic Life." Paper presented at the Annual Meeting of the Midwest Political Science Association.

Sigel, R. S., and N. L. Whelchel. 1986a. "Assessing the Past and Looking Toward the Future: Perceptions of Change in the Status of Women." Paper presented at the Annual Meeting of the American Political Science Association.

―――. 1986b. "Minority Consciousness and a Sense of Group Power Among Women." Paper presented at the Annual Meeting of the Midwest Political Science Association.

―――. 1986c. "Changing Gender Roles: Male and Female Reactions." Paper presented at the Annual Meeting of the International Society for Political Psychology.

Simon, R. J., and J. M. Landis. 1989. "Women's and Men's Attitudes about Women's Place and Role." *Public Opinion Quarterly* 53: 265–76.

Sinnott, J. D. 1987. "Sex Roles in Adulthood and Old Age." In *Current Conceptions of Sex Roles and Sex Typing: Theory and Research,* edited by D. B. Carter, pp. 155–77. New York: Praeger.

Spence, J. T., and R. L. Helmreich. 1978. *Masculinity and Femininity: Their Psychological Dimensions, Correlates and Antecedents.* Austin: University of Texas Press.

Spitze, G., and J. Huber. 1980. "Changing Attitudes toward Women's Nonfamily Roles: 1938–1972." *Work and Occupations: Sociology of Work and Occupations* 7: 317–35.

Stanley, L., and S. Wise. 1983. *Breaking Out: Feminist Consciousness and Feminist Research*. New York: Routledge and Kegan Paul.

Steckenrider, J. S., and N. E. Cutler. 1989. "Aging and Adult Socialization: The Importance of Roles and Role Transitions." In *Political Learning in Adulthood: A Sourcebook of Theory and Research*, edited by Roberta S. Sigel, pp. 56–88. Chicago: University of Chicago Press.

Stewart, D. W., and P. N. Shamdasoui. 1990. *Focus Groups: Theory and Practice*. Newbury Park, CA: Sage Publications.

Stouffer, S. A., et al. 1949. *The American Soldier: Adjustment During Army Life*. Princeton: Princeton University Press.

Tajfel, H., ed. 1978. *Differentiation Between Social Groups: Studies in the Social Psychology of Intergroup Relations*. London: Academie Press.

Tanur, J. M., ed. 1992. *Questions about Questions: Inquiries into the Cognitive Bases of Surveys*. New York: Russell Sage Foundation.

Tavris, C. 1982. *Anger: The Misunderstood Emotion*. New York: Simon and Schuster.

Taylor, S. E., and H. T. Falcone. "Individual Difference Determinants of Sex Categorization and Stereotyping." Undated Mimeo.

Terkel, Studs. 1972. *Working*. New York: Ballantine.

Thornton, A., and D. Freedman. 1979a. "Changes in the Sex Role Attitudes of Women, 1962–1977: Evidence from a Panel Study." *American Sociological Review* 44: 831–42.

————. 1979b. "Consistency of Sex Role Attitudes of Women, 1962–1977," Working Paper Series, Ann Arbor, Michigan: Institute of Social Research.

Tolleson Rinehart, S. 1992. *Gender Consciousness and Politics*. New York: Routledge.

Tolleson Rinehart, S., and J. Perkins. 1986. "Change and Stability in Feminist Attitudes: 1972–1984." Paper presented at the Annual Meeting of the American Political Science Association.

Traugott, M. 1992. "The Use of Focus Groups to Supplement Campaign Coverage." Paper presented at the Annual Meeting of the American Political Science Association in Chicago.

Traugott, S. 1993. Review of a book by J. Tanur. *American Political Science Review* 87: 223–24.

Unger, Rhoda K. 1990. "Imperfect Reflections of Reality: Psychology Constructs Gender." In *Making a Difference: The Social Construction of Gender*, edited by R. Hare-Mustin and J. Maracek, pp. 102–49. New Haven: Yale University Press.

————. 1979. "Toward a Redefinition of Sex and Gender." *American Psychologist* 34: 1085–94.

Verba, S., and N. H. Nie. 1972. *Participation in American Political Democracy and Social Equality*. New York: Harper and Row.

Verba, S., and G. R. Orren. 1985. *Equality in America: The View from the Top*. Cambridge, MA: Harvard University Press.

Von Baeyer, C. L., D. L. Sherk, and M. P. Zanna. 1981. "Impression Management in the Job Interview: When the Female Applicant Meets the Male

(Chauvinist) Interviewer." *Personality and Social Psychology Bulletin* 7: 45–51.

Walker, L., and T. F. Pettigrew. 1984. "Relative Deprivation Theory: An Overview and Conceptual Critique." *British Journal of Social Psychology* 23: 301–10.

Weiss, Robert S. 1987. "Men and Their Wives' Work." In *Spouse, Parent, Worker: On Gender and Multiple Roles,* edited by F. J. Crosby, pp. 109–38. New Haven: Yale University Press.

———. 1985. "Men and the Family." *Family Process* 24 (March): 49–58.

Welch, S. 1977. "Women as Political Animals? A Test of Some Explanations for Male-Female Political Participation Differences." *American Journal of Political Science* 21: 711–30.

———. 1975. "Support among Women for the Issues of the Women's Movement." *Social Science Quarterly* 16: 216–27.

Welch, S., and L. Sigelman. 1982. "Changes in Public Attitudes Toward Women in Politics." *Social Science Quarterly* 6: 312–22.

Whelchel, N. L. 1987. "Sex-Based Respondent-Interviewer Interaction Effects on Gender-Sensitive Questions." Paper presented at the 42d Annual Conference of the American Association for Public Opinion Research in Hershey, PA.

Whelchel, N. 1992. "Feminist Consciousness and Sympathetic Feminism: Sex Differences in Origin and Effects." Ph.D. diss. submitted to the Department of Sociology at Rutgers University, New Brunswick, NJ.

Williams, J. E., and D. L. Best. 1982. *Measuring Sex Stereotypes: A Thirty Nations Study.* Newbury Park, CA: Sage Publications.

Williams, R. 1983. *Culture and Society, 1780–1950.* New York: Columbia University Press.

Wilson, E. O. 1978. *On Human Nature.* Cambridge, MA: Harvard University Press.

Wrong, D. H. 1961. "The Oversocialized Conception of Man in Modern Sociology." *American Sociological Review* 26: 183–93.

Wylie, P. 1942. *Generation of Vipers.* New York: Ferrar, Rinehart.

Zaller, J., and S. Feldman. 1992. "A Simple Theory of Survey Response: Answering Questions versus Revealing Preferences." *American Journal of Political Science* 36: 579–616.

Zanna, M. P., F. Crosby, and G. Loewenstein. 1987. "Male Preference Groups and Discontent among Female Professionals." In *Women's Career Development,* edited by B. Gutek and L. Larwood, pp. 28–41. Newbury Park, CA: Sage Publications.

Zukin, C., and R. Carter. 1982. "The Measurement of Presidential Popularity: Old Wisdoms and New Concerns." In *The President and the Public,* edited by D. Graber, pp. 207–41. Philadelphia: Institute for the Study of Human Issues.

14.32